Motorcycle Guide to Historic Route 66

© 1995, 1996, 1997, 1998, 1999, 2000, 2001 HHJM, Inc. All Rights Reserved

A Personal Note

In the Fall of 1994, I was glancing through a mail order catalog and came across an offer for a book about Route 66. They also offered a coffee cup with the Route 66 logo and a T-Shirt. Something clicked.

Kirk Woodward

"Gosh, that would be a heck of ride. Two thirds of the United States, 2,400 miles, right through some of the best riding in the world. And it's historic, too." (I also remember the television series).

I wondered if any other motorcyclists would like to make that trip, "Get their kicks on Route 66?" How to find out?

Well, I subscribe to a half dozen or so motorcycle magazines, so I hunted up the address for their editorial offices and pulled together a simple news release about what I called The Mother Road Ride/Rally©. To be perfectly honest, I really kind of forgot about it. Making a living *does* intrude on what a person would like to do, doesn't it?

But then, in January, 1995, the phone started to ring. *Cycle World* magazine ran a short item on the rally. The rest, as the saying goes, is history. We rushed an advertisement into the *American Motorcyclist* magazine and started running classified ads under *motorcycles* around the country. The other magazines we had mailed the news release to also made mention of the event.

And so it came to pass that early in the morning of June 10, 1995 two groups of motorcyclists headed down the Mother Road of the United States. One group started in a light rain from Columbus & Jackson streets in Chicago and the other group started from the Santa Monica Pier in the Los Angeles Basin.

Motorcycle Guide to Route 66 is a direct descendent of The Mother Road Ride/Rally© and owes its creation to the massive interest in this historic route. The Mother Road Ride/Rally© has been established as an annual event.[1] You are invited to convert this "armchair" trip down Route 66 into the real thing any year that you can clear a few days to: *"Get Your Kicks on Route 66."*

Organization of this Manual

Most Route 66 literature organizes along the lines of states that the route passes through. That seems logical to us and we have maintained that system.

The Appendices include motorcyclist information, such as "Route Laws" and motorcycle dealer listings.

Best wishes!

Kirk G. Woodward

---

[1] Second Saturday in June.

Table of Contents

History of Route 66 9

Westbound - Turn-by-Turn 12
    *Directions for riding Route 66 if you are traveling **from** Chicago to Los Angeles.*

Eastbound - Turn-by-Turn 41
    *Directions for riding Route 66 if you are traveling **from** Los Angeles to Chicago.*

Chicago 50

Springfield, IL 52

You Can *Still* Get Your Kicks on Route 66 54
    Jim Seay of Mahomet, IL runs from Chicago westward.

Dwight, IL 61

Oklahoma Route 66 Museum 71

Cadillac Ranch 74

Oatman, AZ 78

Los Angeles 86

Laws Along the Mother Road/Riding Safe 89
    Helmets, etc., road riding tips from those who made the trip

Motorcycle Dealers Along the Mother Road 91

Campgrounds Along the Mother Road 97

Essential Extras for the touring Motorcyclist 100

Motorcycling Diaries 101
    *Joe Miller, Lew Bellinger, Kirk Woodward, Roger & Jane Holm, Graeme Ware, Mitch Boehm share great adventures and **mis**adventures with you. Great reading!*

Route 66 Resources 130
    Books, maps, and much more about America's Favorite Road

Highway of Dreams, Parts 1, 2, 3 133
    Greg Harrison & J. B. Norris share thoughts, fun and pictures from their Los Angeles to Chicago run in 1994. Reprinted from the American Motorcyclist Magazine

History of Route 66

The **only** road with a Pulitzer Prize to it's credit.

Travelers along Route 66 who are questioned about the "why" of their journey usually say something along the lines of: "People are tired of fast food, fast times. The effort and feeling that people had gave a heart and soul to old 66. People are starting to realize that again."

Travel on the mythic highway of John Steinbeck, of Doorthea Lange's stark Dust Bowl photographs, and of the television buddies, Martin Milner and George Maharis, has been steadily increasing, fueled most notably by Europeans, some on vintage motorcycles, in hot pursuit of the "real" America.

It is no longer possible to drive the route uninterrupted. But Tom Snyder, founder of the Route 66 Association[2], says that this year, 20,000 die-hards will travel most of the roughly 2,400 mile route, through eight states from Chicago to Santa Monica.

Those visitors represent an estimated $20,000,000 in revenue for the gas stations, motor courts, eateries and other businesses along the route. That's up from $10,000 in 1984.

Route 66 was conceived in the 1920's by Cyrus Stevens Avery of Tulsa,

Cyrus Avery, "Father of Route 66."

Oklahoma as an effort by local boosters to link the former Indian Territory with Chicago and Los Angeles. Avery, a highway commissioner, envisioned diverting traffic from Kansas City and Denver when he was asked by the U.S. Bureau of Public Roads to help develop a new system of interstate highways. Avery spent most of 1925 working with an appointed committee to stitch together hundreds of existing roads into the new system. Avery wanted U.S. 60 for his "road to California" but bowed to political pressure in accepting the "66" designation on November 11, 1926.

The road was later promoted through Phillips 66 gasoline, which appropriated the magic numbers and logo, and by the United States Highway Association, based in Clinton, OK. Both touted Route 66 as the Main Street of America.

Perhaps due to it's Oklahoma origins, Route 66 has become the state's single "most tourists" attraction. Tom Myers, the economic development director for the state tourism office estimates that the state's Route 66 tourists could spend more than $40,000,000 provided they can find the road. Jim Ross, of Ghost Town Press says that about 80 percent of the original paved sections across the country are driveable, but some are abandoned fragments leading nowhere. Improvements and bypasses to the road began almost immediately after its completion in 1926 when engineers sought to straighten out its hooks, elbows and hairpin turns. Navigating Route 66 can be baffling because the road contains many dead ends and sections that have been taken over by city roads or the interstates.

Route 66 travelers have made a fetish out of tracing authentic pieces of the highway.

---

[2] Route 66 Association, Oxnard, CA is one of two national, eight state and ten international groups devoted to preserving Route 66.

They have been aided in their quest by the dramatic resurgence of **Historic Route 66** signs, complete with the legendary shield, that began appearing in June of 1995 in all eight states. The signs resulted from persistent lobbying by the statewide Route 66 Associations, which held car rallies, foot races, peanut brittle sales and box suppers to raise money to supplement the states' investments.

The signs represent "democratized history," according to Michael Jackson, chief architect for the state historic preservation office in Illinois where approximately 600 signs went up in the Summer of 1995. Jackson said they were the result of a grass roots effort.

Route 66 is being viewed now as a means to infuse towns along the route with some of their lost prosperity. Many smaller communities - particularly those in the "oil patch" - are trying to rebound from the double whammy of being bypassed by the interstate highway system and from the oil bust. Combined with the decline of the family farm and rural flight, these blows have resulted in population losses approaching 10 percent in the decade between 1980 and 1990.

Like Route 66 itself, preservation efforts along the route have been patchy. But steadily, in towns along the route a palpable rebirth has occurred by nursing what old timers are calling the memory route.

It begins in Grant Park on the shore of Lake Michigan in downtown Chicago, Illinois and ends at the Santa Monica Pier in the Los Angeles Basin of California. Enroute it passed through eight states. Illinois, Missouri, Kansas[3], Oklahoma, Texas, New Mexico, Arizona and California.

Route 66 was the first highway of such length to be paved from one end to the other. Earlier there were long stretches of dirt, or planks floating on sand. The road brought the nation to California - twice. Once in the 1930's and again after World War II.

Along the original road travelers drove along Main Street(s) of the USA at eye-level with pedestrians instead of skirting towns on freeways.

But why **this** level of interest?

Stuart Kellogg, writing in the *Victorville Daily Press* said: "Because of the kitsch, of course. The snake farms and curio stands, the 40's motel cabins and 50's burger shacks, the [places] `cooled by refrigeration.'

"And everywhere, the gas stations -- some squat as chapels, others exuberant as Chartres."

The freeway system put the nail in the coffin of Route 66: the mom-and-pop motels, the hamburger stands, Americana. Now interested parties - headed mainly by dedicated volunteers in the small towns along the route who recognize the value of Route 66 preservation - are pulling together to maintain much of the magic of the route.

"Why in the WORLD would someone want to ride a motorcycle down Route 66?"

---

[3] The few miles the road covered in Kansas were bypassed when the Interstate Highway system was created.

I[4] wasn't aware that anyone knew the secret. Someone has been spying. The vulgar truth is out. I once spent three years on two wheels. I've tried to hide it, somewhat like AIDS or a loony aunt you never owned up to, but someone has obviously squealed and the cat - not to mention the wheels - is out of the bag.

To ride on two wheels, as opposed to four - the fate of most of the innocent population - is an experience devoutly to be wished. This was best expressed in one of the surprise best-sellers of our time. It was Zen and the Art of Motorcycle Maintenance. It was published in 1974. It went into 10 printings. It was by Robert M. Pirsig. No one had ever heard of him before. No one has ever heard of him since.

It was a tale of how Pirsig, a man in search of himself, rode across the U.S. and A. with a young son on the back of his siccle and discovered himself. No one has said it better:

"You see things vacationing on a motorcycle in a way that is completely different from any other. In a car you're always in a compartment, and because you're used to it you don't realize that through that car window everything you see is just more TV. You're a passive observer and it is all moving by you boringly in a frame.

"On a cycle the frame is gone. You're completely in contact with it all. You're in the scene, not just watching it anymore, and the sense of presence is overwhelming. That concrete whizzing by five inches below your foot is the real thing, the same stuff you walk on, it's right there, so blurred you can't focus on it, yet you can put your foot down and touch it anytime, and the whole thing, the whole experience, is never removed from immediate consciousness."

Good stuff, familiar to anyone who has fallen for the open-road enchantment of two-wheel travel. James Dean knew all about it, though he didn't die on a motorcycle as is legend; it was a dull Porsche that did him in. Marlon Brando, in his black leather jacket in The Wild One, spawned an entire generation of Harley-Davidson freaks, and Tokyo's Kawasaki - operating under the principle that if young North Americans wish to kill themselves, they might as well do it stylishly - now markets machines that look out of a Buck Rogers cartoon strip.

Your agent spent three years in Europe on a Vespa, an Italian invention that doesn't go as slow as a motorbike or as fast as a motorcycle, but just fast enough to get you into serious trouble. Survived is more the operative word than spent. It's absolutely amazing, the number of small European villages that have cobble-stone streets that, when rained upon, can separate driver from steed faster than you can blink. It's astounding how swiftly the slip-stream of a transport truck on a German autobahn, where there are no speed limits, can deposit you in an adjacent ditch. Simply remarkable what you can learn on two wheels.

There was the cow in Poland that did a cutback just as the driver gunned it. Cows, even Polish cows, weigh more than a Vespa, and you would be absolutely dumbfounded

---

[4] We are indebted to Allan Fotheringham for this candid explanation why sane people make fantastic journeys in the **relative** discomfort of motorcycles. The article was originally published in *MacLean's*, January 22, 1990, page 48.

at how much blood can ooze out the end of 10 fingertips when they are the first things that hit rough Polish pavement.

As Pirsig indicates, there's no better way of seeing the countryside of Spain or feeling its texture than on two wheels. Or exploring Rome. And you can't beat the parking.

The joys of two-wheel travel, while the rest of the world cowardly resorts to four, is accompanied by the realization that you are riding in concert with the law of averages. The longer you continue your youthful fetish for speed and wind in your hair, the shorter become the odds. It is a fact, for example, that in rainy Vancouver, on Friday and Saturday nights in December and January and February, hospitals bring in extra transplant doctors, knowing that body organs from healthy young males are likely to be available.

It is why those of us who have fallen off these machines too many times look forward, with nervous finality, to the day when the steed is shipped to the barn for the last time. This jockey had his wind in his hair from Sweden to North Africa, from Warsaw to Ireland, from Athens to Copenhagen. On the last jaunt, a run from Gibraltar to Britain, the final relay from Paris to London was carefully nurtured in midwinter in an atmosphere of fear mixed with frigidity. Plus a resolution that never again, supposedly a semi-grown man and no longer a boy, would this precious body be placed on anything as dangerous as a two-wheel machine. I still look at bicycles, at some distance, with distrust.

The kind motorcycle people advertised the 11th anniversary MAX (Motorcycle Awards of Excellence) presentations: "Canada's motorcycle Oscars" in over 30 categories. Thanks a bunch for the invitation, youse guys, but I take a pass.

Westbound (Illinois to California on Route 66 - Turn by Turn

From Chicago to Gardner

The start of Route 66 has moved a few times. Currently Adams Street at Michigan Avenue is the starting point. Until Jackson Boulevard became one way it was the Route 66 starting point. Some regard the Intersection of Jackson Blvd. and Lake Shore Dr. as the starting point also, and follow Jackson, turn right onto Michigan Av, and left onto Adams St.

The ending point on Jackson Blvd. is currently at Lake Shore Drive although it once was at Michigan Avenue. [changed in 1933 for the world exhibition, when Grant Park was constructed and Jackson Blvd. elongated.]. Jackson now is one way, east bound, so the beginning of Route 66 sign is on Adams street, just west of it's intersection with Michigan Ave.

For purposes of these directions, the "start" is presumed to be on Adams Street, just west of Michigan Avenue, at the "Beginning of Route 66" sign.

Head west on Adams.
After crossing Ashland Avenue, turn Southwest (=left) onto Ogden Avenue.

Cicero
Fans of the television series "The Untouchables" know that Cicero was pretty much the bad guys hometown.

Berwyn

Lyons

In Lyons, turn south (=left) onto Harlem Avenue (SR 43), after about 0.5 mile, turn southwest (=right) onto Joliet Road. After passing the I294 (Tri State Tollway) Joliet road disappears under the I55, continue on the I55 southwest.

ALTERNATIVE 1 : The old way through Joliet. Exit I55 onto Joliet Road at exit 269. At exit 267 (locally known as Welco's Corner). After about 2.5 miles join the SR53 and continue southwest.

Bollingbrook
Follow SR53

Romeoville
Follow SR53

Joliet

Continue on SR53 which becomes a 4 lane at the exit of the town. Just north of Elwood, pass the bridge, 1.5 miles later, turn left and right to change from the 4 lane alignment to the older 2 lane alignment. Follow Manhattan Road, Mississippi Road and Elwood Road. A lot of the bad guys in Cicero eventually forwarded their mail to Joliet, actually Stateville - the state prison.

Joliet approved river boat casinos some years ago. The Empress, south of the city, is one of the most elaborate and boasts a "dockside" hotel roughly 5 times bigger than the casino.

Elwood
Follow Douglas until it rejoins SR53 on the southern end of the town

ALTERNATIVE 2 : Following Interstate 55

One could stay onto the I55 and continue until Gardner or until the Wilmington exit. This way one would still be following the Route 66, but a later (less interesting) alignment. This deviation was created in 1940.

The I55 bypass of Plainfield had an older alignment using SR129 and SR59 to pass through Plainfield itself. When using SR129 to get from about Wilmington to Gardner, one would still be following one of the alignments of Route 66.

ALTERNATIVE END

Wilmington
Continue on SR53 through Wilmington, there is a right turn onto Baltimore Street. At the Launching Pad Drive, see the Gemini Giant (on your right).

Braidwood
Continue on SR53.

Godley
Continue on SR53.

Braceville
Continue on SR53.

Gardner
Continue on SR53. If coming from SR53: Right at Main street, left at second stop sign. At the intersection of SR129 and SR53 (both are Route 66 alignments), use the Frontage Road Southeast of I-55.

From Gardner to Bloomington

Route 66 is stuck between the I 55 and the railroad.

Dwight

The Marathon Oil Station is a well maintained Route 66 relic, constructed in 1932, and still intact. The city has also preserved a historic windmill in the city center.

There are thee options for passing Dwight:
- 4 lane detour
- 2 lane detour
- straight through

- take Dwight Rd. to SR47 South
- when SR47 turns left, go straight to Waupansie St.
- cross SR17 to old 66
- at stop sign south of Dwight, turn Left.

Odell
Turn left on Odell Rd. into town

Cayuga

Pontiac
Before Pontiac: Meramec Caverns Barn 44/66 on the right hand side of the 4 lane road.

Alternative 1: Continue on the 4 lane road

Alternative 2: Left on Pontiac Rd., to Lincoln, to Ladd and then make a right turn onto Reynolds St. Rejoin the 4 lane at Reynolds and the 4 lane 66 (turn left(=South)) to . . .

Chenoa
Left on 3150 north, which turns into Morehead St. Turn right onto US25, then turn left onto 4 lane 66

Lexington

Towanda
Follow 66, at stop sign: South: the 4 lane 66, or right: I 55 to Bloomington.

Normal
Named for the early college.

Bloomington
Right on Pine, left to Linden, right to Willow, left onto Main Street. Right on Business 55 pass Morris Rd. First street past Parkway Inn, Right on Springfield Rd. left on Beich Rd., then Cross I-55. First Left (=still Beich).

Like Beer Nuts®? They are all produced here. Shipped all over the world.

From Bloomington to Springfield (IL)

Shirley

Funk's Grove
Founded in 1825 by Isaac Funk, actually very small as there were never more than 50 inhabitants. The famous "Sirup" is produced here. The Interstate rest stop is a delightful place to take a break. You'll see the land much as it was before the area was settled.

McLean
Curve right onto E. Carlyle, left onto Main. Goto US 136

The first truck stop was founded here in 1928 by J.P. Waters and J.W. Geske. It is always open, 365 days a year, 24 hours a day. It was closed only one day due to a fire. The Dixie Truckers Home features also the Hall of Fame of the Route 66 Association of Illinois. It is truly a "hall." The hall between the restaurant and the souvenir shop. Neat stuff about Route 66 but not very extensive.

Head west on US136 to the railroad tracks. Turn left **before** the tracks and head for Atlanta(IL).

Atlanta
Use Atlanta Rd.

Lawndale

Lincoln
While entering Lincoln, stay on your road or use Business Loop 55 through Lincoln. Lincoln is the only town named for Abraham Lincoln while he was still alive.

Sites:
- The Tropics (eat)
- The Mill (eat: famous for its schnitzel)

South of town, left on the Frontage Road

Broadwell
North of Broadwell, left at another Frontage Road sign

Site:

- The Pig Hip used to be here (closed in '91 due to too much success!)

Elkhart

Sites:

- F.L.Bears Truck Stop
- House by the Side of the Road Restaurant

Williamsville
Turn right at the stop sign, Cross I55. Left onto Frontage Road. At the 3 way intersection: turn left, cross I55, first right follow through Sherman.

Sherman

Site:

* For about 6 miles, the first 4 lane portion of Route 66 straight through the town. 2 of the 4 lanes are closed now, but the effect is still visible.

Springfield
Abraham Lincoln lived here until he departed in 1861 for the White House. You can visit his home in the downtown area and New Salem is where he lived and worked before practicing law in Springfield proper. The Lincoln Tomb & Memorial is in Oakwood Cemetery.

Follow Business Loop 55 into Springfield.

Alternative 1: Left on Dirkson Pkwy. Right on Stevenson Dr. Left on Business Loop 55. Everett Dirkson and Stevenson (a twice defeated Presidential candidate) are icons of Illinois politics.)

Alternative 2: Follow BL55 on Peoria Rd.

Site:

- Marathon Station owned by Bill Shea
- Cozy Drive Inn on 6th St.

Due to the different alternatives to go from Springfield to E. St. Louis, one has different options in Springfield itself. One alignment of original Route 66 is now beneath the waters of Lake Springfield.

Alternative End

From Springfield to Mitchell
Use SR4. After entering Springfield on BL55 (9th street), turn east onto South Grand then turn south onto Mac Arthur Blvd. Turn west on Wabash Avenue.(actually Mac Arthur Blvd. Blends into Wabash Av.) Turn

south(=left) on Chatam Road(SR4). Go west on Spaulding Orchard Rd., then south onto SR4.

Chatman
Continue on SR4.

Auburn
Continue on SR4.

Thayer
Continue on SR4.

Virden
Continue on SR4.

Girard
Continue on SR4.

Nilwood
Continue on SR4.

Carlinville
Continue on SR4.

Gillespie
Continue on SR4.

Benld
Continue on SR4.

Sawyerville
Continue on SR4.

Staunton
Continue on SR4.

ALTERNATIVE 2 : 4 lane road Continue on BL55, use Chatam exit (exit 88), use western frontage road.

Glenarm
There is a route 66 alignment on the western side of I55. After Glenarm, turn at SR104, get on I55 south. Take Exit 80 off of I55, turn Right and Left onto the Frontage Road.

Divernon
There is a route 66 alignment on the western side of I55.

Thomasville
There is a route 66 alignment on the western side of I55.

Farmersville
There is a route 66 alignment on the western side of I55.

Sites:

- Art's Motel and Restaurant
- Our Lady of the Highways

Waggoner
There is a route 66 alignment on the western side of I55. Turn left at 1600 North, cross I-55, take Eastern Frontage Road into Litchfield.

Litchfield
There is a route 66 alignment on the eastern side of I55. Niehaus Cycle Company, a large motorcycle dealership with a booming, world wide mail order business is located directly on Old Route 66 in Litchfield. The second generation of Niehaus'es operate the business.

There are 2 options for passing Litchfield:

- stay on the 4 lane
- 2 lane

Sites:

* Skyview Drive Inn
* Ariston Cafe
* Route 66 Cafe
* Route 66 Motel

Mt. Olive

In Mt. Olive, follow Mt. Olive Rd. Soulby's Station (the Shell Station on your right) came to life the same year as Route 66 (1926).

Sites:

● Shell station (1926-1992), closed by the EPA

Go to SR4, and pickup SR157. It still is unclear whether Route 66 passed Livingston, but here are directions:

From Mt. Olive: Continue south to where the road ends, turn right, cross over I55, turn left on the frontage road, after the Kendon Motel Sign, cross IL4 (????) and turn Left onto the frontage road In Livingston, turn Left at the first stop sign, left at Park St, left on the frontage road and then head to Hamel.

ALTERNATIVE END

Hamel

Sites:

●Church of the Neon Cross

Take SR157 South.

Edwardsville

Follow SR157 till just before I270, turn onto Chain of Rocks Road westbound (=right).

From Mitchell to St. Louis

Mitchell

ALTERNATIVE 1 START: To the (closed) Chain of rocks bridge. There is a move afoot to "restore" the bridge to a park for foot traffic. Periodically the bridge is opened to pedestrians. Call Trailnet, Inc. 314-416-9928 for specific information.

The original Route 66 : Continue on Chain of Rocks Road till the closed Chain of Rocks bridge.

Sites:

* Mustang Corral: At the crossing of SR111 and Chain of Rocks Road is a large lot with about 200 Mustangs waiting for a second life.
* Chain of Rocks Bridge: Constructed in 1927 it is a remarkable bridge with a 135 degrees turn in the middle, closed to traffic, accessible on foot only.

ALTERNATIVE 2 : Over Mc Kinley Bridge

At Mitchell, turn south (SR 203, Nameoki Road)

Granite City

Turn west onto Madison Avenue, which becomes Broadwalk in Venice, cross 4th street, cross the Mc Kinley Bridge (toll)

* The area in Venice you're passing is rumored (?) to be rather unsafe.
* Mc Kinley Bridge is the only currently in use bridge that once supported an alignment of Route 66, all others have been closed. WARNING: Mc Kinley Bridge is in real bad shape, an average speed of about 5 MPH is advised by locals.

ALTERNATIVE 3 : Using I270

Follow I270 and skirt the city. Locals advise that construction has been a way of life for years on I-270. Taking I-55 east of St. Louis to its join with I-44 is faster and will give you a look at the St. Louis Arch and the nicely restored river front area of St. Louis.

ALTERNATIVE END

Route 66 - Missouri - Detailed directions

From St. Louis to Sullivan

St. Louis
Through the city there are many different options.

ALTERNATIVE 1 : I 270 or Chain of Rocks Bridge

One chooses this way for a late Route 66 alignment, skirting St. Louis.

Sites:

* Chain of Rocks Bridge (closed), Rumor has it that on the Missouri side of the Chain of Rocks bridge, one can walk onto the bridge (crossing a closed fence), the bridge should be rather intact except for some graffiti, and one should be able to walk the entire length. Do so at your own risk. Following the rape and murder of a local college student the bridge was closed off.
* The access road paralleling the Interstate has a few old motels left.

Hazelwood

At Hazelwood one leaves the I 270 onto Lindbergh Rd. (US 67) and continues on this road until:

Kirkwood
Where the road is also known under the name Kirkwood Rd.

ALTERNATIVE 2 : Mc Kinley Bridge

Coming from Venice(IL) one crosses the Mc Kinley Bridge, the only still in use bridge that once carried Route 66 into St. Louis. After crossing the bridge turn left onto Salisbury, then left onto Florisant and continue on Florisant onto 13th St. Follow onto Tucker Blvd. and follow onto Gravois Av. Follow onto Chippewa St. Follow onto Watson Road.

Sites:

- Ted Drewes Frozen Custard
- Historic Coral Court used to be here, has made place for a new subdivision.

ALTERNATIVE 3 : Mac Arthur Bridge

This is the original bridge for Route 66, but it is closed for vehicles. One can use the bridge for I55 & I64 instead. Follow the Interstate system towards I-44 and exit at Tucker Blvd. Turn back underneath the interstate and follow Tucker southwest. Follow onto Gravois Av.

ALTERNATIVE END

Out of the city, there are also two different options:

ALTERNATIVE 1 : Manchester Rd.

Manchester Rd. (SR100) is the oldest way out of the city, it passes:

Maplewood
Continue on Manchester Rd. (SR100)

Brentwood
Continue on Manchester Rd. (SR100)

Rock Hill
Continue on Manchester Rd. (SR100)

Warson Woods
Continue on Manchester Rd. (SR100)

Kirkwood
Continue on Manchester Rd. (SR100)

Des Peres
Continue on Manchester Rd. (SR100)

Manchester
Continue on Manchester Rd. (SR100)

Winchester
Continue on Manchester Rd. (SR100)

Ballwin
Continue on Manchester Rd. (SR100)

Ellisville
Continue on Manchester Rd. (SR100). When Manchester Road splits from SR100, stay on Manchester Rd into Grover.

Grover
Continue on Manchester Rd. (not SR100)

Pond
Continue on Manchester Rd. 2 miles after Pond, follow Manchester Rd., continue straight on, crossing SR100, when they intersect again (less than 1 miles later), reconnect for about 2.3 miles with SR100 westbound. Turn right onto a loop that reconnects with SR100 after 2 miles.

Hollow
Continue on Manchester Rd. (SR100).

Gray Summit

ALTERNATIVE 2 : Watson Rd.

Using Watson Rd. to exit the city has its advantages, one passes . . .

Marlborough
Continue on Watson Rd.

Crestwood
Join I-44.

Peerless Park
Continue on I-44.

Eureka
Continue on I-44.

Allenton
Get off the I-44 and onto the BL-44 at exit 261 and cross the I-44. Follow Outher Road (BL-44).

Pacific

Gray Summit
Connect with SR100.

ALTERNATIVE END

Gray Summit
Cross I-44 to the south side (coming from SR100) and use the south service road. Pass over I-44, at the intersection with US50, go straight then cross back to the south side of

I-44 (less than 1 mile later). Take south access road west into St. Clair.

St. Clair
Just past junction with SR30, turn north to cross I-44 (at exit 239), then left onto north access road and cross to the south side at junction with road JJ (at exit 230).

Stanton
Take the south access road to Sullivan. The Meremac Caverns are here.

Sullivan
Turn right on Elmont then turn left at stop sign just before the overpass.

From Sullivan to Waynesville

Bourbon
Continue on south access road. *A picture of that watertower proclaiming "Bourbon" is in many Route 66 scrapbooks.* In actual fact, this is wine country.

Hofflins
Continue on south access road.

Cuba
Continue on south access road.

Fanning
Continue on south access road.

St. James
At intersection with SR68 (Jefferson) cross I-44 and continue on north access road for about 8.5 miles. Turn left at the junction with US63 (Bishop Av.) then cross the I-44 and continue into Rolla.

Rolla

US63 becomes BL44. At Kings Highway right (stay on BL-44A) then left onto south access road just before Kings Highway junctions with I-44. Continue west trough Doolittle. The college in Rolla has constructed a small version of Stonehenge

Doolittle
Continue to the I-44 crossover at exit 176 (Sugartree). Three miles more of south access road to Arlington, but you'll have to return to I--44 at exit 176.

Arlington
Return to I-44 at exit 176. Follow I-44 till exit 172, then take the north service road westbound. Move to the south access road at first opportunity (Clementine). South access road becomes a divided highway (for 3 miles). Turn left just before the Big Piney River to drive through Devil's ELbow.

Devil's Elbow
Turn left onto the 4 lane. Pass over I-44 west of St. Robert.

Waynesville
At the junction with SR17 continue straight (=west) for 5.5 miles.

From Waynesville to Springfield

5.5 miles after Waynesville, cross to the south side on I-44 (at exit 153) then right onto SR17 to junction with road "P" and road "NN" (1.5 miles). Turn right onto road "P" then left at the fork onto road "AA" through Laquey. Turn right at the T-intersection with road "AB" and continue west to Hazelgreen.

Hazelgreen

Continue west to the junction with road "F" at exit 135. Cross I-44 and take north access road into Lebanon.

Lebanon

At the T-intersection with Mill creek Rd. turn right. Turn left at the Y-intersection onto Elm (BL-44). West of town at the junction with road "W"(at exit 127), go right, then left to stay with north access road for 9 miles. Cross to the south side of I-44.

Phillipsburg
Take road "CC"

Conway
Take road "CC"

Niangua
Take road "CC"

Marshfield
Take road "CC" then left onto Road "OO."

Northview
Continue on road "OO."

Holman
Continue on road "OO."

Strafford
Continue on road "OO."

Mulroy
Continue on road "OO."

Springfield
Road "OO" is Kearney St. and SR 744 in Springfield. Turn right onto Chestnut Expwy. or better yet, St. Louis St., College St., and then Chestnut Expy. Cross I-44 and continue on SR266.

Springfield is the "gateway" city from the Interstate to Branson, MO - the country music capital to rival Nashville, TN. Branson is said to be the number one tour motorcoach destination in the United States.

From Springfield to Joplin

Haseltine
Continue on SR266.

Elwood
Continue on SR266.

Halltown
Continue on SR266. West of town, at the end of SR266 and the SR96 go left, continue straight on the old pavement until it intersects with SR96. Continue straight for 0.5 mile and then turn right to take the historic loop trough Spencer.

Spencer
At the next stop sign turn left onto SR96 and head due west.

Albatross
Head due west.

Phelps
Head due west.

Rescue
Head due west.

Log City
Head due west.

Stone City
Head due west.

Avilla

Head due west.

Carthage
Follow SR96 across Spring River and follow SR96 over the railroad tracks to Central Av. then turn left onto Garrison and right onto Oak. Continue toward US71 and take US71 southbound.

Webb City
Follow US71 to Joplin.

Joplin
Left on Madison and follow onto Rangeline. Turn right at 7th St. and go west onto SR66. After 5.5 miles you will have the option to continue straight on SR66, or turn right to the historic route to Galena(KS).

Route 66 - Kansas - Detailed directions

From Joplin(MO) to Quapaw(OK)

Kansas has only 13 miles of route 66, but they are well preserved and worth the time.

Galena
While entering from Missouri, one has the option of staying on SR66 (KS66 and MO66), or using following older alignment:

Coming from Joplin(MO), use SR66, at the sign "old route66, next right" hook right onto the original road and follow this road into Kansas. Continue west toward Galena.

Sites:

* Eagle Picher Plant at "Hell's half acre", named after land damage caused by the mining activity, site of piles of mining debris known locally as "chat."

Use Front St. and turn left onto Main till the junction with SR66.

Site:

* The Galena museum, located at the train depot on SR66

Follow SR 66 to Riverton.

Riverton
After the bridge over the Spring River, join US 69 ALT westbound. A half mile later, US 69 ALT turns south, continue straight on (actually jog right and left) and continue westbound. Cross the Rainbow Bridge over Bush Creek.

Site:

* The March Rainbow Bridge is the last remaining Rainbow Bridge on Route 66, built in 1923, and saved by the Kansas Route 66 Association.

Continue Southbound towards Baxter Springs. Cross Willow Creek.

Baxter Springs
Swing left (=east) onto 3rd St. Continue South on Military Av. (US 69 ALT). At Roberts Rd, turn left then immediately right onto 30th St., reconnect with US 69 ALT after the commercial building and continue south toward Oklahoma.

The Kiwanis Park in Baxter Springs is a nice place to take a break.

Sites:

* Baxter Springs Historical Society Museum (at 8th St.)

Route 66 - Oklahoma - Detailed directions

From Baxter Springs(KS) to Vinita
Enter Oklahoma on US 69 ALT. Follow US 69 ALT to Quapaw.

Quapaw
Follow US 69 ALT to Commerce.

Commerce
Follow Mickey Mantle Blvd[5]. (US 69). Head South on US 69 to Miami.

Miami
Enter Miami on Main St., turn right onto Steve Owens Blvd. and cross Noesho River. Turn south following US59/69.

Dotyville
Follow US 59/69

Narcissa
Follow US 59/69. After crossing I-44, join US60 (follow US69, leave US59).

Afton
Follow US 59/69. Note the Route 66 Cafe on the west side of the road.

Vinita
Follow US60/69. Turn left at the light at Wilson then continue out toward White Oak.

From Vinita to Tulsa

Join SR66[6] just before White Oak.

White Oak
Continue on SR66.

Catale
Continue on SR66.

Chelsea
Continue on SR66.

Foyil
Continue on SR66. At the flag poles on the east side of the highway you'll see the memorial to Foyil's Andy Payne who won the "Bunion Derby" (a foot race from Los Angeles to New York - much of it along Route 66). North of the city see a sign directing you to the "World's Largest Totem Pole." It is four miles east of the highway

Sequoyah
Continue on SR66.

Claremore[7]
Pass Claremore on Lynn Riggs Blvd.

Verdigris

Catoosa
Right onto Antry, left onto Cherokee. Beyond the school at the T-intersection, left onto 193th Av. and then pass under I-44. Right onto 11th St. The Blue Whale, decay-

---

[5]
Yes, Commerce is the birthplace of the Yankee's Hall of Famer. Sadly, the "city dads" (beyond naming the street) did not value the "Micks" heritage sufficiently to avoid having his boyhood home moved to Branson, Missouri.

[6]
The "locals" call this the Free Road. The Interstate in this portion of Oklahoma is a toll road.

[7]
Claremore is where the Will Rogers Memorial is located. The Annual Mother Road Ride/Rally® participants report it as a "must see." Because Rogers traveled Route 66 many times while appearing in motion pictures, it was often referred to as The Will Rogers Highway.

ing symbol of an early day water park, calls Catoosa home.

Tulsa
Stay with 11th St. and follow as it flows into 10th St. Rejoin 11th St. at Boulder. Go straight at Denver and follow curve left. Turn right onto 12th St. Turn left onto Southwest Blvd. and cross the Arkansas River. You can see the original route's bridge next the new one . . . at least for the time being.

From Tulsa to Davenport

Follow Southwest Blvd.

Oakhurst
Follow Southwest Blvd. Turn right at intersection with SR66

Sapulpa
Follow SR66 (Mission). Right onto Dewey. Right at the sign for Old 66. Reconnect with SR66 at intersection of SR33 and I-44.

Kellyville
Follow SR66. Nice state park with camping space and lake is south of the city.

Bristow
Follow SR66, enter on Main St. Right at the light with 4th St. and follow curves out of town.

Depew
Follow SR66.

Milfay
Follow SR66.

Stroud
Follow SR66.

Davenport
Follow SR66.

From Davenport to Oklahoma City

Follow SR66.

Chandler
Follow SR66. Right on Manvel Av. Right at south end of town to stay with SR66

Warwick
Follow SR66, pass under the railroad.

Wellston
Pass under I-44. Right at Y-intersection into Wellston and then rejoin SR66. This is only place on all of Route 66 that you will see a 66A and 66B option.

Luther
Follow SR66.

Arcadia
Follow SR66. Watch for the Round Barn on the north side of the highway. Rock cafe is a bit east of the Round Barn and on the south side of the road.

Edmond
Follow SR66, enter on 2nd St. and follow to Broadway (US 77), turn left and exit at Memorial Rd. Left at the stop and left onto Memorial Rd. Pass under Broadway and immediately turn right onto Kelley.

Oklahoma City
Follow Kelley Av. (for about 5 miles) and then enter I-44 Westbound. Exit (almost immediately) at the Lincoln Blvd. overpass to follow Lincoln south to 23th St., then turn

right[8] onto May Av. After crossing 36th St., use left lane and enter I-44 westbound. Take the exit for SR66 (War Acres/Bethany)

Taking I-44 to it's join with I-40 skips urban traffic and offers easy access to the Murrah Building Memorial (now known as the Oklahoma City National Memorial) - exit I-40 at Robinson Ave and go north to 5th street.

From Oklahoma City to Hydro

Follow SR66.

War Acres
Follow SR66.

Bethany
Follow SR66. West of town, just before Lake Overholser Bridge, turn left and leave the 4-lane and turn right over the old bridge. Follow to the west side of the lake. When the road curves steadily left, bear right at the Y-intersection to follow Mustang Rd. into Yukon.

Yukon
Enter on Mustang Rd. and turn left at the intersection then immediately right onto the 4-lane. Follow SR66.

El Reno
Follow SR66 onto Rock Island Rd. Left onto Wade and right onto Choctaw. Left onto Sunset and follow SR66. West of the city, SR66 ends as it curves toward I-40, just before the curve, turn right onto the 2 lane towards Fort Reno.

Fort Reno
Continue on the 2-lane for about 5 miles then right onto US-270. Follow US-270 to Calumet.

Calumet
Follow US-270.

Geary
Enter on US-270 then turn left onto US-281. Bear right at the Y-intersection to cross the Canadian River(=newer alignment).

Bridgeport
Enter on US-281, continue west at Hinton Junction when US-281 turns south. Use north Service road.

Hydro
Use north Service road.

From Hydro to Hext

Use north Service road.

Weatherford
Use north Service road, bearing left at the Y-intersection onto E. Main St. then left onto Washington and right onto Main. Use right lane before 7th St. and go straight when the road curves left. Astronaut Thomas Stafford is memorialized across the street from City Hall. Turn left onto 4th St. and cross the railroad. Right onto the north service road for 6 miles (ignore SR54). At the T-intersection, left and cross I-40. Continue west and bypass next change to cross over the I-40. At the next stop sign (road ahead dead-ends), cross I-40 and continue west to Clinton.

---

[8] Yes, that is the state capitol building, complete with it's infamous oil derrick.

Clinton[9]

Right at the yield sign onto Gary Blvd. Left onto 10th St. Follow 10th St. south until I-40. The Route 66 Museum will be on your right at the west edge of town, across the street from the Tradewinds Motel. Right at the Y-intersection out of town. Ignore 2 chances to cross I-40 and cross to the north side (under the I-40).

Foss

Continue straight at the intersection with SR44. Cross to the south side at the next opportunity then cross to the north side at the next opportunity. Cross to the south side at the next opportunity (again!).

Foss Lake has a state park and camping facilities.

Canute

Right at the 4-way stop in town. Right again at the crossroad 1 mile west and pass under the I-40. Turn left to continue west.

Elk City

Entering Elk City, left then right onto SR34i (BL-40). Follow BL-40 left onto Van Buren and follow BL-40 into 3rd St. (Ignore SR6). Past the junction with SR34, right onto the 2-lane and continue west. At the T-intersection, cross I-40 to the south side and cross I-40 at the next opportunity to the north side. Use the north service road toward Sayre.

Sayre

---

[9] Clinton is home to - arguably - the finest (certainly the most expensive, $1 million invested) Route 66 museum. Annual Mother Road Ride/Rally® participants rate it a "must see."

Right at the stop sign then left onto 4th St. (US-283) and pass through town. Cross the river, then right onto the 2-lane just before the I-40 overpass. The courthouse was seen in the motion picture "The Grapes of Wrath."

Hext

From Hext to Shamrock(TX)

Erick

The 100th Meridian Museum is in Erick, limited operating hours. *(The 100th meridian is the border between Oklahoma and Texas.)*

From Texola to Amarillo

Use the south frontage road.

Shamrock

South frontage road becomes BR-40 when entering the city. Continue through the city.

Site:
* U-DROP-INN Restaurant and service station (with tower): at the intersection with US-831, dating from 1936, an example of art-deco. Sadly, the restuarant has been closed for several years. Preservation/restoration efforts are being made.

At the west end of the city avoid the I-40 and use the south frontage road. The I-40 campground is at the far west edge of the city. Nice facilities, but it is very close to the interstate . . . lots of highway noise.

Lela

Continue on the south frontage road.

Site:

* Rattlesnake sign.

Continue on the south frontage road. At county line road (exit 146), cross I-40 to the north frontage road.

Mc Lean
Follow the curve around the off-ramp of exit 143 and turn right onto the divided highway into Mc Lean.

Site:

• Devil's Rope Museum, admission is free, Route 66 display maintained by the Old Route 66 Association of Texas.
• The first (restored) Phillips 66 gas station.
• Cactus Inn (west side).

Through town westbound traffic follows 1st St., eastbound traffic would follow Railroad St. Cross SR273 and after 1.1 miles, turn left (=south) to avoid entering I-40. Turn left again (=east) and follow through the U-turn underneath the I-40. Continue on the south frontage road (heading west). From Mc Lean to Alanreed, there still exists an old (used till 1932) dirt road, it is located more to the south.

Alanreed
Follow south service road.

Site:

• Oldest Cemetery on Route 66 in Texas.
• Oldest Baptist Church on Route 66 in Texas.
• 66 Super Service.
• Remains of the Reptile Ranch.

West of Alanreed, beyond the I-40 off-ramp, route 66 becomes unpaved for about 1 mile (part of the infamous "Jericho Gap" (not bypassed till the late 1930's) with car trapping mud, the complete Jericho Gap was 18 miles long)

Option: (needed when the weather is bad!) return to SR291, cross I-40, join I-40 to exit 124.

At the Johnson Ranch Road underpass (exit 132) pass under I-40 and enter I-40. There is an hard to reach (unpaved?) piece of Route 66 more to the south, featuring "rockledge." Exit I-40 at exit 124.

Jericho
At exit 124, cross I-40 to the south side and follow the frontage road.

Groom
Follow south frontage road.

Site:

* Leaning water tower, designed so to attract visitors, and still successful at it.
* Route 66 Court - closed and decaying but an excellent example of the "motor courts" along Route 66.
* Largest cross in the Western Hemisphere.

Follow south frontage road.

Lark
Follow south frontage road.

Conway
Follow south frontage road. At exit 89 (7 miles west of Conway), cross I-40 (could be you need to join I-40 sooner). Use the north

Motorcycle Guide to Route 66

frontage road. At exit 85 stay with the frontage road as it curves away from I-40 go straight across the 4 lane BR-40 onto Farm Market Road (2575) and follow this road into 1912 (turn right). Proceed to US-60 (Amarillo Blvd. and BR-40) and turn left

This to avoid the airport which covers part of old 66:

Option:

In the late 1920's, Route 66 zig-zagged south from Conway using dirt roads till Washburn, from there it followed present day US-287 and 10th St. into Amarillo.

Palo Duro Canyon is south of Route 66 :

Palo Duro Canyon is well worth the trip if you have the time. A spectacular canyon with horseback riding, hiking trails, and a musical performance in an outdoor setting every evening in the summer ("Texas"- you should call (806) 655-2181 for reservations).

Amarillo
Enter Amarillo on Amarillo Blvd. (US-60 & BR-40) at the intersection with US-287 left onto Pierce St. (major intersection). Cross the railroad (bridge) and turn right onto South 6th St.

Site:

- Golden Light Bar and Grill
- Bronco Lodge at Bell and Route 66
- 6th St. has many antique shops trying to recapture the old 66 days.
- Cadillac Ranch, built in 1974 and relocated in 1997 by Stanley Marsh, 10 Cadillacs buried nose down in concrete, at the angle of the great pyramids, each of the models from 1948 to 1964. West of the city at exit 60, take south access road back toward Amarillo 1.3 miles.

- The Texas Trading Company at the same exit is new and has a nice selection of Route 66 items and motorcycle jewelry.
- Big Texan Steak House, get your huge free steak (if you can eat it fast enough)

From Amarillo to Glenrio

From south 6 th. St., just past Belleview, turn left onto Bushland (=southwest) just past Western, turn right onto 9th St. (=west) pass underneath Amarillo Blvd. Turn left at BR-40 and follow BR-40 past the city limit. At the S-curve, turn right onto Indian Hill Rd. (=west). At the T-intersection, turn left and cross the railroad.

Turn right onto the service road (north of I-40) and continue on the northern service road.

Bushland
Continue on the northern service road.

Wildorado
Continue on the northern service road.

Vega
Continue on the northern service road and then follow BR-40 through Vega. Continue on the northern service road. There was an unpaved version of the road north of the railroad, watch for concrete culverts near both Vega and Adrian (standing rather lonely in the field)

Adrian

Continue on the northern service road. See the Midway Cafe on the south side of the highway. Their window says that it is precisely 1,139 miles to Chicago or to the Santa Monica Pier.

Gruhlkey
At exit 18 (Gruhlkey Rd.), join I-40.

Site:

* Old Caprock gas station

A dirt road version ran close to the railroad more to the south, past a railroad section house at "boise".

Glenrio
Take exit 0 on I-40 (half mile before the border with New-Mexico, to visit the ghost town). Cross to the south side and turn right to enter town.

Site:

* First/Last Motel in Texas. Glenrio straddles the state line.

Route 66 - New Mexico - Detailed directions

From Glenrio(TX) to Santa Rosa
If coming from Glenrio, the old road can be driven all the way to Saint Jo (passing Endee), if road conditions permit it. If not, follow I-40, use exit 369 (Endee) and turn right at the stop and turn left onto the north frontage road. At Bard (exit 361), large vehicles ought to take I-40 till exit 356, otherwise, stay with the northern frontage road as it passes a tunnel under I-40 then take the south frontage road

Saint Jo
Follow southern frontage road (the southern Frontage road is the second road counting from the I-40).

Tucumcari
At the east end of the town (exit 335), cross I-40 and turn left onto Tucumcari Blvd. West of the city, follow signs for I-40 and join I-40 at exit 329. Larger vehicles continue till exit 311 (Montoya), smaller vehicles exit at exit 321 (Palomas). Cross I-40 to the south and turn right onto the frontage road. Follow the frontage road through the tunnel under I-40 and turn west to Montoya on the north frontage road.

Sites:

• Blue Swallow Motel, at east edge of the city. Closed and for sale in 1997, but the neon sign - featured in many Route 66 videos and books - was still intact. In 1998 the Bakke family purchased and moved to the property and are upgrading and renovating the motel. Nice, inexpensive place to stay right on the Old Road.
• Route 66 Monument. West edge of city, at the Convention Center. Erected in 1997 it is destined to become a modern day icon for the road.

Montoya
Cross to the south frontage road. After 5 miles, the road passes I-40 and the road parallels the railroad through Newkirk. Follow the road parallel to the railroad tracks.

Cuervo
Rejoin I-40 (exit 291), exiting at exit 277 (Santa Rosa). Turn right at the exit stop sign

and follow the boulevard westward into town.

Santa Rosa

Site:

* The Silver Moon Restaurant.

Cross the Pecos River and bear right at the junction with US-54. Pass under the railroad and continue towards exit 273 of I-40. Take the I-40 westbound to exit 256.

A very early alignment (prior to 1937) of Route 66 went north from Santa Rosa to pass through the state capitol . . . and one of the oldest cities in North America . . . Santa Fe, NM. It is a beautiful city and the central business district (on the square at the Governor's Palace) will give you a feel for the early squares of Old Mexico.

Santa Fe has a significant "arts" community, including an internationally recognized opera company that performs in the summer months.

From Santa Rosa to La Cienega/Tijeras

ALTERNATIVE 1: the Santa Fe loop

Take exit 256 on I-40. Take US-84 north

Dilla
Continue north on US-84.

Note: there was a road straight from Santa Rosa to Dilla, but it's not usable anymore

Los Montoyas
Continue north on US-84.

• Charles R Ranch

Continue north on US-84

Romeoville
Continue north on US-84 and cross over I-25. Turn left onto US84/85, while avoiding the I-25 on-ramp.

Las Vegas
Somehow (how?) Route 66 passed through here once, but the route is now unknown.

Sites:

● Las Vegas - San Miguel Chamber of Commerce, 727 Grand Ave., Las Vegas, NM 87701. (505)425-8631

Serafina/Bernal
Continue on the US84/85 on the north side of I-25.

Ribera/San Jose
Continue on the US84/85 on the north side on I-25.

Ilfed/Sands
Cross to the south side at exit 320.

Rowe
Continue on the south side of I-25, then cross I-25 to the north side and head north on SR63.

Pecos
Turn left onto SR50.

Glorieta
Take I-25 at exit 299.

Canoncito

Use exit 294 (Canoncita). Follow the north frontage road towards Santa Fe.

Santa Fe

Follow the northern frontage road as it becomes Old Pecos Trail, then follow Old Pecos Trial as it becomes Old Santa Fe trail. Cross the Santa Fe River and turn left onto Water St. Turn left onto Cerrillos Rd.

Sites:

- The Wheelwright Museum has Native American pottery exhibited. Also the International Folk Art Museum is nearby. Admission is either nominal or by donation. Downtown is the "oldest" dwelling in the US, from the early 1600s.

- Palace of the Governors/city square.

La Cienga

Follow Cerrillos Rd. to the I-25 at exit 278 and take I-25 south until exit 276.

From La Cienega to Grants

At exit 276, take the south(east)frontage road. At exit 267(Waldo), rejoin I-25 till the Aldogones exit (248).

Algodones

Turn right(=south) at exit 248 onto SR313 and follow SR313 southbound.

Bernalillo

Follow SR313 southbound.

Alameda

Follow SR313 southbound.

Albuquerque

Follow SR313 southbound and continue to follow as it turns into 4th St. Turn left onto Lomas Blvd. Turn right (=south) onto 3rd St. Cross Central Av. (=also a route 66 alignment!)

Sites:

- The Albuquerque Museum 2000 mountain Rd. NW. Admission: donation.
- Indian Pueblo Cultural Center 2401 12th St. NW. Admission: $2.50
- National Atomic Museum Kirkland Air Force Base, Building 20358 Wyoming Blvd. It includes a replica of the atomic bombs dropped on Japan during World War II.
- 66 Diner (1405 Central Ave, NE (505)247-1421). Just west of the University of New Mexico Campus, on Central Avenue (Route 66). The original building was destroyed by fire, but the owners re-build in full fledged Art Deco style. Lots of neon and shiny tile . . . the wait staff dresses in retro uniforms. See it at night for the full effect of the neon.
- Sandia Crest Road. East of the city, exit is clearly marked from I-40. Go from 6,000 to 10,000 feet over paved, beautiful drive in 19 miles of twisties with terrific scenery. At the top, the view is 150 miles on a clear day.
- Turquoise Trail. Exit from I-40 east of the city. Trail leads to the Sandia Crest turnoff and continues on north to Santa Fe. Interesting scenery and little towns.

Turn right at Silver Av. Turn left(=south again) at 4th St. and then right onto Bridge Blvd. Cross the Rio Grande on the Barelas Bridge and continue on Bridge Blvd. Turn left onto Isleta Blvd. (SR314).

Pajarito

Continue south on SR314.

Los Pallidas
Continue south on SR314. South of Los Pallidas, turn left onto SR147.

Isleta
Turn right onto SR47 and continue south on SR47. Turn right at SR6.

Los Lunas
Continue west on SR6 until it meets I-40 at exit 126.

ALTERNATIVE 2: the 1937 cut-off

Continue on I-40 past exit 256

Clines Corners
Continue on I-40.

Edgewood
Use exit 204 and take north frontage road. Cross to the south side (at exit 197). Follow BR-40 into Moriarty.

Moriarty
Follow BR-40 through Moriarty. At the west end of town , just before the I-40 interchange, take the SR333 westbound.

Edgewood
Continue on SR333.

Barton
Continue on SR333.

Sedillo
Continue on SR333.

Zuzax
Continue on SR333.

From Tijeras to Grants

Tijeras
Just before Tijeras, make sure to stay on SR333 as it intersects with SR337 and SR14. After Tijeras, the road curves under I-40. Continue west.

Carnuel
Continue west entering I-40 at exit 170.

Albuquerque
Take exit 167 (Central Av./Tramway). Turn left to the south side of I-40. Turn right into Central Av. and stay with Central Av. as it bends right. Stay with Central Av. as it swings left at the intersection with Lomas. Cross the Rio Grande (old town bridge) and continue on Central Av. At the junction with I-40 (exit 149), cross to the north frontage road and continue to Rio Puerco. Cross the old bridge and join the interstate at exit 140. Continue on I-40 till exit 126.

Site:

• Tramway is the route to the tramway that ascends Sandia Peak's western slope. It is a terrific ride, whisking you to the Crest in less than thirty minutes. There is a restaurant at the top. Neat side trip.

ALTERNATIVE END

Correo (Suwanee)

Laguna
Addresses:

• The Governor of the Pueblo, Box 194, Laguna, NM 87026. (505)552-6654

Either continue on I-40 westbound to exit 117 (Mesita) or go south on SR6 for 2 miles to:

Cuerbo
Turn right at the intersection after the railroad overpass (if road conditions permit) and cross I-40. Follow at the old alignment becomes the north frontage road and passes exit 117. Continue west on the north frontage road. Turn right onto SR124 (around exit 114) and follow SR124.

Laguna
Follow SR124. Cross the railroad tracks and continue to follow SR124.

New Laguna
Follow SR124.

Paraje
Follow SR124.

Cubero
Follow SR124.

San Fidel
Follow SR124. Crossing over I-40 at exit 96 (McCartys). Large vehicles ought to join I-40 till exit 89.

Mc Cartys
Continue on the south frontage road following it through the tunnel to the north side of I-40 (=right). Continue onto SR117 west at exit 89.

Sky City
Eighteen miles east of Grants. Casino, convenience store and gas . . . all exempt from Federal tax. It is on the Acoma Indian reservation and the tribe's real Sky City is south of the Interstate exit.

Grants
Enter on Santa Fe Av. West of town, cross over the railroad and follow SR 122.

From Grants to Sanders(AZ)

Follow SR 122.

Milan
Follow SR 122.

Bluewater
Follow SR 122.

Prewitt
Follow SR 122.

Thoreau
Follow SR 122. Enter I-40 at the continental divide (exit 47) and leave I-40 at exit 36 (Iyanbito). Take the north frontage road to Gallup.

Continental Divide
Waters flow to the Missippi or Pacific here. A "genuine" Indian hogan has been built here and there is a neat "photo op" with the covered wagon.

Gallup
Cross I-40 to the south side of I-40 at the eastern end of town and follow the railroad tracks through town.

Sites:

- Red Rock State Park 8 miles east on I-40. Admission: park:free museum:donation dance:$4

Continue west on SR118, 3 miles after the west I-40 overpass, turn left and pass under I-40 to take the south frontage road (SR 118). After 3 miles cross I-40 at exit 8 to curve around the intersecting road and turn right to cross the railroad tracks. Continue on SR118 through:

Manuelito
Continue on SR118.

Route 66 - Arizona - Detailed directions

From Gallup(NM) to Winslow

Leave New-Mexico on the north frontage road and cross to the south I-40 frontage road just west of the state line at exit 359. Turn right (heading west). In October, 1997 the Interstate was badly in need of repair. The frontage road might be in better shape than the Interstate. Unquestionably the most garish "tourist trap" strip of shops on Route 66 is right here at the New Mexico/Arizona border.

Lupton
Continue west to exit 354 (Hawtorne Rd.) and join I-40. Continue on I-40 westbound.

Houck
Continue on I-40 westbound to 346 (Big arrow Rd.) then either stay on I-40 to exit 339 (sanders) or take north frontage road west. Continue as it becomes a dirt road to cross Box Canyon. Pass Old Querino Canyon Trading Post. Pass over the Querino Canyon Bridge and join I-40 at exit 342 (Cedar Point).

Sanders
Use exit 339 (Sanders) from I-40 and follow the north frontage road.

Chambers
At the junction of the north frontage road and US-191, turn left to reconnect with I-40 (exit 333) and continue westbound on I-40.

Navajo
Continue westbound on I-40.

Sites:
- Painted Desert: colored sand, beautiful views.
- Petrified Forest: 225 million years ago, these trees grew here, now they are colorful stones. *(As a child it was **most** disappointing to me to find that the trees were no longer standing upright. I fully expected a forest scene . . . not of wooden trees but stone. kgw)*
- The "long logs" area is the most interesting.
- There is a 28 mile drive showing many aspects of the park.
- It is illegal to remove anything from the park except yourself..

Continue westbound on I-40 using exit 289 and then turn right onto Navajo Blvd.

Holbrook
Pass under I-40 at the edge of the city and turn right onto Hopi Drive follow Hopi Dr. through the city.

Sites:

- Holbrook Petrified Forest National Park Camber of Commerce 100 E. Arizona, Holbrook, AZ 86025, (602)524-6558

- Wigwam Motel. Sleep in a concrete teepee for $30 or so. 520-524-3048.

Continue on Hopi Drive till the I-40 at exit 285 then join the I-40 till exit 277. Then get off the I-40 and take the north frontage road.

Joseph City
Continue on to north frontage road and cross the I-40 at exit 274. Continue on the south frontage road.

Site:

- Jack Rabbit Trading Post, west side of the highway.
- Mormon memorial is east of the interstate, take the city route exit from the Interstate.

Cross to the north side of I-40 just west of Jack Rabbit and join I-40 at exit 269. Continue on I-40 till exit 257 and then cross to the south side. Turn right onto BR-40.

Winslow
Route 66 westbound is 3rd St., Route. 66 eastbound is 2nd St.

- The corner referred to in the Eagle's song "Take It Easy" *("Standin' on a corner in Winslow, Arizona and such a fine sight to see...etc.")* ... is at 2nd & Kingsley, the eastbound one way street. The Old Trails Museum is between 2nd and 3rd on Kingsley. It is a modest but interesting stop.

From Winslow to Flagstaff
West of Winslow, turn right at the access to I-40 to join I-40 at exit 252.

Site:

- Meteor Crater, south at 9 miles from I-40 at exit 233. The Crater is one of the few stops in Arizona that is not Government owned. It has been in private hands for nearly 100 years.

Leupp Corner
Continue on I-40.

Winona
Use exit 211 and turn right onto Camp Townsend-Winona Rd.

Flagstaff
At the junction with US-89, turn left and enter Flagstaff on Santa Fe Av. (nicely labelled as Route 66). Stay with Santa Fe Ave. Flagstaff is a dramatic contrast to the surrounding desert. Higher altitude, trees and mountains.

Sites:

- Museum of northern Arizona. On US 180 (Fort Valley Rd.). Admission: $4.
- Museum Club. A country and western nightclub born in the 1920's as a 'believe it or not' type museum. Lots to see even if you don't stay for the music and boot scootin'.
- Walnut Canyon National Monument: admission $3.
- Sedona and Alt 89 towards it, passing through Oak Creek Canyon. You'll pass the highest point in Arizona. Taking Highway 89 north from Flagstaff takes you through a really beautiful forest area and to the Grand Canyon. You can return from Grand Canyon to Williams, AZ, skipping only a small portion of Route 66 between Flagstaff and Williams.
- There is a annual Route 66 festival, in June.

Turn left onto Sitgraves St. and pass under the railroad. Pass Malpais Dr. and turn right onto Old Highway 66, (leaving US-89).

From Flagstaff to Seligman

Continue on Old Highway 66 to the I-40 at exit 191 and then join I-40.

Bellemont
Exit I-40 at exit 185. Conditions permitting, follow north frontage road through Branning Park.

Site:

- Highest point on old 66: 7320 feet.

Turn west as the pavement resumes into Parks, conditions not permitting, follow I-40 till exit 178

Parks
Continue west on the north frontage road, join I-40 at exit 171, or continue on graveled road (Deer Farm Rd.) and join I-40 at exit 167.

Williams
Exit I-40 at exit 165 and cross to the south side. Turn right towards Williams and pass under the railroad. Route. 66 westbound is Railroad Av. Route. 66 eastbound is Bill Williams Av. West of Williams, join I-40 at exit 161

Sites:

• Twisters, The Route 66 Place, 417 East Route 66 (Bill Williams Ave). If you are Westbound, look to your left in the 400 block of Railroad Ave. Twisters is on Rte 66 Eastbound, but you can see their sign if you are Westbound..

One of the more dramatic down hill runs of Route 66 takes you from the 7,000+ feet of Flagstaff and Williams to Ash Fork and Seligman.

Ash Fork
Exit I-40 at exit 146 and turn right onto Lewis Av. Join I-40 west of town at exit 144 and leave I-40 at exit 139. Turn right and curve around to head west onto Crookton Rd.

Seligman
Enter town just beyond the east overpass by turning right, then left. Note the newly reconstructed segment of Route 66. Knowledgeable people feel that further destruction of Route 66 is unlikely. This reconstruction is an encouraging sign.

From Seligman to Needles(CA)
Leaving Seligman, pass under the western overpass and continue on SR66.

Site:
Grand Canyon Caverns: 21 story elevator descent, always 56 degrees F. Admission: $7.50. What may be the only motel and gas station on this 150+ mile loop of Route 66 is here.

Nelson
Continue on SR66.

Peach Springs
Continue on SR66.

Truxton
Continue on SR66.

Valentine
Continue on SR66.

Hackberry
Continue on SR66.

Site:

• Old Route 66 Visitor's Center and Bio Regional Center. North side of the highway, west edge of Hackberry. Bob Waldmire sold the property to John & Kerry Pritchard in December of 1998.

Val Vista
Continue on SR66.

Site:

• An oasis of golf course, retirement community and multi family housing.

Kingman
Entering Kingman, pass under I-40. Route 66 becomes Andy Devine Blvd all the way through town.

Site:

• Quality Inn Motel in Kingman on the local 66 route...the entire place is dedicated to Route 66...breakfast area, front desk, lobby are full of 66 memorabilia. Also each room in the hotel is named/tagged for a person that was/is tied to the '66 legend.
• Lewis Kingman Park. No camping, but a beautiful place to take a break.
• Power House. Kingman got its electricity from this formidable building until the 1930's. An interesting Visitor's Center now occupies the building.

Follow BR-40 (Andy Devine Blvd) and turn left at the Y-intersection (away from BR-40). Follow the path of the Railroad through the narrow canyon and turn right at I-40 exit 44 (McConnico). Pass under the I-40 and continue past the on-ramp. Turn left onto Oatman Rd.

The road to Oatman is one of the most dramatic of Route 66. Ten mile-per-hour hairpin curves abound. The road is closed to any vehicle over 30 feet in length.

The dramatic Boundary Cone is on your right at the rudimentary rest stop. Exit slowly, the rest stop is gravel.

Oatman
Ghost town . . . sort of. It is a very popular motor coach destination and the T-shirt shops are side by side down the 7 blocks of main street. The people who live there think it's **great**. The burros you see in the town were brought to the area by early miners. They are surprisingly tame for "wild" burros and the people of Oatman will be **most upset** if you harm or attempt to take them as a souvenir.

Site:

• Oatman Hotel - no longer rents rooms, said to be where Clark Gable and Carole Lombard stayed on their honeymoon. Which would give you a feel for how far Oatman is from civilization.

Two miles west of Oatman, bear left at the Y-intersection and join I-40 at exit 1, some 15 miles south of the Y.

Route 66 - California - Detailed directions

From Topock(AZ) to Barstow
Enter California on I-40, use the second exit (Five Mile Station Rd.). Cross I-40 and continue till US-95. Turn right(=north) onto US-95. Cross I-40 at the US-95 exit.

Needles

Enter Needles on Front St.

ALTERNATIVE 1:newer alignment

Turn left into Broadway.

ALTERNATIVE 2:older alignment

Avoid Broadway, stay with Front St. Go one block left on F St., right towards G St. one block later, right again (on G St.). Turn left onto Front St. Turn left onto L St. Turn right onto Broadway.

ALTERNATIVE END

Follow Broadway over the railroad overpass. Turn left onto Needles Highway, follow as it crosses I-40. Follow as curves northwest. Cross I-40 at the interchange and continue on River Rd. Turn left at the Y-intersection onto National Old Trails Highway. Turn left onto Park Rd. and then join I-40 westbound.

ALTERNATIVE 1: original route

Use the US-95 exit. Head north for 6 miles on US-95. Turn west on Goffs Rd.

Goffs
Continue for 14 miles west on Goffs Rd. Cross the railroad tracks, then turn left to keep on Goffs Rd. (=southwest).

Fenner
Continue on Goffs Rd. Cross the I-40 and join the National Old Trails Highway.

ALTERNATIVE 2: 1931 bypass

Exit I-40 at the Mountain Springs Rd. exit. Cross to the south of I-40 and turn right onto the National Old Trails Highway.

ALTERNATIVE END

Continue on National Old Trails Highway.

Essex
Continue on National Old Trails Highway.

Cadiz
Continue on National Old Trails Highway.

Amboy
Continue on National Old Trails Highway.

Site:
Roys Cafe. Once a hub of activity, the Interstate reduced it to what you see now, a virtual ghost town. Sometimes gas is not available. Fill up in Needles or Ludlow.

Bagdad
All that is left of the Bagdad Cafe is the sign in the picture and a few pieces of concrete. The Bagdad Cafe of the motion picture is at Newberry Springs.

Continue on National Old Trails Highway

Ludlow
Continue on National Old Trails Highway. Turn right onto Crucero Rd., pass under I-40 then turn left to parallel the I-40. Turn left at Lavic Rd. (after 8 miles), cross the I-40 and

turn right to stay with the National Old Trails Highway.

Newberry Springs
Continue on National Old Trails Highway. West of town, cross I-40 and continue west paralleling the I-40. The Bagdad Cafe and Motel - where the movie was filmed - will be on your right.

Daggett
Continue west paralleling the I-40, join the I-40 at the Nebo Rd. exit, a marine base blocks old 66. After 2 miles, use the exit for the Marine Corps Logistics Base and turn left from the off-ramp, pass under I-40. Turn right onto E. Main St. You'll see signs about the Calico Ghost Town ten miles north of Daggett. Pretty commercial, but a few original buildings still stand and they do stage gunfights.

Barstow
Turn right at Montara Rd., cross under I-40. Turn left to stay with E. Main St., cross over I-15 and follow BR-15 (Main St.). Leaving the city, Main St becomes National Old Trails Highway. Interstate 40 ends at Barstow.

From Barstow to San Bernardino

Lenwood
Continue on National Old Trails Highway.

Hodge
Continue on National Old Trails Highway.

Helendale
Continue on National Old Trails Highway.

Oro Grande
Continue on National Old Trails Highway.

Victorville
Continue on National Old Trails Highway. Pass under I-15 and turn right onto 7th St. Follow 7th St then join I-15 southbound at the Palmdale Rd. Continue on I-15 for about 20 miles and take the Cleghorn exit. From the off-ramp, turn right, then turn left onto Cajon Blvd (half of a once 4-lane divided section). Join I-15 at the Kenwood Ave. exit and use left lanes immediately to access I-215. Leave I-215 at the Devore exit, turn right, then left onto Cajon Blvd.

Site:

- Route 66 Museum, on D Street in downtown area.
- Roy Rogers & Dale Evans Museum. North of downtown area, exit I-15 at Roy Rogers Blvd, turn left (=south). You'll see the stockade type structure of the museum on your left on Civic Center Drive.

Devore
Continue on Cajon Blvd. At the Y-intersection, turn right and continue under the railroad. At the next Y-intersection, left to stay with Cajon Blvd.

San Bernardino
Continue on Cajon Blvd., pass under Highland Av. Follow right turn toward intersection with Mount Vernon Av., turn left(=south) onto Mount Vernon Av. Turn right(=west) onto 5th St., follow the curves as 5th St. becomes Foothill Blvd. (SR 66)

From San Bernardino to Santa Monica(END)
Subpart1: from San Bernardino to Upland

Follow Foothill Blvd. (SR 66).

Rialto
Follow Foothill Blvd. (SR 66).

Fontana
Follow Foothill Blvd. (SR 66).

Rancho Cucamonga
Follow Foothill Blvd. (SR 66).

Upland
Follow Foothill Blvd. (SR 66).

Subpart2: from Upland to Pasadena
Follow Foothill Blvd. (SR 66)

Upland
Follow Foothill Blvd. (SR 66).

Claremont
Follow Foothill Blvd. (SR 66).

La Verne
Use the left lanes to pass under I-210 and stay with Foothill Blvd.

Glendora
Follow Foothill Blvd. (SR 66). (Foothill Blvd. changes into Alosta Av.)

ALTERNATIVE: turn right onto Amelia Av., left onto Foothill Blvd.

Continue across the intersection with Citrus Av., follow as Alosta changes back into Foothill Blvd.

Azusa
Follow Foothill Blvd.

Irwingdale
Cross the San Gabriel River, follow as Foothill Blvd. turns into Huntington Dr.

Duarte
Continue on Huntington Dr.

Monrovia
Continue on Huntington Dr.

Sierra Madre
Continue on Huntington Dr.

Arcadia
Continue on Huntington Dr., on the west side of Arcadia, turn right at the Y-intersection onto Colorado Place. Follow to the Rosemead Blvd. and follow it as it changes into Colorado Blvd.

Pasadena
Continue on Colorado Blvd. Turn left at Arroyo Parkway (also known as the Pasadena Freeway, first freeway in the United States - it is now on the Register of Historic Places) and follow it southbound. Colorado Blvd is where the Beach Boy's *Little Old Lady from Pasadena* put the pedal to the metal.

Subpart3: from Pasadena to Santa Monica

Pasadena
Follow the Pasadena Freeway. It is America's first true freeway and the engineering mistake of those ultra short exit and entrance ramps is clearly evident. It is virtually impossible to enter or exit anywhere except at the beginning and end of the road.

Los Angeles
Follow the Pasadena Freeway, after 7 miles, use the far right lane and exit at Santa

Monica Blvd. From the off-ramp, turn left and cross the freeway. Turn right onto Figueroa and one block later, right onto Sunset Blvd. After 3 miles, turn left onto Manzanita Blvd., follow as it changes into Santa Monica Blvd.

West Hollywood
Continue on Santa Monica Blvd.

Beverly Hills
Continue on Santa Monica Blvd.

Santa Monica(END)
Continue on Santa Monica Blvd. Route 66 ends here at Ocean Av. As you look across Ocean Blvd and to your left (=south), you will see the Santa Monica Pier. Its entrance is from Ocean Blvd and Colorado Blvd. The building on the south side of the Pier houses the carrousel featured in the movie *The Sting*. The Annual Mother Road Ride/Rally® begins it's eastbound run on the Pier and the westbound riders end there.

Site:

• Ocean & Santa Monica: A bronze plaque mounted on a stone base notes that Route 66 was called the Will Rogers Highway. Roger's ranch - visitors invited - is in the hills above the highway. He lived there while making movies in Hollywood. The plaque was placed in conjunction with promotion of the motion picture *The Will Rogers Story*. The movie company placed eight such plaques during promotion of the movie. One in each of the 8 states Route 66 passed through. The Santa Monica plaque is believed to be one of two that survive to the present day.

Eastbound (California to Illinois) on Route 66 - Turn by Turn

This set of instructions was compiled for those of us who wish to travel Route 66 from Los Angeles to Chicago. I started with the directions provided on the Route 66 web site, and transcribed them backwards. Where there was a choice of alignments, I generally tried to take the oldest possible road. This was a good start, and I tried to make some notes to refine the steps as I traveled the mother road.

I traveled the road by motorcycle, so I generally tried to avoid dirt and gravel sections. Some weren't bad, and I've made notations where it's okay to ride a street bike on the unpaved sections. There's a bad 17 mile section just west of Glenrio. My friend lost a tire on his bike there due to some baling or barbed wire. (we hadn't intended to travel THAT far on dirt, we'd expected it was only two miles long)

I'd be glad if anyone traveling Route 66 corrects any errors or adds clarifications to these directions. It's my hope that after a few revisions this document will be comprehensive. No doubt I'll update it the next time I travel it, but that won't be for at least another year.

Have a good trip, and remember to take lots of film with you! -Kelly Cash

Editor's Note: Because Route 66 - in a technical sense - doesn't exist anymore, no governmental unit is charged with it's maintenance and upkeep. **It would be a mistake for anyone to follow *any* "directions" to Route 66 with anything less than a great deal of caution.** If the road ahead doesn't look safe **you really do travel it at your**

Motorcycle Guide to Route 66

own risk. Don't let pride or "directions" interfere with your safety.

Directions from Santa Monica to Topock via Route 66

Start at intersection of Ocean Ave. and Santa Monica Blvd.
Head east on Santa Monica Blvd. Through Beverly Hills and West Hollywood
Right onto Sunset Blvd. south.
110 Freeway North. It ends on Arroyo Parkway.
Follow it North, It runs into Colorado Blvd.
Take Colorado Blvd. East; It curves around Santa Anita racetrack.
Follow to Huntington Dr. East, through Arcadia, Monrovia, Duarte.
Turns into Foothill, then Alosta, back into Foothill.
Follow Foothill East through La Verne to Rancho Cucamonga.
Follow Foothill East through Fontana, Rialto
Foothill becomes 5th Street. Follow east
Left onto Mount Vernon Ave.
Right on Cajon Blvd., follow it North.
It dead-ends, get on 215 North to 15 North.
Exit I-15 at Kenwood Ave., go under freeway.
Turn Right on Cajon Blvd. again, follow it about 5 miles. (One half of the
divided highway is open- looks like CalTrans gave up on half of the road!)
Get on I-15 North
Get off at 7th Street North.
Take National Trails Highway North (left).
Follow it east to Barstow, it becomes Main Street.
Main Street becomes National Trails Highway again.
Follow it East.
At Marine Corps Logistics Base, get on I-40 East.
Exit Nebo street, turn Left to National Trails Highway.
Take National Trails Highway East. (Right) Almost to Ludlow, take a quick left onto Lavic, then Right back onto
National Trails Highway.
Roy's Cafe: Lots of Route 66 Memorabilia, absolutely killer milkshakes! Doing things the legal way requires you to hang a Left on Kelbaker to I-40 east past Amboy, Get off at Essex Road Southeast (Right), then Left onto National Trails again. However, if you tip Roy well, you'll find that the locals simply drive AROUND all the barricades, and never leave Route 66. There's a blocked bridge in the middle of the barricaded section, but there's a PAVED path around it! One thing to note, however- as soon as I went around the barricades, my RADAR detector went berserk from X-band, and didn't shut up until I passed the final barricade on the other side. I saw no police, and was beginning to wonder if the barricaded section was radioactive!
At Essex, turn Left on Goffs Road. Cross I-40.
At Goffs, the Goffs road Bears Right. Stay with it.
Take US-95 South
Take I-40 South
Take US-95 South to Five Mile Station Road. It's unmarked, but it's there.
Turn left at the 'Y' in the road.
Take Five Mile Station Road East to I-40.
Take I-40 East into Arizona. Avoid signs telling you to exit for Route 66
before you get to Arizona. They're for old alignments that no longer exist.

Directions from Topock to Lupton via Route 66
Enter Arizona on I-40.

Take the first exit from I-40 onto SR66 East and follow the signs.
When you get to Golden Shores, go straight to Oatman.
Follow SR66 to Oatman
Take Oatman Road East out of Oatman
Turn Right onto BR-40 (It's Andy Devine Blvd., though not marked as such)
Pass under I-40
Turn Left at I-40 exit 44 (McConnico)
Follow path of railroad through narrow canyon
At 'Y' intersection, turn Right to remain on BR-40
Follow into Kingman
Quality Inn in Kingman is dedicated to Rt. 66. Don't miss it, it's quite a place. It has more memorabilia than the Route 66 Hall of Fame in Illinois.
Head East out of Kingman on SR66 through Valentine,
Truxton, Peach Springs, Nelson, Seligman.
Exit Seligman to the East on Crookton Road (SR66)
Crookton Road intersects I-40 before Ash Fork. Older alignment?
Follow to Ash Fork
Enter I-40 East
Leave I-40 at Exit 161
Follow Bill Williams Blvd. East
Pass under railroad
Enter I-40 at Exit 165, follow to Exit 171.
Head East on North Frontage Road
Re-enter I-40 at Exit 178
Leave I-40 past Bellemont at Exit 191
Take Old Highway 66 East
Turn Left onto Sitgraves Street
Pass railroad
Turn Right onto Santa Fe Ave. (labeled Route 66) at Flagstaff
Walnut Canyon- Ancient cliff dwellings

Santa Fe Ave. dead-ends into Walnut Canyon.
You have to get back on I-40. I couldn't find the frontage road. Besides, there's a lot of dirt road on Route 66 at this point.
At Junction of US 89, bear right onto Camp Townsend-Winona Road
Enter I-40 at Exit 211, through Winona, Leupp Corner
Point of Interest: Meteor Crater, 9 miles south of I-40 at Exit 233 Leave I-40 at Exit 252 West of Winslow.
Take 2nd Street (Rt. 66) East, go through Winslow
Find BR-40, Follow East(ish)
Turn Left onto frontage road on south side of I-40
Enter I-40 at exit 257
Leave I-40 at exit 269, Take south frontage road East
Follow frontage road East (to north of I-40)
Just West of Jack Rabbit, cross to South side frontage road
Point of Interest: Jack Rabbit Trading Post
Continue East on south side frontage road
At Exit 274, cross to north side frontage road
Enter I-40 at Exit 277
Leave I-40 at Exit 285
Take Hopi Drive East through Holbrook
Turn left onto Navajo Blvd.
Pass under I-40 at far edge of city
Enter I-40 at Exit 289
Point of Interest: Petrified Forest, Painted Desert
Leave I-40 at Exit 333
Do NOT follow north side frontage road East, it dead-ends.
At Sanders, enter I-40 at Exit 339
If you can travel extensive unpaved roads, follow this next section.
Leave I-40 at Exit 342

Note: May want to stay on I-40 through Houck and Lupton. 66 is dirt road between Exit 342 and Exit 339. But has Querino Canyon Bridge, Old Querino Canyon Trading Post points of interest.

Take north side frontage road East, onto dirt road, passing Querino Cross Box Canyon Dirt road becomes 346 (Big Arrow Road). Take it East to I-40, and enter I-40. Leave I-40 at Exit 354 (Hawthorne Rd.) Take south side frontage road East into New Mexico

Directions from Manuelito to Glenrio via Route 66
Enter New Mexico on SR118 from Arizona frontage road
Go through Manuelito on SR118
Cross railroad tracks
Turn Left, curve around intersecting road, cross over I-40 at Exit 8
Go about 3 miles on the south frontage road (SR118)
Pass under I-40, take north frontage road
Pass the I-40 overpass, continue East on SR118

Red Rock State Park
Follow Railroad tracks through Gallup
At East end of Gallup, cross over I-40 to north frontage road
Follow frontage road East, enter I-40 at Exit 36 (Iyanbito)
Leave I-40 at other side of Continental Divide (Exit 47)
Take SR122 East through Thoreau, Prewitt, Bluewater, Milan
Follow SR122 into Grants. Cross over railroad tracks
Find Sanders Avenue, follow out of Grants.
Find & follow SR117 East

Cross over I-40 at Exit 89, follow frontage road through tunnel
May want to take I-40 from Exit 89 to exit 96 if road is bad.
Take SR124 East through McCartys, San Fidel, Cubero, Paraje
Around I-40 Exit 114, turn left onto North frontage road, follow East
Follow east, pass Exit 117, cross I-40
Road conditions are bad. Should take I-40 to Cuerbo. Route 66 is dirt, and severe "washboard" which is quite hard on street motorcycles. It's not well marked, either. It's no fun at night.
Turn Left, pass railroad overpass, go into Cuerbo
Exit Cuerbo on SR6, go North on SR6 for 2 miles to Laguna
Follow SR6 (may need to ask directions) to Correo
Continue on SR6 to Las Lunas
Go two lights, Turn Left on 314 (Luna Ave.)
Continue on SR314 North through Pajarito
SR314 becomes Isleta Blvd. in Albuquerque.
Turn right onto Bridge Blvd., cross the Rio Grande on Barelas Bridge.
Turn Left (North) onto 4th St.
Turn Right onto Silver Ave.
Albuquerque Museum
Turn Left onto 2nd St.
Turn Left onto Lomas Blvd.
Turn Right (North) onto 4th St.
4th Street becomes SR313, follow it North.
Follow SR313 through Alameda, Bernalillo
At Algodones, enter I-25 at Exit 248.
Leave I-25 at Exit 267 (Waldo).
Take South (East) frontage road North.
La Cienega
Rejoin the I-25 at Exit 276, go for two miles to Exit 278.

Follow Cerrillos Road way up, it becomes Gallisto.
Turn right onto Water Street.
Turn Right onto Old Santa Fe Trail, cross the Santa Fe River.
Old Santa Fe Trail becomes Old Pecos Trail.
Cross the Pecos River.
Old Pecos Trail becomes northern frontage road of I-25.
Follow frontage road, enter I-25 at Exit 294.
Leave I-225 at Exit 299 at Glorieta
Take SR50 at Pecos, turn right onto SR63 South.
Take US84/85 South through Rowe
Cross to south side of I-25 at Ilfed/Sands
Continue on US84/85 on north side of I-25
Pass Riberia, Serafina/Bernal to Las Vegas
Take US84/85 south through Romeoville, Charles R Ranch, Los Montoyas,
Dilla. (84 is also I-40)
Leave I-40 at Exit 273. (by Santa Rosa)
Pass under Railroad, and bear Left at US54 junction
Cross Pecos River
Silver Moon Restaurant (East end of town)
Follow the boulevard East through Santa Rosa
Enter I-40 at Exit 277, leave I-40 at Exit 291 at Cuervo
Follow I-40 frontage road parallel to railroad tracks to Newkirk
Follow frontage road through Montoya, cross to north frontage road
Enter I-40 at Exit 321 (or at Exit 311 if you don't want to ride on gravel)
Leave I-40 at Exit 329 (Tucumcari Blvd)
Follow South frontage road to San Jon
Take old road (frontage?) past Endee to Glenrio-

But when you see the sign stating that "Pavement Ends", get back on I-40 East or you'll go on 17 miles of dirt road. The dirt is deep, and there's glass and wire scraps in it. NOT for street motorcycles.
Take I-40 East to Texas

Directions from Glenrio to Texola via Route 66
Can leave I-40 at Exit 0 to see a Ghost Town
Leave I-40 at Exit 18 (Gruhlkey Rd.)
Head East on northern service road (May be BR-40?)
Follow service road through Adrian, Vega, Wildorado, Bushland **The Midway Cafe in Adrian bills itself as half way (1,139 miles) between Los Angeles and Chicago. True or not, it is a neat place to take a picture . . . they have the mileage on their window and cut a great piece of coconut cream pie.**

Cadillac Ranch: On south side of I-40, West of Amarillo, take exit 60 from I-40, go toward Amarillo on the south access road 1.3 miles.

Get to Indian Hill Road, turn Left onto BR-40
Follow BR-40 into Amarillo, pass underneath Amarillo Blvd.
Turn Right onto 9th Street (east)
Just before Western, turn Left onto Bushland (northeast)
Just before Belleview, turn right onto South 6th Street
Cross railroad bridge, and turn Left onto Pierce Street
At intersection with US-287, turn right onto Amarillo Blvd. (US-60 & BR-44)
Turn Right onto Road 1912

Motorcycle Guide to Route 66

Turn Left onto Farm Market Road (#2575)
Get on frontage road, cross BR-40. Road curves towards I-40
Follow Northern I-40 frontage road east. Cross to south frontage road at Exit 89
Follow south frontage road Through Lark, Groom
See Leaning Water Tower East of Amarillo

Follow southern frontage road to Jericho, Enter I-40 at Exit 124
Lots of unpaved sections here, "Jericho Gap" Stay on I-40 to Alanreed
Follow south frontage road east, cross I-40 to Northern frontage road
Follow into McLean
Devil's Rope Museum, Rt. 66 Display, First Phillips 66 station (restored).
Cactus Inn
At County line road (exit 146) cross I-40 to south frontage road
Rattlesnake Sign
Continue on south frontage road past Lela into Shamrock
Frontage road becomes BR-40 in the city. Continue through.
U-Drop-Inn, Texan Route 66 Motel
Continue on south frontage road to Texola in Oklahoma

Directions from Texola to Baxter Springs via Route 66

Continue on south I-40 frontage road through Erick
Halfway to Hext from Erick, frontage road crosses to northern side of I-40
Heading to Sayre, cross river, take 4th street (US-283)
Bear right on BR-40 through Sayre
Take Northern Service Road towards Elk City
Service road will jog south of I-40 once towards Elk City
As soon as the road jogs, hang a left past the Texaco station across I-40.
In Elk City, Get to 3rd Street.
Follow BR-40 to Van Buren, BR-40 is also SR34i
(Weak directions here)
Follow northern frontage road East, cross to south side, to Canute
Follow southern frontage road East, cross to north, south, north again.
Past Foss, cross to south side. Ignore 2 chances to cross north.
Cross North, at I-40 take 10th St. North into Clinton
Turn Right onto Gary Blvd.
At Yield sign (may not be facing you!) turn Left onto frontage road (?) East
Follow North Frontage Road East, cross over I-40 to South Frontage Road
Skip next opportunity to cross I-40
Cross I-40, at |-- intersection , turn Right
Take North Frontage Road 6 miles (Ignore SR54) to Weatherford
Turn right on Rainey
Left onto 4th Street, Cross the Railroad
Go left onto Main Street
Left onto Washington
Right onto E. Main Street, Follow onto North I-40 Frontage Road
Bear left before the freeway
Follow North Frontage Road through Hydro, to Bridgeport
Take US-281 North to Geary
Take US-270 East to Calumet
Continue on US-270 (it bears South) back to North Side I-40 Frontage Road
Follow Frontage Road East for about 5-6 miles to Fort Reno
Follow SR66 East to El Reno. Becomes Sunset [Rd].

Right onto Choctaw
Left onto Wade
Right onto Rock Island Rd. This becomes SR66
Follow SR66 East through Yukon
Exit Yukon on Mustang Rd.
Follow East, over Old Bridge (Not Overholster)
(It's not easy to get to the old bridge, so Overholster may have to do)
Get back on 4-Lane SR66 East through Bethany, to War Acres
SR66 becomes 39th Street
Take 39Th Street East, Into Oklahoma City, Right onto Western Ave.
Left onto 23rd St., Left onto Lincoln Blvd.
Right onto 50th Street, left onto Kelley Ave. for approximately 5 Miles
Kelley dead-ends into Memorial Road. Take Memorial Road, then a quick right turn.
Left onto US77 North, 77 is also named Broadway. Go on it a few miles.
Get back on SR66 East, go through Edmond, Arcadia
Turn right on SR66, go through Luther
Follow through Wellston, Pass under I-44
After Wellston, pass under railroad
Continue East on SR66 to Chandler
Follow SR66 East through Davenport, Stroud, Milfay, Depew
Follow curves into Bristow
Follow SR66 East to Kellyville
Follow SR66 to Intersection of SR33 and I-44.
SR66 becomes Dewey, Left onto SR66 (Mission) into Salupa
Follow SR66 NE to Southwest Blvd. in Oakhurst
Follow 66E. It joins 44E. Stay on 66/44E. When they split apart again, follow 66E.
Follow it through Catoosa, into Verdigris

Take Lynn Riggs Blvd.
SR66 NE through Claremore, Sequoia, Foyil, Chelsea, Catale, White Oak
Take US60/69 East to Vinta
66 becomes 66E.
In Vinta, 60/66 turns right on Illinois Ave., and becomes 59/66/69.
Take US59/69 SE through Afton
Cross I-44, follow US59/69 through Narcissa, Dotyville
When approaching Miami, Take Steve Owens Blvd.
Turn Left onto Main Street.
Take US69 North to Commerce
US69 is Mickey Mantle Blvd. in Commerce. Follow it.
Take US-69 Alt North through Quapaw, into Kansas

Directions from Baxter Springs to Galena via Route 66
Enter Kansas on US-69 North
At Baxter Springs, Connect to 30th Street before commercial building
Left onto Roberts Road,
Immediately Right onto Military Avenue (US-69 ALT)
Take 3rd Street West
Cross Willow Creek
Rainbow Bridge is one way, north to south. 3rd street parallels the bridge.
Pass the bridge, then cross it from north to south over Bush Creek.
Rainbow Bridge
Follow US-69 North (jogs a little left & right), then East
Join SR66, cross Spring River to Riverton
At Galena, Take Main Street, Left on Jefferson, Right onto Front Street
Continue East past Galena
Follow road East, take "Old Route 66" hook to SR66

Follow SR66 East to Joplin, MO

Directions from Joplin via Route 66
Enter Missouri on SR66 East
Becomes 7th Street into Joplin
The following is a deviation from the signs:
Turn Left (North) onto Rangeline, becomes Madison
Turn Right on MacArthur Blvd. (US-71)
Follow US-71 East / North to Webb City
At Carthage, Take Oak
Left onto Garrison, right onto Central Ave.
Instead, we took:
66 East, past Rangeline, to 71 north.
Leave at 3rd Carthage Exit.
Turn Right onto SR96 East.
Follow SR96, go over Railroad tracks, across Spring River
Head due East on SR96 through Avilla, Stone City, Log City, Rescue, Phelps, Albatross
At Spencer, take Historic Loop, head towards Halltown
(we missed the historic loop entirely)
At the West end of Halltown, go from SR96 to SR266 East
Continue on SR266 through Halltown, Elwood, Haseltine
Enter Springfield on SR266, becomes Chestnut Expressway East
At 'Y', bear right onto College Street.
Left at the next 'Y' in the road.
Take St. Louis Street East.
Turn Left onto National, then Left onto Kearny Street.
Kearney Street becomes County Road 00. Follow it straight.
County Road 00 bends Right. Follow it out of Springfield,
Follow 00 NE through Mulroy, Strafford, Holman, Northview.

In Marshfield, take road "CC" North (it branches left)
Follow Road CC through Marshfield, Niangua, Conway, Phillipsburg.
Take Road "W" North, cross I-44. Follow Road W 9 miles.
Go towards 'W' fork
Road 'W' dead-ends into Elm. Turn Left onto Elm.
Elm becomes Mill Creek. Follow it straight.
Left on Outer road past Lebanon, cross over I-44
Turn left on frontage road
When Road 'MM' splits right, bear left to stay on the frontage road.
Join County Road "F" at I-44's Exit 135, go through Hazelgreen
Take County Road "AB" East through Laquey
Connect to Road "AA"
Right onto Road "P"
Left onto SR17
At I-44 Exit 153, cross to north side of I-44 on SR17
Follow SR17 through Waynesville
The following section was too hard to find, we wound up going
40 miles out of our way. We were running short of time and daylight, so we
just jumped on I-40 for awhile. Okay, it's blasphemy, but hey- Sue me. I'll
go back and do the road again later.
Cross over I-44 before St. Robert, head to Devil's Elbow
Take South Outer Road (I-44 frontage road) to Arlington
Cross I-44 at Clementine
Enter I-44 at Exit 172, then leave I-44 at Exit 176
Follow South Outer Road past Newburg and Doolittle

Follow BR-44 East through Rolla
BR-44 becomes US63 (Bishop Ave.).
This section was hard to find at night, nothing to see in the dark anyway.
Follow it across I-44, go onto North Outer Road
Follow North Outer Road about 8.5 miles
Cross I-44 at intersection of SR68 (Jefferson)
Continue North on south outer frontage road through:
St. James, Fanning, Cuba, Hofflins, Bourbon, Sullivan.
Road jogs Right at Sullivan, left onto Elmont
Back onto south outer road heading North
Follow North through Stanton, cross to north outer road
Cross to south outer road around St. Clair
Cross north, then south again before Gray Summit
Connect to SR100, pass through Gray Summit, Pacific
Take BR-44 to I-44, enter I-44 at Exit 261
Continue on I-44 through Allenton, Eureka, Peerless Park
Leave I-44 to join Watson road.
Continue on Watson Road through Crestwood, Marlborough.
At St. Louis,
Bear left onto Chippewa Street
Bear left onto Gravois Ave., onto Tucker Blvd.
Follow to 13th Street, to Florissant (Jefferson?),
Right onto Salisbury,
Cross McKinley Bridge (TOLL). The bridge was reported to be in bad shape, but it's fine. A fully functioning, working bridge.

Directions from St. Louis to Chicago via Route 66

After crossing McKinley Bridge, take Madison Ave. NE Actually, it's rather hard to get to Madison Ave., so take Spur 3 to Chain of Rocks Road.
Area was reported to be unsafe. It's a bit depressed, but not bad.
Madison Ave. becomes SR203. Take it NE to Chain of Rocks Rd.
Sidetrack- Hang a left on Chain of Rocks Rd, follow over first bridge. The road dead-ends to packed gravel. 1/2 mile of gravel to the Chain of Rocks bridge. Not bad for motorcycles. The bridge is impassable to vehicles.

Mustang Corral is supposed to be right by there, but we didn't see it.
Head East on Chain of Rocks Rd., turn East on Old Poag Road.
It becomes SR157.
Follow SR157 through Edwardsville
SR157 becomes Old Route 66.
Take SR157 North past Church of the Neon Cross, past Hamel.
There are lots of older original alignments of Route 66 which criss-cross over SR4. Most are reasonable to travel on, though some are dirt.
Left onto SR4 North through Sawyerville, Benld, Gillespie, Carlinville, Nilwood, Girard, Virden, Thayer, Auburn, Chatman
From SR4 North, connect to Spaulding Orchard Rd. East.
Go North on Chatam Road (SR4)
Turn Right on Wabash Ave., it then blends into MacArthur Blvd.
Head North on MacArthur, turn Right (East) onto South Grand
Turn Left onto 9th Street. (BR55)

Turns into Peoria Rd.
Head out of Springfield on BR55 North.
Follow BR55 through Sherman.
First 4-Lane section of Rt. 66
Take East side frontage road (of I-55) North.
Take I-55 to Williamsville. Frontage road becomes BR-55, and is still Rt. 66.
Signs clearly mark the route.
Follow east frontage road through Elkhart, Broadwell, Lincoln
The Mill: famous for schnitzel
Cross I-55 to west side frontage road
Follow west frontage road north through Lawndale, Atlanta
First Truck Stop- Always open. Dixie Truckers Museum, Rt. 66 Hall of Fame. Located in McLean.
Follow north through McLean, Funks Grove, Shirley
Cross I-55, continue NE. Becomes Beich rd.
Right on Springfield Road. Exit right for Main Street.
Left onto Main Street
Right on Willow, Left on Linden, Right on Pine
Pine becomes Henry. Follow it, then turn right on Shelbourne.
Follow NE to East side I-55 frontage road
Pass Bloomington, Normal, Towanda, Lexington, Chenoa, Pontiac,
Continue through Odell, Dwight
Marathon Oil Station - Rt. 66 relic
Take SR53 NE, Continue through Gardner
Riviera Restaurant
Continue on SR53 NE through Braceville, Godley, Braidwood
Gemini Giant mascot at Launching Pad Drive In
Becomes Baltimore Street, then Left (North) onto SR53 again.

Follow SR53 North into Elwood, SR53 may be called Douglas also.
Cross Des Plains River, Follow SR53 through Joliet, Romeoville, Bollingbrook, SR53 runs into Joliet Road North. (SR53 veers away from Joliet road)
Follow to I-55, enter I-55 at Exit 269.
Leave I-55 at Exit 276C
Take Joliet Road Northeast, turn Left on Harlem Ave. (SR43)
Turn Right on Ogden Ave. Follow it a long way.
Turn Right (East) on Jackson Blvd.
Follow to Lake Shore Drive.

Route 66 - Town by Town

Chicago, Illinois *(Population: 3,100,000)*

So, just **where** does Route 66 start in downtown Chicago? It all depends on which book or map you are consulting.

Old Route 66 originally began on Jackson Boulevard at Michigan Avenue, a few blocks north of the present-day Interstates 55, 90 and 94. After the 1933 World's Fair provided some reclaimed land, the start was moved farther east to Lake Shore Drive . . . at the entrance to Grant Park. In 1955, Jackson Boulevard became an **eastbound** (toward the Lake) one-way street. In other words: To be precisely correct, you would have to travel several miles the wrong way on a one-way street to be on the "original" Route 66.

Adams Street, the Westbound "paired" street to the Eastbound Jackson . . . is as close to the original as it is possible to get[10]. All of which is to say that **all** variations on the theme of: "Route 66 begins (or ends) at Lake Michigan & Lakeshore Drive" are close enough for highway work.

And, so, Just how far is it? Again, it depends on which resource you are consulting. In June, 1995, "all-the-wayers" participating in The Mother Road Ride/Rally© consistently logged more than the "traditional" 2,200, 2,300, 2,400 miles reported in various guides to Route 66. We submit the following table as a reasonable "real miles" gauge and will continue to incorporate reported mileages as they are made available to us.

From:	To:	Miles:
Chicago, IL	St. Louis	299
St. Louis	Miami, OK	310
Miami, OK	Clinton, OK	288
Clinton, OK	Santa Rosa, NM	310
Santa Rosa, NM	Chambers, AZ	329
Chambers, AZ	Needles, CA	330
Needles, CA	Santa Monica, CA	340
	Total:	2,206

Chicago's demotion from 2nd City to 3rd City has left it's many attractions undimmed. As with Los Angeles - or any large metropolitan area for that matter - one really needs to ask "Which Chicago do you want to see?"

Sears Tower (largely vacated by Sears Roebuck in favor of getting closer to their stores and customers) is five blocks West of The Mother Road Ride/Rally©'s start point. The **Museums** would take weeks to really see fully.

In that Grant Park is where Route 66 beings/ends (depending on your direction of travel), you may want to focus your sightseeing (pun intended) on the "Loop" and near Northside. **The State Street Mall,** (four blocks west of Grant Park) and Michigan Avenue (two blocks West) are a shopper's paradise.

A boat ride on the **Chicago River** will give you an interesting perspective on the city - as well as bringing you close by the Wrigley Building (built entirely on the profits from those little packages of gum). You'll also pass under the grid bridges so feared by motorcyclists and the main reason the "surface street" route suggested for motorcyclists is not recommended. I-55 to Joliet Road is the preferred route.

The **Shedd Aquarium** and **Adler Planetarium** are less than a mile South of the Route 66 starting point (on that long causeway jutting out into Lake Michigan). Both are world class attractions. **Field Museum of Natural History** is just across the street west and it is one long block north of Solider's Field - home to the NFL's Chicago Bears.

Adams Street intersects Ogden avenue (Rt 34) which feeds onto I-55 and the original Route 66 disappears. It re-emerges at Joliet

---

[10] The 1995 run of The Mother Road Ride/Rally© started in light rain conditions at Chicago. The route the participants took crossed steel grid bridges that are very little fun for motorcyclists in any weather and may be actually dangerous when wet. Organizers now favor arriving and departing downtown Chicago via the Interstate system in all but the very lightest traffic conditions and ideal weather.

Road (Illinois Route 53).South of Joliet Route 53 becomes four-lane. In 1943, Illinois authorized construction of what would be considered a high-speed, divided highway between Chicago and St Louis. It was designed to by-pass towns and provide a faster, more direct route. The Interstate Highway system followed through on that concept with a vengeance.

Funk's Grove, Illinois

The Funk family has sold maple syrup/sirup here since 1825. The 5th generation is now minding the store. Actually "store" overstates the case. The store is a small building out behind their house. Motorcyclists traveling the Mother Road have told us the Funks welcome one and all to their small corner of the Route 66 world. And such people, places and products are the warp and woof of Route 66. They make it a totally unique way to wend one's way across the country.

Springfield, Illinois
(Population: 120,000)

175 miles South of Chicago, 75 miles North of St. Louis on Interstate 55. State Capitol of Illinois.

Lincoln Home, Springfield, IL

A personal note from Kirk Woodward: In the early 1960's, I traveled to Springfield on business a number of times. Over the course of several visits, I was able to tour many of the Lincoln landmarks in the city. I found the Lincoln Home (8th & Jackson in downtown Springfield) and the Lincoln Tomb (Oakridge Cemetery) to be impressive counterpoints to Lincoln's life. The Home celebrates his life, and you can stand where he stood when he learned that he had been elected President. The Tomb is a truly awesome tribute - vastly richer and more elaborate than his home. It was built in the years following his death with public donations, so it provides an interesting insight into how the public regarded him. I see from the materials received from Springfield that considerable work has been done to enhance the blocks around the Home (now closed to vehicles) and I heartily recommend the stop.

The Lincoln Home

A great starting point for your tour of Spring field. The Quaker-brown residence where the Abraham Lincoln family resided for seventeen years (1844-1861) is a national treasure. It's located at Eighth and Jackson streets in the midst of a restored four-block neighborhood. Your tour of the only home the Lincolns ever owned will be conducted by National Park Service rangers. Free tickets are required and may be obtained at the Visitor Center near the Lincoln Home on a first-come, first-serve basis. The Lincoln Home, 8th and Jackson, Springfield, Illinois, (217) 492-4150. Hours of Operation: 8:30am-- 5:00pm daily, extended spring, summer and fall hours. Closed on Major Holidays.

Lincoln Tomb

The final resting place for Abraham, Mary Todd, Tad, Eddie and Willie Lincoln. (Oldest son, Robert, is buried in Arlington National Cemetery). Abraham Lincoln was buried in Springfield's Oak Ridge Cemetery at the request of Mrs. Lincoln after his assassination in 1865. The monument was designed by sculptor Larken Mead, completed in 1874, and paid for with public donations. The original receiving vault in which Abraham Lincoln was buried, as well as monuments to four Illinois governors, poet Vachel Lindsay, and Lincoln's law partner, William Herndon, can be seen on a tour of the cemetery. Ask about the Civil War Retreat Ceremony held at the Tomb each Tuesday evening during the summer. The Lincoln Tomb, Oak Ridge Cemetery, Springfield, Illinois, (217) 782-2717, Free Admission. Hours of Operation: March through October 9:00am-5:00pm Daily, November through February 9:00am-4:00pm Daily, Tuesdays (June through August) 7:00pm-8:00pm. Closed Holidays.

Lincoln's New Salem
Springfield, Illinois

20 miles NW of Springfield near Petersburg on Route 97. This reconstructed log cabin village contains 23 authentically reproduced buildings. Abraham Lincoln arrived here at age 22. As the town developed, so did Lincoln and his career. He worked as a laborer, store clerk, merchant, county surveyor, postmaster and captain of the local militia. It was during his six year stay at New Salem that he studied law and was elected to the State Legislature. A donation is suggested.

Bloomington, Illinois
(Population: 52,000)

There is a seamless division between Bloomington, IL and Normal, IL on the Main Street that traverses both cities. And there's a school at both ends of this Main Street. Illinois State is in Normal, Illinois Wesleyan in Bloomington.

BEER NUTS® Outlet Shop
Bloomington, Illinois

Shirk Products sells **four million pounds** of these every year all over the world. Their retail store has **free samples** (open Monday-Friday, 8AM-5PM. They'll also show a fifteen minute video on the production process if you ask. If you've ever eaten a package of these, they came from here. It's the only place in the world where they are manufactured. The snack originated in the mid-1930's as "Virginia Redskins" peanuts.

HISTORY OF ROUTE 66 IN ILLINOIS

1915:
>Pontiac Trail.

1918:
>Start of the paving the Pontiac Trail.

19xx:[11]
>Renamed to State Bond Issue 4 (SBI4).

1926:
>Completion of paving of SBI4.

1927:
>Route 66 Signs are posted.[12]

1933:
>Chicago: terminus at Cicero moved to entrance of Grant

---

[11] The exact date for this is unclear. We will value any information regarding this event.

[12] The original Route 66 was accomplished by "stitching" together existing roadways under the Route 66 signage.

1955: Park at Jackson Boulevard on Lake Shore Drive.

Jackson Boulevard became one way, terminus moved to Adams on Michigan Avenue.

1995: New Historic Route 66 signs have been put up, documenting the different historic alignments.

YOU CAN STILL GET YOUR KICKS ON ROUTE 66![13]

It rose from the shores of Lake Michigan, not far from Navy Pier at the intersection of Columbus and Jackson, angled through Chicago's big shoulders, followed old Indian trails through the 'burbs and then flowed across the Illinois prairie through what the poet Carl Sandburg called "the little soft cities" to the Father Of Waters at St. Louis.

Seven states later (Missouri, Kansas, Oklahoma, Texas, New Mexico, Arizona and California) it emptied into the Pacific Ocean at the Santa Monica Pier running, some say, from pier to shining pier. I first traveled it before I was a year old in a Model T Ford truck with all our worldly belongings loaded into the bed, as my family desperately sought work during the gut-wrenching poverty of the Great Depression, not terribly unlike the Joads and their fellow Okies did in The Grapes of Wrath.

Frank Lloyd Wright called it, "a great chute down which everything loose in the rest of the nation is sliding into southern California." Bobby Troup and Woodie Guthrie sang about it. John Steinbeck wrote about it and named it "The Mother Road." And everyone knew it as America's Main Street. It was the carrier of people, freight and dreams. It was the world's most famous and beloved road. It

---

[13]

Reprinted by permission from *Wing World* - the Gold Wing Road Riders Association magazine and Jim Seay of Mahomet, Illinois. *Wing World* is Gold Wing specific, but contains much material of interest to any touring motorcyclist. Annual membership for Gold Wing owners is $65, subscription is $30. *Wing World* GWRRA, PO Box 42450, Phoenix, AZ 85080-2450 - 1-800-843-9460.

was the tangible evidence of the ever-restless American Spirit. It was the paving of our Manifest Destiny. It was, of course, U.S. Route 66.

Jenkin Lloyd Jones, editor and publisher of The Tulsa Tribune once said of it, "Historians of the 26th Century should know that American kitsch and bad taste may have reached their height in 66's old alligator farms and 'Indian' trading posts. But 66 did indeed span the nation, give birth to the motel[14] age, and the winds that blew up its dust also blew up fundamental changes in America."

For a wonderful half century starting in 1926, U.S. Route 66 embodied and embraced the United States. Every week, television glorified it as Marty Milner and George Maharis headed their Corvette down its pavements and through our living rooms. Who cared that many of their adventures took place hundreds of miles away from the real Route 66? It had become a national icon rather than just a mere road. Nat King Cole and Bing Crosby sang Bobby Troup's romantic description of it on juke boxes and radios everywhere. And, of course, it was America's great storyteller, John Steinbeck who immortalized The Grapes of Wrath as the Joad family and the other Okies, displaced persons in their own country, drove it out of the dust bowl in search of the mythical promised land of California.

There is scarcely an American alive who is over the age of 40 who has not at one time or another dreamed of setting wheel to pavement along its way. But then, in 1976, the interstate highway system began replacing Route 66. By 1984, the job was done. Route 66 was no longer a part of our national highway system. Its signs came down, it disappeared from the road maps of America-and passed into the realm of legend. The Mother Road did not disappear from the hearts and minds of the American people. Nor did it pass from the hearts and minds of other fans throughout the world who had become fascinated with its mystique.

There are Route 66 Associations in Germany, France, Belgium and The Netherlands, as well as in each of the eight United States[15] through which it passed. One wonders why. Other U.S. highways were replaced by the interstate system and some are being replaced even as you read these words. But none of them have so captured the imagination of the people, many of whom have never even seen it, as has U.S. Route 66. Somehow, it has become more than just a few million cubic yards of concrete.

It was a 2,400-mile-long community, a continent-spanning celebration of the American spirit and character. And though it was taken off the maps, the spirit and character still thrives and can still be celebrated along that legendary pavement of the former Main Street of America, the Mother Road. Yes, even though the bureaucrats have declared it a nonentity, for the most part, the old pave-

---

14

People interested in the history of the American Motel will want to read about the evolution of two properties in Albuquerque, New Mexico in that section of this Guide.

15

The addresses of those Associations are in the Appendix of this Guide.

ment is still there and can still be traveled by the adventurous.

Here in my native Illinois, for example, 90% of the old road still survives. A rider can travel the 297.1 miles from Old Mile One to St. Louis, Missouri with less than 18 miles of interstate "detours." My wife, Priscilla, whom some of you know as "Big Bird," and I decided that we wanted to make that tour down the Old Road. It holds a secure place in our hearts. I was born on it. I also went to undergraduate school on it. Priscilla traveled it from her ancestral home in northern Illinois to her adopted home in Springfield many times. We met each other only half a block from the old City Route 66 in Springfield 35 years ago.

A ride down 66 would be a ride down our history as well as our nation's. We thought we might share the route through Illinois on the Mother Road so that you, too, could follow the first 300 or so miles of the Highway of Dreams; so that you, too, could still get your kicks on Route 66! The route we followed was from north to south, beginning at Old Mile One in Chicago. Whenever possible, we favored the older "alignments" or paths which Route 66 took, as it changed channels many times during its career as does any strong-currented stream.

If you use the following route sheet in conjunction with an official Illinois highway map, you should have no trouble retracing our route. Last year, under pressure from the Route 66 Association of Illinois and other groups devoted to the preservation of the Mother Road, the Illinois Department of Transportation placed Historic Route 66 signs all along its passage in Illinois making following of the Old Road even easier. Don't worry if you should travel several miles between instructions or signs-you are on the right road.

Take your time. Some of the Old Road is pretty rough from neglect, but you are not making this tour to make time. If you wanted to do that, you'd be blasting south down Interstate 55 to St. Louis, rather than traveling the Mother Road. (Do you think for one minute Bobby Troup could have written something like "Shuck and Jive on I-55?") Also, watch out for new construction and other road work. There may be a few detours not noted in this story. Remember, 90% of the old pavement is still in daily use. Join Big Bird and me, now, for a nostalgic ride down the Main Street of America.

1. In Chicago, turn off Lake Shore Drive onto Jackson Boulevard. At Columbus Avenue, you are at Mile One of U.S. Route 66. Turn right on Michigan Avenue, then left on Adams Street and left again on Ogden Avenue.

2. In the town of Berwyn, turn left on Harlem Road, then right onto Joliet Road. This blends into I-55 just after I-294.

3. At Exit 269 of I-55, take Joliet Road south to Illinois Route 53. Follow Illinois 53 through the "little soft cities" of Joliet, Elwood, Wilmington, Braidwood and Godley. An interesting side trip would be to see one of the few remaining bits of barn art, advertising Mail Pouch Tobacco. To get to the Mail Pouch Tobacco sign, simply turn left on Manhattan Road in Elwood and curve right immediately onto Mississippi Road. This

may be one of your last opportunities to view a vanishing American icon.

4. In Gardner, turn right on Main Street, and left at the second stop sign. Then angle onto East Frontage Road.

5. In Dwight, turn left onto Illinois Route 47 South. When 47 turns left over the railroad tracks, go straight on Waupansie Street. At the stop sign south of Dwight, turn left. (If you are a veteran, stop for some refreshment at The Beachhead-the local V.F.W. post-and ask for John, Sweet Old Bob, or Mudflap and tell them Jim sent you.)

6. Turn left on Odell Road. Be on the lookout for a classic Sinclair gas station on the right. This would be a good place to stop to take a photo of you and your Wing next to a another bit of vanishing Americana. You'll not have many other opportunities. At the stop sign south of Odell, turn left.

7. Proceed through Cayuga, Pontiac, Chenoa, Lexington and Towanda to Normal. Should you prefer an alternate route through Pontiac, turn left on Pontiac Road. This will become Lincoln Street and then Ladd Street. Turn right at the stop light and then left at the stop sign and back onto Old 66. (For an alternate route through Chenoa, turn left on County Road 3150N north of town. This road becomes Morehead Street. Turn right at the stop sign, then left on to County Road 2800E.

8. In Normal, turn right on Pine Street, left on Linden Street, right on Willow Street and left onto U.S. Route 51 which is Main Street at this point. You may, if you wish, nod at my Alma Mater, Illinois State University, as you pass by. A unique curiosity about the twin cities of Normal and Bloomington-it is the only pair of cities in the country which share a street with a university at either end-Illinois State University in Normal and Illinois Weslyan University in Bloomington. At any rate, follow U.S. 51 through Normal and Bloomington or, as an alternate route, you could follow Business Loop 55 through these twin cities.

9. On the south side of Bloomington, turn right on Business 55, then right again on Morris and left immediately onto Springfield Road. After that, take a right on Beich Road, cross I-55 and take the first left, which is still Beich Road.

10. Just south of the tiny towns of Shirley and Funks Grove, stop at the Funks Grove Maple Sirup (please note: it is NOT syrup!). The store is on your left. You'll have to drive back a ways off Old Route 66, and you'll probably have to honk your horn a few times, but you'll be rewarded with some of the best pure maple sirup (sic) you have ever put on your pancakes, along with a plethora of Old Route 66 stories.

11. In McLean, curve right onto East Carlyle, then left onto South Main. You are now at the Dixie Truckers Home and Truck Stop which also houses the Route 66 Hall of Fame of Illinois. Established in June of 1990, the Route 66 Hall of Fame of Illinois commemorates the people, places and events that gave Route 66 its special character in the state of Illinois. It features plaques and displays honoring each member of the Hall of Fame, as well as many other exhibits of historic and unusual interest. It is open year round and admission is free. Induction cere-

monies for new members of the hall of fame are held the second weekend of June each year. This year four new members were inducted. They are the Edward Bauize family of Eddie's Pure/Union 76 Truck Stop in Towanda, the Old Log Cabin Restaurant in Pontiac, Irvin Brothers, Inc. of Bloomingon, and Wilton Rinkel of Hamel. Together, their ties with Route 66 total 221 years and they bring to 27 the number of Hall of Fame members in Illinois.

12. At Illinois Route 136 in McLean, turn west, then left onto the road before the railroad tracks. Turn right onto Atlanta Road and continue through Atlanta on Southwest Arch Street. At the Frontage Road, again turn right.

13. North of the town of Lincoln (the only town in the country named for Honest Abe before he became president, and which he personally christened with the juice of a watermelon!) turn left onto Business 55 and follow its signs to Washington Street and turn left. Follow this back to Business 55, which is the old four-lane Route 66, and turn left. Alternatively, you may stay on the original road instead of turning on Business 55, a Johnny-come-lately in the development of the Mother Road in Illinois.

14. South of Lincoln, turn left at the Frontage Road Entrance sign. Just north of the town of Broadwell, look for the old Pig Hip Restaurant on the right. On our trip down Old 66, Priscilla and I were saddened to see that the restaurant, not only famous for its special ham sandwiches, but also for its clientele, is now closed. Ernie Edwards, the owner/chef of the Pig Hip was cutting his grass at the time and we stopped to talk to him. He is still as cheerful as ever, even though he told us that he is suffering from colon cancer.

With the state of his health and 51 years of business behind him, Ernie decided to give up the restaurant business. "Fifty-one years is long enough," he explained, "I don't owe it anything." Ernie and Priscilla knew each other pretty well in the old days when Priscilla worked at the Illinois State Library with Ernie's second, now deceased, wife. They began to exchange old stories. I listened. "I've had three good wives," Ernie told us, "and three good mothers-in-law. A fellow can't do much better than that." He then invited us into his den to look at his collection of Route 66 and Pig Hip memorabilia collected over those 51 years.

"The day I closed the restaurant, I had an inventory of $800 worth of Pig Hip T-shirts. Sold 'em all before close and had people begging me to order more," he said. "This is my dream, but I don't think it will ever come true," he told us, pointing to a large floor plan of the restaurant thumb tacked to the wall. "See these cubicles? Well, they'd be displays of famous people who I met on the Highway [the Highway becomes a proper noun when talking to people like Ernie!].

It would be a sort of hall of fame, although the people up at the Dixie beat me to that idea. Over here would be video terminals -we've got a lot of videos about the Highway, plus, of course, episodes of the television program. But I'm afraid I'm running out of time. I've been taking chemo and the doctor says I'm on the downhill side of things now, and, of course, they opened up that Hall of Fame up at the Dixie a couple of years ago."

He loaded us down with Route 66 Association of Illinois literature and one of his old business cards and thanked us for stopping to chat. He then prepared to return to his grass mowing. "You need a riding mower, Ernie," I told him. "Had one," he answered. "Sold the s---------! This is how I get my exercise. Can't get any exercise sitting on a riding mower!" He certainly does not look like a man taking chemotherapy for colon cancer.

He even made his special Pig Hip sandwiches for everyone who attended the Route 66 Association of Illinois picnic last September. We left Ernie mowing the grass around his home and his now-closed Pig Hip Restaurant, and headed south toward Springfield on Old 66. It was a happy/sad occasion. I'm sorry so many of my fellow riders will never have the chance to visit the Pig Hip Restaurant as they cruise the Old Road in Illinois.

Back to the route! Just north of Broadwell, turn left at another Frontage Road Entrance sign.

15. In Williamsville, turn right at the stop sign, cross over I-55 and turn left on the frontage road. At the three-way intersection, turn left. Cross over I-55 again and take the first available right. Ride south through the village of Sherman.

16. At the north edge of Springfield (where I was born, grew up, graduated from high school, enlisted in the United States Air Force and, later, met my wife) turn right at the direction signs to 5th Street and the airport. This road curves, becomes 5th Street and takes you through Springfield and, eventually, back on I-55. Just a half a block east of 5th Street on Capitol Avenue, on the south side of the street, is Norb Andy's Ta-BAR-In. The food is great, the fellowship warm, and on Wednesday through Saturday nights, the jazz is cool. And this is where Priscilla and I met for the first time 35 years ago. An alternate (but less interesting) route through Springfield is to merely follow Business 55 through the town, as it is a later path of U.S. Route 66.

17. Take Exit 88 off I-55 and turn right at the end of the exit ramp onto the frontage road on the west side of I-55. Go through Glenarm, turn left on Illinois Route 104, and get back on I-55 South at Exit 82.

18. Take Exit 80 off I-55 and turn right at the end of the exit ramp. Take the first available left in Divernon back on to the West Frontage Road. Continue through Farmersville and Waggoner. Watch for the Our Lady Of The Highways Shrine on a farm north of Raymond. This is another unique sight along the Mother Road, built by a devout farm family to remind travelers to pray for a safe journey and to invoke divine intervention in protecting them.

19. Turn left on County Road 1600N. Cross I-55. Take the East Frontage Road through Litchfield. This is a good place to stop for any need you may have for your Wing, as Niehaus Cycle Sales, a huge Honda/Yamaha dealership, is located right smack-dab on Historic Old Route 66 in Litchfield.

20. Turn left on Mount Olive Road, and proceed through town on Old Route 66 (a.k.a. North 5th Street) which curves left and becomes Illinois Street. Here, we recommend a slight detour. When Old 66 curves south, ride a block north instead, and visit the monument to Mother Jones, a union leader for miners in the turbulent labor movement of the early 20th century and a major figure in the American labor movement. Solidarity forever!

21. Turn left at the Mill Cafe south of Mount Olive. Go under the railroad viaduct. Take the first available right at Tom Cal Contracting. You will cross I-55 almost immediately.

22. Proceed into rural Staunton. Turn left on County Road 2075E. Turn left again on County Road 150N. Turn right on the Frontage Road.

23. In Livingston, turn left at the first stop sign (there is also a Frontage Road sign here) onto Park Street. Proceed through town and turn left at the Frontage Road Entrance sign. Continue on to Hamel. At the stop sign in Hamel, continue south onto Illinois Route 157.

24. Follow Illinois 157 to and through Edwardsville. Immediately north of I-270, angle onto the North Frontage Road. North of Mitchell, angle left onto Illinois Route 203.

25. Proceed through Granite City on Nameoki Road. Curve right onto Madison Avenue by the high school. Follow "McKinley Bridge" signs as Madison Avenue curves and becomes Broadway. Cross the McKinley Bridge into St. Louis, Missouri.

This concludes our nostalgic ride retracing the first 300 miles of Historic Old Route 66 as it cuts across Illinois, the first of the eight states it touches. But it certainly does not conclude Route 66. Much of it is still passable all the way to the Santa Monica Pier.

In fact, there is now a major motorcycle ride/rally each June that takes in the entire route, with participants traveling either east to west or west to east as is their desire. It is the second longest officially sponsored motorcycle ride/rally in the country, second only to the famous (or infamous) Iron Butt Rally.

For those of you interested in learning more about Route 66, I suggest the following books[16]: Searching For Route 66 (both first and second editions) by Tom Teague, Route 66-The Mother Road by Michael Wallis, Route 66 Roadside Companion by Tom Snyder, A Guidebook To Highway 66 by Jack Rittenhouse and Route 66: The Highway And Its People by Quinta Scott and Susan Kelly.

I recently saw a photograph of a sign, somewhere either in Texas or New Mexico, where some Route 66 buffs had replaced a sign on part of the old pavement which read "ROAD ENDS" with one which reads "THIS ROAD

---

[16] Many of these titles can be found at any large book super store . . . certainly they can order them for you. *"Motorcycle Guide to Route 66"* is **not** available in book stores. Purchase it directly from the publishers: HHJM, Inc. 2024 Heatherbrook Drive, Grapevine, TX 76051. 1-800-994-8251.

DOES NOT END!" I think that says it all. Yes, you can still get your kicks on Route 66!

Dwight, Illinois
(Population: 5,100)

Windmill with an Attitude - Dwight, IL

Route 66 enters Dwight from the North and traverses the village. The windmill is five blocks south of Route 66 on Prairie Avenue. It was built on a family estate in 1896.

Dwight has also restored the Pioneer Gothic Church that was built in 1857. They use it for community events and meetings.

The Prairie Creek Public Library is housed in a restored structure. Formerly a carriage house, the building was donated to the library district by the estate owners. The windmill, church and library are all listed on the National Register of Historic Places.

Mount Olive, Illinois

Soulsby's Station, Mt. Olive, IL *Picture from video "Ride Route 66-Illinois," HHJM Video, 817-488-4940*

Soulsby's Station has been here on original Route 66 ever since the road came to life. It is the oldest one still standing on Route 66. At 13 by 20 feet, the original station was smaller than the restrooms in many modern stations. Henry and his son Russell doubled its size in the 1930s, but it was never big enough to accommodate a car. Oil changes and minor repairs were done on a ramp outside. After their father died, Russell and his sister, Ola, ran the station until 1991. Russell finally sold the station in 1997. Its new owner is working with the Soulsby Station Society to maintain the site as a historic and educational attraction for Route 66 cruisers.

St. Louis, Missouri
(Population: 1,100,00)

St. Louis is where we transition from I-55 to I-44 to continue the Southwestward slant toward Oklahoma City. Interstates 55, 64, and 70 all cross the Mississippi River over the Polar Street bridge, just south of the famous arch.

You can see the **Chain of Rocks** bridge if you opt for the I-270 bridge (north of the Arch). Chain of Rocks is to the south of the I-270 bridge and carried Route 66 traffic for decades. It is now closed to traffic although communities on both sides of the river would like to see it become more than a derelict reminder of the past. Take Exit(s) 3AB from I-270 on the Illinois side of the river to reach Chain of Rocks Road and then go west to the bridge over some pretty rudimentary road bed. There is a dirt road turn off from Chain of Rocks Road just before the bridge that will take you down to the bank of the Mississippi and a terrific view of the bridge. In Missouri, take Exit 34 from I-270 for an easy 1/4 mile jog to the bridge entrance.

Why the 24 degree jog in the Chain of Rocks Bridge? Well, Randy Smith, writing in *The*

66 News! (Spring 1997 issue, page 6) says that engineers on the Missouri side were in such a hurry to get their half of the bridge done that they never planned ahead of what they were doing. In the middle of the river they couldn't find a solid rockbed to continue construction.

So, (Smith says) the Illinois engineers went a few hundred feet to the north to find solid rockbed that went out to the half finished bridge. The solution seemed adequate until semi-trailer trucks were allowed to use the bridge. Traffic from the other direction had to stop, in some cases back up to allow those big rigs to pass.

All of which, says James R. Powell writing in *Show Me Route 66/Winter 1997, Page 15* says is **Myth No. 4.** Just not so. Powell writes that the original plan was to build the bridge straight across the the river **but** the Corps of Engineers said that plan would place the bridge at too critical an angle to the flow of the river. River traffic would be endangered by having to maneuver across the current to pass under the main span. Too risky. The "jog" places the main span at 90 degrees to the current. A safer arrangement.

Who to believe? Take your pick. There are at least three other myths about the jog according to Powell. We like the "angle to the current" explanation because we find it hard to believe that such serious money would be spent without determining where the bedrock lay.

Originally **Chain of Rocks** bridge was a toll bridge. The city of Madison, IL charged thirty-five cents to cross. The tolls nearly paid for the entire operation of the City of Madison. When the "no toll" Interstate bridges opened in St. Louis, Chain of Rocks began an abrupt decline culminating in it being closed in 1968. In 1981 *Escape From New York* filmed extensively on and around the bridge.

Gateway Trailnet, Inc., based in St. Louis is trying to raise funds to preserve the bridge as a park and biking-hiking trail. If successful, they may just get the bridge re-opened to at least foot traffic. In June, 1998, Trailnet hosted a wedding and other festivities at the bridge.

The riverboat casinos are moored on either side of the river, downstream at the St. Louis Gateway Arch.. The Gateway Arch, at 630 feet, is the tallest thing in town. If you elect to take the I-270 bridge - approximating original Route 66 - you'll be way north of the Arch and won't see it. Take I-55 east of the river to its join with I-44 and head west. The Arch - and exits to the river front park area - will be on your right. The other factor suggesting the I-55/I-44 route is that I-270 has been "under construction" for years and choked down to one lane each way as late as June, 1998.

At the foot of the Arch is the Museum of Westward Expansion. You can take the passenger tram to the observation room at the top. An authentic slice of old St. Louis is left along the river front. A few blocks north of the Arch lies Laclede's Landing, a covey of red brick and cast iron facaded Victorian warehouses, cut by cobblestone lanes. Trendified into shops, bars and restaurants, the landing nonetheless has the feel of the levee to it, especially on a cool gray day when fog seeps in off the river.

The **Bowling Hall of Fame & Museum** is in the downtown area . . . across from Busch Stadium, 111 Stadium Plaza. The **National Video Game and Coin-Op Museum** is at 801 N 2nd where you can replay classic video games such as Pong, Pac-Man, Donkey Kong and Centipede.

Levee Line buses . . . painted to resemble river boats . . . circle every few minutes between Union Station and the riverfront from mid-May to December and they are free. The largest brewery in the world, the **Anheuser-Busch Brewery** at 13th & Lynch Streets, offers tours of the Clydesdale stables, brewing gallery, bottling plant, aging tanks and hospitality room where complimentary samples are offered.

The **Old Courthouse** @ 11 North 4th street is the 19th Century building where the Dred Scott trial began. Five museum galleries feature history of St. Louis. There are two restored courtrooms and the guided tours are free.

Rolla, Missouri

Kings Highway was the original alignment of Route 66 through Rolla. *(The locals pronounce it: RAH la).* The road east of the city is in good repair and you can follow Route 66 a good piece between Rolla and St Louis.

The University of Missouri at Rolla's civil engineering department has erected a half scale, partial reconstruction of England's Stonehenge at 14th Street and Bishop Avenue. It is oriented so that the rising sun at the summer solstice can be observed through the central trilithon. The school provides **motorcycle parking** at the site and it is an impressive sight. As you see it, ponder how people managed to design and build the full size Stonehenge in 3,000BC.

University of Missouri-Rolla's Stonehenge, 14th & Bishop . . . Business Route 44 in Rolla.
Picture courtesy of University of Missouri-Rolla

Buehler Park, 1300 Kings Highway, has been a favorite place to stop and rest throughout the life of Route 66. The Rolla Chamber of Commerce extends an invitation for motorcyclists to "take a break" at the Park. It can be reached directly from the Interstate 44 by taking **Exit 184.**

Springfield, Missouri

One of twenty-eight (28) *Springfield's* in the United States(!). Springfield, Missouri was a long time stopping place along Route 66. St Louis street was Route 66 in Springfield and in 1926 **serious** money ($300,000 *in 1926 dollars*) was invested in the Gilloiz

Theater in anticipation of Route 66 being at it's front door. The theater still stands. In 1956 - it is said - Elvis Presley watched a Glenn Ford western there before performing to a standing room only crowd three blocks away at the Shrine Mosque.

The Gilloiz closed in 1980 because of declining attendance following the population shift to the suburbs. Deterioration began. A non-profit corporation (Springfield Landmarks Preservation Trust) purchased the theater in 1992 and began restoration. More than a million dollars was raised to bring the theater back to use in Springfield's re-emerging downtown area. Visitors can also stop at a park a half block east. The park marks the location of the Jewell Theater where the ABC-TV Ozark Jubilee, starring Red Foley, was telecast live nationwide every Saturday night from 1955 to 1960. Country music thrives 60 miles south of Springfield at **Branson, Missouri.**

A Sleeper Puzzle
We are indebted to Sophia L. Dembling, a freelance travel writer who lives in Dallas, Texas for this bit of Route 66 information.

The little shop at Sleeper Junction and I-44, on a piece of old Route 66 about 55 miles from Springfield, boasts "The Largest Selection of Jigsaw Puzzles in The Missouri Ozarks." Possibly anywhere. A sign behind the counter lists the number in stock on any given day and the count averages between 1,500 and 2,000. If you are westbound, you'll see the shop on your right before you reach the Sleeper Junction exit from I-44. You then double back to the shop. If you are eastbound, exit at Sleeper Junction and follow the signs to the shop.

The working clock behind the counter is a jigsaw puzzle. The New York skyline above

The Puzzle Source I-44 at Exit 135

the counter is a 7,500-piece puzzle -- it took store owners Keith and Nancy Ballhagen 10 months to put that one together. (Actually, it took about two and a half weeks to work the skyline and water. The rest of the time was spent on the sky.)

The shop carries 3-D puzzles and two-sided puzzles. There's a puzzle of the Sistine Chapel with 8,000 pieces, and the what must be the world's tiniest puzzles, about two-inches square with 99 pieces. There's a puzzle of Amsterdam at night that lights up. There are two-sided puzzles and puzzles with five extra pieces. There are Clint Black puzzles and Reba puzzles and Vince Gill puzzles. A puzzle with an abstract painting by Jackson Pollack is one of the hardest in the store, Ms. Ballhagen says, and the 3-D puzzle of Big Ben is the largest.

The Ballhagens have puzzles from 35 different manufacturers, 10 different countries. The walls of the shop are lined with puzzles, the shelves stacked with them. And the Ballhagens hand-cut custom wooden puzzles. You can provide the photo, they'll cut an 8-inch by 11-inch puzzle with 140 pieces, or an 11 inch by 16 1/2-inch with 330 pieces.

The Ballhagens also make dollhouse miniatures to sell wholesale, and in their spare time, they work puzzles for display in the store. But they aren't what you'd call puzzle addicts. "I don't mind a challenge, but I don't like to get ridiculous," says Mrs. Ballhagen.

For more information, write Ballhagen Woodcraft, 25211 Garden Crest Rd., Lebanon, Mo. 65536. Call (417) 286-3837. The Ballhagens do not have a catalog, but if you know what you're looking for, they will do mail orders.

In June, 1998, the Ballhagens featured several busts - Darth Vader included - that were made up of 1/8th inch slices of hardboard. Scrambled the "slices" would be a formidable, unusual challenge for jig saw fans.

Joplin, Missouri   *(Population: 41,000)*

Exit I-44 @ Hwy 71 and go North to 7th Street - the original Route 66. The buildings located downtown between Main Street and Byers Street, from 1st to 10th are significant to Joplin's History. Eight of these buildings are listed on the National Register of Historic Places.

The original alignment of Route 66 ran Westward from Joplin to Kansas. The **Joplin 66 Speedway** is at 3406 West 7th Street. When Interstate 44 was built it turned more sharply towards the Oklahoma line and Tulsa, thus cutting off the few Kansas miles of Route 66. You may well want to jog off I-44 to the city of Joplin and then cover the few miles of Route 66 in Kansas before turning back in to Oklahoma for Miami and the Will Rogers Freeway.

The city of Joplin is named after the Reverend Harris G. Joplin, who settled in the area and held church services in his home. With the discovery of lead, mining operations began in the early 1800's and were only interrupted when the Civil War began. Joplin was incorporated in 1873.

Joplin celebrates it's mining history in the **Tri-State Mineral Museum.** The Museum, established in 1930 and operated by the City of Joplin was rebuilt and dedicated in 1973. Its purpose is to tell the story of the local zinc-lead mining industry that resulted in the founding of Joplin. Joplin was, at one time, the tenth largest mining town in the world.

Kansas

In all the "literature" on Route 66, there is no discussion of that state dropping off the Route 66 map when the Interstate Highway System was created and Route 66 was officially decertified in the mid 1980's. Given the historic nature of the political battles won and lost regarding highway building, this in itself is surprising.

Obviously the Kansas mileage was a jog over established roads - the original commission of the committee asked to create a national highway system was (more or less) just stitching together existing roads and linking them with a numbering system. Hence the "Ozark Trail," "National Old Trails," etc., that were stitched together under the number 66. In that the new Interstate Highway System was to be all new construction, they didn't face the same constraints as the earlier group. They were free to draw straighter lines of travel.

Three cities, Galena, Riverton and Baxter Springs were thus cut off from the larger plan. The "cutting off" created some unique distinctions. Kansas is the only state where Route 66 is not interfered with by the Interstate. Museums in Galena and Baxter Springs are guardians of the history of mining in the area and can testify to Quantrill's bloody 1863 raid at Baxter Springs.

Quantrill, William Clarke (1837-65), American Confederate guerrilla commander, born in Canal Dover (now Dover), Ohio. Before the American Civil War he was a gambler and, occasionally, a schoolteacher in the West and Midwest. Warrants for his arrest were issued several times on charges of murder, theft, and horse thievery. When the Civil War began in 1861, Quantrill, aided by the notorious outlaw Jesse James, headed a band of Confederate guerrillas in Missouri and Kansas, raiding farms and communities sympathetic to the Union.

In 1862 he was commissioned a captain in the Confederate army; that same year he was declared an outlaw by Union authorities. On August 21, 1863, he led his guerrillas on their most infamous exploit when they burned and pillaged the town of Lawrence, Kansas, killing more than 150 unarmed men, women, and children. In October, they killed about 100 Union soldiers at Baxter Springs, Kansas. Two years later the guerrillas were looting in Kentucky when a small force of Union soldiers surprised them and fatally wounded Quantrill.

Riverton, Kansas
Eisler Bro's Grocery - northside of the Highway - probably has the most extensive collection of Route 66 souvenirs you will see along the Route. This modest establishment is the place to stop to make sure you don't miss the turnoff (west of town) onto original Route 66 pavement. If you stay on the "main" road, you will be whisked on to Baxter Springs and Oklahoma, but you'll miss the beautiful **Rainbow Bridge** the community went to a lot of trouble to restore. You will also miss the Route 66 shield painted directly on the highway.

Baxter Springs
Look for the downtown bike shop on your right, a half block from the stoplight. There was a genuine antique Harley and restored Indian in the window. You also pick up the 'main' road south of the business district. If you are eastbound on Route 66, the turn off the main road in Baxter Springs is well marked . . . harder to see if you are coming into Kansas from Joplin.

Claremore, Oklahoma
(Population: 13,000)

Thirty miles East of Tulsa, Claremore's main claim to fame is it's connection with Will Rogers who in turn is closely identified with Route 66. Route 66 was often referred to as the Will Rogers Highway. A plaque near the end of the highway in Santa Monica, CA mentions it. Roger's ranch - where he lived while making motion pictures - was in the hills above the ocean in what is now Santa Monica.

Will Rogers Memorial & Birthplace
One mile west of Route 66 on West Will Rogers Boulevard. Claremore, OK is on a section of the original Route 66 that parallels

Interstate 44 between Catoosa and Vinita, Oklahoma. One of the early "nicknames" for Route 66 was The Will Rogers Highway. **You can also stay on Route 66 (now known as the *Free Road* by the locals) between Tulsa and Oklahoma City. I-44 is a Toll Road.**

Rogers was without equal in his time as an entertainer and personality. In our era of instant fame - and equally instant obscurity - it's difficult to conceive of a person as well known as Will Rogers. He lectured, wrote a newspaper column, appeared on Broadway, starred in a succession of motion pictures and was heard regularly on radio. No person before or since excelled in so many venues at the same time. A Paul Newman who lectures, sings, appears on television, writes a syndicated column and stars in a series of Broadway shows while continuing to appear in motion pictures might be a rough parallel.

The eight-gallery Will Rogers Museum of Claremore features Rogers early life. He rode horseback on the trail that would become Route 66 from his father's 60,000 acre ranch to Vinita, OK. In later years he travelled on Route 66 from Oklahoma to California. His California home - in Santa Monica, CA - was the toast of Hollywood and was just a few miles from the end of Route 66.

Another 12 miles West is the 400 acre living history ranch where the log house of Rogers birth still stands amid a herd of Texas Longhorn cattle. There are overnight hook-ups available at the 1879 living history ranch overlooking Lake Oologah.

Route 66 "Ribbon Road"

Miami, Oklahoma

Before the Interstates, before the 16 foot wide Route 66 of the 30's, there was the

Ribbon Road, Miami, OK

"Ribbon Road." You can ride a section of the original one-lane concrete highway with six inch border near Miami, OK. Go south of Miami on State Highway 125 to the Vocational/Technical Center on the west side of the highway. The road immediately south of the school is original "Ribbon Road."

Coleman Theater, Miami, Oklahoma

A 1920's era theater built at an original cost of $600,000 when Miami had a population of 10,000. 103 North Main Street, Miami, OK. Exit I-44 at Miami, OK (exit 313). Go West on State Highway 10 two miles to Main Street. Turn right (North) on Main for 4 clocks to corner of North Main and First Avenue, NW. Donations accepted. Tours Weekdays 9-4. The opulent Coleman Theater was on the Orpheum Vaudeville circuit. Will Rogers, Sally Rand, Tom Mix and many others appeared live on the Coleman's stage. The original Wurlitzer pipe organ has been restored and reinstallation into the theater has begun. When complete, this will be the only theater in Oklahoma with its original pipe organ in place.

Catoosa, Oklahoma

Many Route 66 "guides" have taken note of a defunct amusement center dominated by a large blue whale. While we understand that serious money has been made available for restoration of this Route 66 icon, in May, 1995 a sign read: "Danger! Don't mess around. Do not enter. Keep Out. You may be shot."

In June, 1998, the threatening sign was gone but the fence was still up. The Blue Whale did seem to have profited from a

Blue Whale, Catoosa, OK. *Photo courtesy of Roger & Jane Holm*

new coat of blue paint, but nothing further in the way of restoration had been done. It is interesting to see what a "water park" of the 1940's looked like.

Tulsa, Oklahoma
(Population: 504,000)

If the "Oil Bidness" has a capital, Tulsa is it. In June of 1901, a commercial oil-well was set up across the Arkansas River in Red Fork, a toll bridge spanned the river and the population exploded.

I-44 and State Route 66 will loop South of downtown, you would need to head downtown to approximate the original Route 66 although 11th Street (2 blocks South of I-244) and 10th street

Route 66 author lecturer, and Harley rider, Michael Wallis, makes his home in Tulsa. *Photo from video "Ride Route 66 - Texas."*

were also part of Route 66. Tulsa now has a series of one way streets in the central business district that will further confuse the issue of traveling the "original" Route 66. Bob Moore was quite taken with the richness of the art-deco buildings in Tulsa and heartily recommended taking the 'downtown' route through the city. The Art Deco buildings of Tulsa are the legacy of a "million-a-month" downtown construction boom in the 1920s. This distinctively extravagant style was the predominant expression of architecture of that era. Most of the buildings remain, their opulent lobbies and towers make the downtown core an art deco mosaic and mecca for fans of the style.

Plan at least a 'roll through' of the 11th Street alignment of Route 66 in Tulsa. A four-mile stretch of Route 66 is coming back. A ribbon of brick inlaid with ceramic Route 66 shields[17] now livens up the side

---

[17]

Please, again, **look but don't take.** One of the major problems groups re-establishing Route 66 signage face is people stealing the signs about as fast as they can put them up. There are several sources for these

walk as part of a $2,500,000 street and sidewalk reconstruction. The old bridge across the river still stands, although it is no longer in use.

Allen Ranch

Exit I-44 @ Highway 75, go South to 181st Street, then East to Memorial, then South 1.25 miles. Allen Ranch (Paula Allen, 918-366-3010) said that they are " . . . a working horse and cattle ranch offering Western entertainment to the public. Bunkhouse, horseback riding, corporate retreats and summer camp." They have a gift shop and charge according to the various activities. This might be an interesting stop - perhaps an unusual overnight stay in a "real" bunkhouse.(?)

Sapulpa, Oklahoma

Norma told Roger & Jane Holm that one of her patrons had been eating breakfast and lunch at her cafe every day for the past 37 years.

Norma of (naturally) Norma's Cafe in Sapulpa, OK. *Photo courtesy of Roger & Jane Holm.*

Frankoma Pottery is also located in Sapulpa, OK. They've been right on Route 66 for decades. One can visit their plant and see pottery in the making as well as shopping in their gift shop. The shop includes many Route 66 specific items.

Kellyville, Oklahoma

Watch for a "pocket park" and lake south of Kellyville. **Heyburn State Park** has camping space, mature trees, parking, etc., an altogether nice place to take a break.

Between Sapulpa and Oklahoma City you'll see a number of abandoned stretches of older Route 66. Most dead end and, because the right of way was returned to property owners, the signs have been taken down. They are now private property and there hasn't been any maintenance done.

Stroud, Oklahoma

The **Rock Cafe** has been hosting Route 66 crusiers 24 hours a day for many years. Don't be mislead by the sleepy nature of Stroud. Way back when, it was a Tough Town. Cattlemen shipped from here and a string of bars sold a lot of whiskey to them and visitors from the nearby Indian Territory.

Chandler, Oklahoma

The distinctive redstone **Lincoln County Museum** is an interesting stop both for the history of the county and Route 66. A bit further on see the movie theater on your left. It continues in business - somewhat surprising for a central business district theater although "improvements" to the structure have not improved the appearance of its elaborate exterior.

Arcadia, Oklahoma

---

reproduction signs priced from $10-$50.

The Round Barn in Arcadia has a distinctive history. That history includes a "grass roots" effort on the part of the citizens to keep the highway from dipping south of their city and the restoration of the barn itself. A plaque commemorates those efforts and the interior of the barn has a variety of interesting displays.

Oklahoma City, Oklahoma
(Population: 445,000)

Oklahoma City is where the Mother Road switches between I-44 and I-40. To bypass the central city, one would use I-44 Westbound, **I-44 Westbound most closely approximates an early alignment of Route 66.** In the Northwest section of the city (West of I-235) I-44 is designated the 39th Expressway. The bombing of the Alfred P. Murrah Federal Building in 1995 brought unwanted attention to Oklahoma City. The site of the building - now a memorial to the people who died (now known as the Oklahoma City National Memorial) - is in the downtown area of the city. The Memorial is most easily reached by taking I-35 south to its join with I-40. Head west on I-40 and exit at the Robinson Street exit to downtown. Work your way north to 5th street. The building stood between Robinson and Harvey Avenue.

Round Barn, Arcadia, OK
Picture Courtesy of Arch Archuletta

Oklahoma City was born in a single day: April 22, 1889. When a cannon was fired that day thousands of men and women raced into two million acres of the Unassigned Lands to stake their claims. The people who entered before the cannon blast stepped into immortality as **Sooners**. A nickname that persists to the present day: The Sooner State.

Oklahoma City also plays an integral part in the history of Route 66. Oklahoma City has ten historic markers along the existing stretches, and a number of businesses in the Bethany area (West Oklahoma City) have a strong Route 66 connection. According to the Oklahoma Route 66 Association, some of the places along Route 66 in Oklahoma City are . . .

Carlyle Motel - 3600 NW 39th Expressway, 405-946-3355

Snacks With Love - (snacks, souvenirs, etc.) 4625 NW 39th Expressway, 405-787-8558.

Mickey's Route 66 Restaurante - 4533 NW 39th Expressway, 405-789-8766

Ann's Chicken Fry House - 4106 NW 39th Expressway, 405-943-8915.

And Don't Forget to Feed the Meter

The first parking meter was used on July 16, 1935 in Oklahoma City.

Clinton, Oklahoma

Route 66 Museum, Clinton, Oklahoma. Located at 2229 West Gary Blvd, it is open Tuesday-Saturday, 9AM-5PM and Sunday 1-

5PM. Closed on Monday. Admission is $3 for adults, $1 for children. The phone number is: 405-323-7866. Joe Morgan, a retired engineer with the Oklahoma Department of Transportation told a reporter that "The Museum is good for Clinton but it'd be good anywhere they put it. A lot of broke people went over that road and became millionaires."

Route 66 Museum, Clinton, OK
(Photo courtesy of Oklahoma Historical Society)

Clinton is the home of the **Oklahoma Route 66 Museum**. They opened it with much fanfare on Saturday, September 23, 1995.

Oklahoma, by virtue of the slantwise course Route 66 took through the state, has more Route 66 mileage (396 miles) than any of the other eight states the route passed through.

The Oklahoma Route 66 Museum in Clinton is expected to draw 50,000-60,000 per year. It is the most visible sign yet of the revitalized interest in what people around Clinton still refer to as "the old road." The museum was built by the Oklahoma State Historical Society, a state agency, with $250,000 in contributions from the citizens of Clinton (population: 10,000) and an $850,000 Federal grant given for highway enhancement. It continues the grand tradition of Route 66 roadside attractions. There are also plans for the museum to serve as the flagship in a string of nine satellite exhibits to be sprinkled in small towns along the route. The museum includes a zany re-creation of a 1950's diner and the display of a 1928 International Harvester truck, the type depicted in the movie *The Grapes of Wrath*.

Hedrich Blessing writing about the museum from an architectural point of view noted that the building was designed by a native of Clinton, David Elliot. Blessing also termed it " . . . a superb regional specimen." He went on to write that "The museum's flat billboard facade and bright neon banding give it proper roadside panache, while its low, befinned roof resembles the back end of a 1959 Cadillac Coupe de Ville.

"The exhibits are arranged chronologically from the 1920s, when the highway began, to the 1970s when it finally succumbed to the interstates and lost its designation as a U. S. highway.

Sayre, Oklahoma
(Population: 3,000)

While Sayre is proud of their Southwestern Oklahoma State University campus (established in 1938) their major connection to Route 66 is their courthouse.

The Beckham County Courthouse was pictured in the movie *"The Grapes of Wrath."* The film makers chose Sayre to film a scene with the courthouse in the background because it was the only one at the time situated on Route 66, which was the road traveled by nearly everyone seeking their fortunes in California.

In 1910, a bond issue - which carried by a huge majority - of $70,000 was voted to build a courthouse and jail. It was erected at the end of East Main Street. The cornerstone was laid on April 19, 1911, only a few months after the election. An early day photo shows literally hundreds of people turning out for the eventful day. Construction was completed in late September, 1911 and by October it was occupied by county officers who were delighted to be moving to the most modern building known to western Oklahoma.[18]

On the dome's exterior was a place for a huge clock, but money was not available at the time of construction for that feature. For some reason, funding for the clock was never made a priority, and the courthouse has stood all these years without the clock. The elevator was added in 1949, central heat and air conditioning in 1964

The **Shortgrass Country Museum** and Historical Society is located in the former railroad depot right next original Route 66.

Texola, Texas

Texola Department of Corrections
From the Video: Route 66-Texas

As the name suggests, Texola sits squarely on the Texas/Oklahoma border. Entering the town from the east, watch on your right for an old time frontier jail. It is a favorite photo op for Route 66 cruisers.

Shamrock, Texas
(Population: 3,000)

At the time the Chicago, Rock Island and Gulf Railroad built its line across lower Wheeler County this city was called Wheeler. In 1902, a sale of town lots was celebrated by a barbecue at the site and in 1903 the railroad officially named the stop "Shamrock." A school was opened in 1904 and the town of Shamrock began to grow as a market and trade center. It incorporated in 1911.

U-Drop Inn, Shamrock, TX

There can be no doubt that Interstate 40 - which runs exactly on top of Historical Route 66 in this part of the Texas panhandle - is the "river" from which Shamrock draws a lot of water. Shamrock has right at 400 motel rooms available.

McLean, Texas
(Population: 850)

McLean's Route 66 Association led by Delbert Trew, a re-

The first Phillips 66 "filling station." Restored by McLean, TX residents. *Photo courtesy of Roger & Jane Holm.*

---

[18] Sayre led the way in Oklahoma road construction as well. The first paved road in the state was the New Liberty Road.

tired rancher, recently preserved the state's earliest surviving Phillips 66 station. Four years ago, they opened their own private Texas Route 66 exhibit as part of the Devil's Rope Museum, which displays more than 1,000 varieties of historic barbed wire in an old brassiere factory. In August of 1995 1,091 people visited the museum.

Trew told a reporter that: "The interstate bypass just devastated us. We wanted to do something to revive our little town. So we just gathered everything up." That includes a 15 foot tall Cobra head from the Regal Reptile Farm, once a prime Route 66 attraction, but now defunct.

Groom, Texas
Groom is home to two Route 66 icons. One old, one new. The old: That leaning water tower. The new: The Largest Cross in the Western Hemisphere. To accept that definition you have to believe that somewhere there is a repository of cross measurements, but, for SURE, it **is** a very big cross. Standing 190 feet tall and constructed of 50,000 pounds of reinforcing bar and 1,200 tons of concrete, the cross is impressive by day and awesome by night. It is a work in progress. Eventually a church will be a part of the project.

Big Texan Steak House, Amarillo, TX. If you can eat a 72 oz steak in an hour (with trimmings) its free.

Amarillio, Texas *(Population: 160,000)* Name is from the Spanish word for "yellow." The yellow was seen on the banks of Amarillo Lake and the many yellow wild flowers.

Sixth Street was Route 66. Traveling West from 6th & Taylor will give you a good feel for the original route. The free steak at The Big Texan Steak Ranch you've been seeing so many billboards about as you approach Amarillo used to be on Amarillo Blvd during the years that street was Rt 66. After I-40 opened, they moved South to the Interstate.

Palo Duro Canyon

Billed as "The Grand Canyon of Texas," it is 27 miles South of Amarillo off I-27 East of Canyon, TX. As you approach Palo Duro it is impossible to believe that such an impressive canyon is so near. You will see nothing but board flat
Texas all around you until you reach the rim. Then it's twisties and descent the equal of any canyon. There are over 116 campsites for tents and RV's of all types, plus riding stables, numerous picnic areas and miles of hiking trains. **For more information: 806-488-2227.**

Musical Drama: "Texas!"

Performed under the stars in a natural amphitheater, a 600 foot cliff serves as the backdrop as 80 singers and dancers take you back to the Old West. The sound effects are so convincing that people reach for their umbrellas during the thunderstorm scene. More than two million people have seen the production. "Texas!" is performed nightly **except Sundays**, from mid-June through late August. They also serve a "chuck wagon" meal before each performance. Call 806-655-2181 for information/reservations. (Or just show up, always looked like there was room for a few more when we visited.)

Historic Route 66 District
Amarillo, Texas

Amarillo Blvd, 806-374-0459. According to the Amarillo Chamber of Commerce, old San Jacinto is becoming one of the premier antique centers of the Southwest. Buildings that once housed theaters, cafes, and drug stores are now the homes of shops specializing in antiques, collectibles, crafts and other nostalgic specialty items. The Historic District is the mile between Georgia and Western Avenues.

Cadillac Ranch

Ten Cadillacs buried nose down in a field at the same angle as the Cheops Pyramids. In the spring of 1997, it moved from its original location further west of Amarillo. Leave I-40 at exit 60 and go toward Amarillo on the south access road 1.3 miles. Graffiti artists are welcome at the Cadillac Ranch.

Cadillac Ranch *Photo from video "Riding Route 66 - Texas"*

Tucumcari, New Mexico
(Population: 6,900)

Tucumcari was named after the flat topped mountain to the south of the city. A derivative of the Comanche word "Tukamukaru." By virtue of it's location, Tucumcari is often a stopping point forraffit travelers as their slogan: "2,000 motel rooms" attests.

Virtually every video producer has been intrigued by the flapping wings of the Swallow Motel in Tucumcari, NM. The motel is at 815 East Tucumcari Blvd (original Route 66). In June, 1998, Ken Lato, a participant in the 4th Annual Mother Road Ride/Rally stayed at the Blue Swallow and reported it clean and comfortable but not to be mistaken for a Four Seasons resort. The Bakke family now owns - and occupies - the property. They are making steady progress in their plan to renovate, renovate and preserve the motel.

Swallow Motel in Tucumcari, NM. *Photo Courtesy of Bill Mikesell, South Elgin, IL.*

Certainly there can be no question about the Route 66 monument erected on the west edge of Tucumcari... at their Convention Center. Dedicated in 1997 it features tail fins, hubcaps and a salute to the old road.

Seven miles west of Tucumcari, at the bluffs of the Llano Estacado, you are at the western edge of the Staked Plains that stretch from there into Texas.

The name "Staked Plains" developed because the land is so flat that early travelers drove stakes in the ground at watering holes.

The Santa Fe Connection

Early in it's life Route 66 looped northward from the Interstate 40 alignment in order to pass through the state capital of New Mexico: Santa Fe.

Santa Fe is one of the oldest cities in the United States. The Spanish explorations of the southwest noted the existence of the city as an important trading center. The city has preserved many of it's older buildings and the Palace of the Governors still hosts native artisans who display and sell their wares directly from the south portico on "market days."

In winter, Santa Fe is "ski country" and the mountains that make the skiing possible make for interesting "twisties" and scenery that is some of the most dramatic in the southwestern United States. Take exit 256 from I-40 (Highway 84) to follow the route to Santa Fe, or, if you are eastbound, take I-25 north to Santa Fe (I-25 is almost exactly on top of the old road) then pick up Highway 84 to Las Vegas, New Mexico and then south and east back to I-40.

St. Francis Cathedral in downtown Santa Fe, New Mexico. *(Picture courtesy of Alan F. Hill)*

Albuquerque, New Mexico
(Population: 400,000)

In Albuquerque, New Mexico, much of Central Avenue was a dirt road until the early 1930s, but was soon to be the city's section of Route 66. It would eventually be "crowded with commerce- car lots, chicken and burger joints, gas stations, and countless motor courts and motels."

The "Main Street of America" entered New Mexico at Glenrio, on the Texas/New Mexico border. In 1946 the town had a population of 84, a store, a gas station, but had no tourist facilities. Two-hundred miles later, westbound motorists entered Albuquerque, the state's largest city.

66 Diner, 1405 Central Ave NE, Albuquerque, just West of the University of New Mexico. A faithful reproduction of the roadside diner of early Route 66 days. *Picture courtesy of Jim Ross, Ghost Town Press.*

"Suburban growth had already begun to occur in subdivisions near the University of New Mexico in the 1910s and 1920s, and a small commercial strip extended along Central Avenue as far as Girard Avenue. With the realignment of Route 66 onto Central Avenue, the East Mesa began to transform. In 1937 federal monies were used to begin constructing buildings at the new State Fair grounds on East Central. At the same time

Central was widened to six lanes all the way to the grounds" (Kammer 1992: 70).

In 1937 Route 66 was "widened from the `Dip' [located in front of The Modern Auto Court] to a point 2.5 miles east. New paving was 60 feet wide with six traffic lanes as far as the entrance to the new Fairgrounds and a 4-lane road for the remainder of the distance" (Albuquerque Progress, December 1937: 5).

"Many improvements attracted commercial developers along the new highway. A commercial block including the Lobo Theater began east of Girard Avenue. Farther east, beyond the commercial strip catering to the area's new suburbs, roadside businesses catering to tourists began to appear. Although the Aztec Court had been built in 1931, catering to tourists coming into Albuquerque from US 60 at Willard and then through [Tijeras] canyon on what was then US 366, it wasn't until 1937 that large numbers of tourist-related businesses began to fill the roadside"

The opening of Route 66 along Central Avenue in Albuquerque in 1938 brought much-needed business to the Nob Hill area, the city's first suburb. The Modern Auto Court, opened just the year before at 3712 East Central Avenue, saw an increase in business prompted by the first New Mexico State Fair, held on October 9th through 16th, 1938. Visitors to the Duke City could also take in a movie at the newly-opened Lobo Theater on Central Avenue in the Nob Hill area.

Visitors were coming to Albuquerque from such foreign cities as Peking, London, Rio de Janeiro, Paris and Tasmania. The New Mexico State Tourist Bureau met this onslaught with state road maps and brochures and a keen awareness of the benefits of tourist dollars. The city of Albuquerque continued to grow with a 1940 population of 35,449. The entire Albuquerque metropolitan area blossomed to hold over 69,000 residents at the time. Motel building represented a boom in related industries as well. Sales increased for the suppliers of plumbing, furniture, linen, and electrical equipment.

According to New Mexico State Highway Department surveys, the average daily traffic count on Route 66 at the Texas line rose from 211 in 1928 to 300 in 1936-7 to 970 in 1940. In the decade of the 1930s traffic on Route 66 increased at least 300%. The increased number of tourist and commercial vehicles resulted in undue wear and tear on the already strained roadbed and necessitated ongoing maintenance. However, road traffic declined by one-third to one-half during the years of World War II. But as soon as the war ended tourist automobile traffic bounced back to even higher numbers. New Mexico was now known as the land of "ancient pueblos, volcanic lava flows, the Continental Divide, Indian reservations...and many Indian trading posts."

Following the war a boom in tourist-related businesses along Route 66 occurred. The expansion of roadside restaurants and tourist courts in the late 1940s and early Fifties attracted so many vehicles that New Mexico residents recall a "traffic jam" along the highway. But these "overcrowded conditions and the drivers themselves began to make Route 66 a dangerous road" (Kammer, 1992:88).

Route 66 was widened at the eastern and western limits of Albuquerque but the consequences of a transcontinental highway running through the middle of the state's largest city created serious problems in traffic flow. As a result of these "dangerous" conditions, improvements to the pavement and the straightening of the roadway took place and subsequently lured an increasing number of travellers to New Mexico. Average daily traffic along Albuquerque's Central Avenue climbed from 20,000 in 1949 to nearly 24,000 in 1952.

The construction of the Interstate Highway System through Albuquerque in the 1960s and Seventies marked the beginning of the end for Route 66. A new freeway was built which carried traffic away from the roadside businesses of the old highway. At some points along the new road the Interstate Highway was separated from Route 66 by almost two miles.

Albuquerque's annual Balloon Fiesta, first week in October every year, is the largest balloon event in the world.

Business owners were faced with either moving to be adjacent to the new highway exit and entrance ramps, or shutting down. Since the late 1950s and early 1960s the existing roadside restaurants, motels, and automobile service facilities along Central Avenue in Albuquerque were either supported by the local tourist trade or forced to close their doors. In 1985 Route 66 was finally decertified.

But a few of these businesses, opened in the 1930s and serving the needs of tourists for over five decades, still survive. Two examples are the Nob Hill Motel, originally The Modern Auto Court, and the Aztec Motel, the oldest motel on Central Avenue in Albuquerque.

Picnic spots, and scenic vistas abound in the Sandia Mountains east of Albuquerque. **The mountains average 10-15 degrees cooler than the city.** The ride begins east of the city. Exit Interstate 40 at exit 175, marked Cedar Crest and Tijeras. Indian traders, '49ers, and scores of early settlers traveled the same route.

Head north to the twisties, south if you'd like to pick up a detail map from the Ranger Station that is a mile south of the Interstate on your left.

The early inhabitants had many anxious moments during the full moon in September (the "Comanche Moon") when fierce Comanche raiding parties would sweep down this canyon to attack the valley settlements and carry off the harvest.

The mountains on your left are the Sandia Mountains. On your right are the Manzano Mountains. The Sandias were named because of the watermelon-pink glow that lingers on their heights at Sunset, the Manzanos were named for apple orchards planted in their foothills by Spanish settlers. Continue north on 14 to the junction with 536 and take a left. The route from here to the Crest is designated a **National Scenic Byway** by the United States Forest Service. It passes through four life zones and pauses at scenic overlooks on its way to the 10,678 foot Sandia Crest. The road is perfect . . .

two lanes, paved, all the way up. **With the possible exception of the old road from Kingman, AZ to Oatman, AZ this is the finest motorcycle road on or near all of Route 66.** And if it is a hot day when you arrive in the Alburquerque area, then this road is superior . . . will take you to 10,000+ feet and a cool break from the desert heat.

At the Crest, on a clear day, the view is 15,000 square miles - a 100 mile radius. And the weather is dramatically different from the valley below. Average rainfall is less than 10 inches a year in Albuquerque. At the Crest the annual precipitation is 38-40 inches and snowfall averages 111 inches.

Another fun way up to the Crest is on the *west* side of the mountains. You take Interstate 25 north from it's join with Interstate 40 and watch for Sandia Peak Tram signs. The Tram makes the trip to the Crest in about twenty minutes. There is a restaurant at both ends of the Tram.

Grants, New Mexico

Hard to imagine that Grants was a very rough, tough town during the heyday of mining in the area. Santa Fe Avenue was lined with saloons that featured open gambling and other unsavory entertainment for the miners. Today, a monument to Route 66 dominates a peaceful city center park and fountain. It is right next the New Mexico Mining Museum and the city's Chamber of Commerce.

Continental Divide, New Mexico
Here you

pass the highest point on all of Route 66. It is a community as well and there is a quarter mile or so of the Old Road you can ride, but it ends in a dead end. Neat photo opt at the gas station and they have a pretty good selection of Route 66 merchandise.

Oatman, Arizona

There is a loop of Route 66 between Topock, AZ and approximately 12 miles West of Kingman, AZ. At about the mid-point of that loop you'll come to Boundary Cone Road. The huge Boundary Cone, a dome shaped rhyolite rock is visible at some distance away. It was named by Army Lt. Joseph Ives in 1857 because the 35th parallel of latitude aligns through it's center. **Oatman** is a curiosity in itself. It is not

Boundary Cone
Picture from video "Ride Route 66 in Arizona" from HHJM Video, 817-488-4940

uncommon for it - and the Historical Route 66 highway - **not** to appear on highway maps.

It remains one of the most interesting "loops" of Route 66 still accessible in the United States today. As you ride it, imagine 20's and 30's vehicles struggling up the twisties. Several references mention the demands of the climb and that it was common to see abandoned vehicles that gave their last gasp on this stretch of road.

Martin C. Berke visited Oatman, AZ when he prepared his book on motorcycling in the Southwestern United States[19]. "Oatman was named for a migrating pioneer family who was massacred by Tonto-Apache Indians in 1851.

Oatman, AZ's most famous public relations workers.
Photo courtesy of Bill Mikesell, South Elgin, IL

Born in 1906 as a tent camp for gold mining, Oatman produced 1.8 million ounces of gold but nearly died when gold became a nonessential material in World War II. The town itself is well preserved -- the Oatman Hotel is on the National Register of Historic Buildings. Check out the dance floor environs and the room where Clark Gable and Carol Lombard honeymooned. It also serves as local hangout for a cast of characters, literally and figuratively. Mornings bring the inhabitants to the hotel for coffee and conversation. On weekends gunfights are staged in the streets. It's real tough to tell the actors from the residents. Movie makers have used Oatman and its setting for such movies as "How the West was Won," "Foxfire," and "Edge of Eternity."

---

[19] *Motorcycle Journeys Through the Southwest* should be in the library of every touring motorcyclist. It is available from: Whitehorse Press, 154 West Brookline Street, Boston, MA 02118. 1-800-531-1133

"Every day, wild burros enter the town to be fed by the tourists. Their ancestors were used for mining and freight hauling, but they were released into the wild as people abandoned Oatman. Today, they arrive daily around 10:30 a.m.

Kingman, Arizona
*(Population: 28,500)*The city was established in the early 1880s by Lewis

Powerhouse Visitors Center, Kingman, AZ

Kingman who located the route of the Santa Fe Railway. Kingman has been the county seat of Mohave County since 1887. Kingman and its historical downtown shops are part of the Arizona Main Street Program. **Andy Devine Avenue is Kingman's main street and the original Route 66.** It represents the longest remaining preserved stretch (160 miles) of old U. S. Route 66 left in the United States.

The Powerhouse Visitors Center is in the oldest known reinforced concrete structure in Arizona. Desert Power & Water operated the powerhouse from 1907 to 1927. That mass of reinforced concrete made demolition too expensive so it survived to 1986 when it was placed on the National Register of Historic Places. Now the building houses the visitors center, the Chamber of Commerce and a neat little Route 66 museum.

Old Route 66 Visitors Center Hackberry, AZ

On Old Route 66, between mile markers 80 & 81. Bob Waldmire, Prop. (This is the loop north of Interstate 40 between Kingman and Ash Fork, AZ. The longest stretch of the original route still easily accessible). This is a 1934 gas station/general store.

John & Kerry Pritchard with Buffy at Hackberry, AZ

Waldmire maintained it personally along with an intact 1930's "homestead" of 22 acres. It includes the old store, old house, outbuildings, meditation garden, 1/4 mile hiking trail and a home made, in progress museum. There is no admission charge and there is Route 66 memorabilia for sale. In December, 1998, Waldmire sold the property to John & Kerry Pritchard who intend to expand on the exhibits and create other reasons for Route 66 cruisers to stop by for a break.

There are no "chain" motels or hotels on this loop of Route 66. Accomodations are a good bit less than five star although they are available at Grand Canyon Caverns and elsewhere.

The building of Interstate 40, cut off this loop of the original Route 66. The towns of Nelson, Peach Springs, Valentine and Hackberry were not enriched by the change in course, but this does constitute the longest segment of Route 66 in The Mother Road Ride/Rally©.

Flagstaff, Arizona
(Population: 50,000)

Route 66 goes right through the center of town.

Museum Club - Flagstaff, Arizona

3404 E. Route 66, Flagstaff (East end of town). The Visitor's Center tells us that the

building is on the register of Historical Places and that they have Route 66 memorabilia for sale. The cover charge varies but the Museum Club is billed as a "genuine" country & western nightclub with dancing.

Seligman, Arizona

The Historic Route 66 Association of Arizona[20] stages an annual Route 66 Fun Run Weekend in late April of each year. It goes between Seligman and Topock, AZ (via Golden Shores, AZ with the direction of travel varying from year to year) and covers some 160 miles of "original" Route 66 (billed as the longest stretch left in the country).

---

[20] PO Box 66, Kingman, AZ 86402, 520-753-5001

Angel Delgadillo is President Emeritus of the Association and when not performing official duties, he can be found in the barber shop/visitor center right on Route 66 in Seligman. President Emeritus Delgadillo has been quoted in Route 66 videos as insisting that Route 66 will **never die** because people don't want it to die.

Angel Delgadillo's Day Job

And all indications are that it is a weekend jammed with activities. A Queen is elected amongst much celebration and dancing.

Holbrook, Arizona
(Population: 7,000, Elevation: 5,000 feet)

Route 66 goes through downtown Holbrook and you'll want to roll through. Period restaurants, motels and shops still offer the weary traveler old west friendliness. The motel with units shaped like Indian tepees has made every Route 66 tour book and video on the market today.

Perry Owens, local sheriff, is credited with bringing law and order to Holbrook back in 1888. It was the famous shootout with cattle rustlers at the Blevins House. That historic house still stands, as does the Bucket of Blood Saloon. The 1898 courthouse, now on the National Register of Historic Places, is the centerpiece of the town. Between June and August free Native American Indian dances are presented Monday through Friday from 7PM-9PM.

The Petrified Forest & Painted Desert National Parks
The Park and Desert are only a 25 minute drive East of Holbrook. A globally significant frontier for Triassic period paleontologists, it includes a portion of the Painted Desert with its incredible vistas and multi-colored badlands.

Picture from the video "Ride Route 66-Arizona." HHJM Video 817-488-4940

Williams, Arizona
(Population: 8,500)

As the *Motorcycle Guide to Route 66* has become more and more known, there has been increasing pressure to include sights and places not - technically - on Route 66. Because the **Grand Canyon**, Las Vegas, even Los Angeles itself fall in to that category, we have opted to include them and we know for certain why later editions

Dave Pouquett of Twisters in Williams, AZ, a Route 66 favorite. Picture from video "Ride Route 66 - Arizona."

of "niche" travel guides tend to get bigger and bigger.

The city was incorporated in January, 1890. Roughly 50% of the population are members of the Navajo and Hopi tribes. There are nearly 60 tribes represented in the city.
Grand Canyon of the Colorado River is 80 miles North of Williams, AZ. If you haven't seen it, then it certainly is worth the `detour' to see it. To give yourself some variety in the going and coming, you might elect to turn North to the Canyon at either Williams or Flagstaff and then return to Route 66/I-40 through the other city.

The Canyon's **South Rim** is your destination and it **is** a busy and popular place. You might consider stopping on Highway 64 just North of the Grand Canyon Airport to take in the IMAX® Theater's *Grand Canyon - The Hidden Secrets* movie. IMAX® is quite a show all by itself and the film gives you a view of the Canyon that would be impossible to get unless you had weeks to spend, a very strong stomach and a lot of money. After you finish the film, run on up to the Canyon for a "real time" look see.

If you have some extra time, there are numerous activities available to you at Grand Canyon, most of which are open year around. Flights over the Canyon are available or, if you prefer to keep your feet on the ground, there are hiking trails that probe the very depths of the Canyon.

Raft trips through the Canyon via the Colorado River are available from April through October. They originate from Lee's Ferry near Page, AZ. Motor, oar and paddle trips are available from 3 to 22 days in duration.

If you are unfamiliar with the Grand Canyon area, a guided motorcoach tour is recommended to acquaint you with the history, the primary points of interest, and the most outstanding overlooks in the South Rim area. And, if you prefer to park your bike in Williams, you can ride the **steam engine powered Grand Canyon Railroad** to and from the Canyon on an all day trip.

Winslow, Arizona
Business Loop 40 approximates the alignment of the original Route 66 through Winslow which achieved a degree of fame through the rock group Eagle's song "Take It Easy."

That famous corner in Winslow, AZ

("Standin' on a corner in Winslow, Arizona . . . such a fine sight to see . . . there's a girl my Lord in a flatbed Ford slowin' down to take a look at me.)

La Posada was saved from the

La Posada, Winslow, AZ

wrecking ball and re-opened as a place to stay in 1997. It is a beautifully impressive property - originally one of the storied Harvey Houses built to serve a nation that traveled by rail. The front door of La Posada faced the railroad - where Amtrak still stops twice a day. The back door was to Route 66 and it is through that back door that most visitors come to ooh and ahh about the elegance of the property. Before they are done the combination of private and public financing will invest $9 million dollars in restoring the hotel.

Needles, California
(Population: 5,200.)

West bound between Needles and Amboy, California.
Photo Courtesy of Bill Mikesell, South Elgin, IL

Needles is just across the Colorado River from Arizona. If you are Westbound, exit I-40 where Highway 95 and Historic Route 66 branch off. If you are Eastbound, take the J Street exit and cross back under the Interstate to Downtown Needles. Route 66 ran over two streets in Needles during the years. Front and Broadway. Front is the older section, Broadway the newer. Some of the old 'cabin courts' have been restored as bed and breakfasts.

Heading West from Needles means the Mojave. You'll find that the "locals" are reluctant to call it "Desert" because of the negative connotations connected with the word. However, it is rough country and we advise a full tank of gas in Needles or Barstow. If you elect to take the National Trails loop south of Interstate 40 gas is **uncertain** as is the road itself. There have been reports of wash outs and travel restricted to local residents. Certainly there can be no question that the road is **not** maintained to Interstate standards. None the less it **is** negotiable by large touring bikes and it was the original path of Route 66.

Historic Route 66 - Needles - Barstow
Leaving Needles stay on I-40 to the Highway 95 exit. You'll be pointed north towards Las Vegas. Take the Goffs Road turn off and head west to Goffs. You will wend back under I-40 and be on the National Old Trails Highway. Rather than leaving I-40 at Hwy 95 and going north, you can continue on I-40 to the Mountain Springs Road exit and then head to Essex, Amboy, Bagdad and points west. *The movie "Bagdad Cafe" was actually filmed in Newberry Springs.*

Oro Grande Main Street
Picture Courtesy: Joyce Wade

More than one Route 66 cruiser - arriving in Needles amidst triple digit temperatures - has opted to "lay up" in Needles and cross the leg between Needles and Barstow at night. That was certainly the practice during the early days of Route 66.

Oro Grande, CA
(©Copyright 1999, Joyce Wade, All Rights Reserved)

Long ago, before Route 66 passed through Oro Grande, California, the community bustled. In the late 1800's, the Indians established a trading post with the adventurous Mormons, who passed through here while making their way from Salt Lake City, Utah to San Bernardino, California. Oro Grande is 3000' high in the Mojave Desert of southern California, about 45 miles north of San Bernardino and 90 miles from Los Angeles.

During the period of gold discoveries, one of the mines was named Oro Grande, or Big Gold. Miners flocked to Oro Grande and established homes and a post office. Soon, the railroad was built through the Cajon Pass to Oro Grande. For awhile the town was named Halleck, however, eventually it was changed back to Oro Grande.

In those days, a weekly stage coach from the Butterfield Company brought passengers along the dry Mojave River bed though Oro Grande on their way to the Panamint; a range of mountains about 200 miles north. The lure of gold and silver in the Panamints brought miners in search of their fortune. The old stage stop

Antique Station, Oro Grande, CA
Picture Courtesy: Joyce Wade

in Oro Grande was replaced by a more modern structure in the early 1900's.

The railroad brought a great change to the desert and helped the small town to grow. Enormous deposits of silica and lime were discovered in Oro Grande and that began a new type of mining. In 1907, a cement plant was started near the rail line running through Oro Grande. Using cottonwood from the riverbank as fuel, a crude lime was used in mixing the mortar.

Today, the cement plant in Oro Grande had its origins from that frugal beginning. It was this plant that brought people to the community. Who would have thought that British pound sterling helped to develop the plant?

Mrs. Potts, the original owner, was able to prove to English investors that in quarrying limestone for the cement plant, rich deposits of gold ore would be uncovered. Therefore, the investors would reap a double return on their investment; gold and cement.

The community of Oro Grande has had its ups and downs. At one time, the plant provided company houses for their workers. The homes are still there but now are privately owned. Abandoned buildings are ghostly reminders of the little towns' history. Driving the National Trails Highway, it's easy to spot the abandoned buildings standing as ghostly reminders of another time. A few miles beyond Oro Grande, on old Route 66, stand three rock buildings; one said to be an old stage stop.

Route 66 brought over two million cars over the National Trails Highway in 1961 on their way through the Victor Valley to the blue waters of the Pacific. Today cement dust still swirls around the mill, dusting the sleepy little community of Oro Grande, on old Route 66.

Submitted by Joyce Wade 1999 All rights reserved

Victorville, CA
(Population: 61,000)

Victorville is situated 100 miles North and East of Los Angeles and 35 miles North and East of San Bernardino.. The city is just North of the San Bernardino Mountains, at the edge of the Mojave Desert.

Prior to the establishment of the Santa Fe Railroad through the Cajon Pass, Victorville served primarily as home to Native American Indians and as rest stop for Mormon and Spanish Missionaries as well as exploration expeditions. There was some mining and apple growing (the city of Apple Valley adjoins Victorville to the East) but it was the discovery of an underground water supply by an oil wildcatter that brought real growth to the Victor Valley. Victorville was incorporated on September 21, 1962.

With an elevation of 2,875 feet, Victorville is termed "High Desert." The annual rainfall is a sparse 4 inches per year.

The Roy Rogers & Dale Evans Museum is a major tourist stop in Victorville. Although Roy died in 1998, Dale is said to put in an appearance now and then at the museum in a wheelchair. Trigger, Buttermilk and Trigger II are all on display, thanks to the miracles of modern taxidermy.

The Roy Rogers Museum moved from Victorville to Branson, Missouri, in the spring of 2003. The Route 66 Museum, however, is still in Victorville and well worth a stop!

In November of 1995, The Old Town Victorville Property Owners Association celebrated the "Turning on the Lights in Old Town." The centerpiece of Victorville's Old Town is the Route 66 Museum smack dab in the downtown area on the old Route 66. **Exit from Interstate 15 at Victorville, D Street is South of the Interstate.** Victorville pulled together motorcyclists and classic cars for the event.

San Bernadino County, CA has more than 100 miles of original Route 66 roadbed - more than anywhere else in the nation, according to Beverly Pfrommer who heads publicity for the city's museum. The famous black and white Route 66 shield is prominently displayed across D street from the museum.

Audrey Burgess & Roy Rogers, May 29, 1997
(Picture courtesy of Audrey & Carroll Burgess)

The California Route 66 Museum at Victorville - "Where the trails meet" - is at 6th & D Streets in Downtown Victorville. Opened in the Fall of 1995 the museum seeks to present the best in both historic and contemporary displays regarding Route 66. The museum is made possible by the volunteer services and contribution of its members and patrons.

Old Route 66 - known here as the National Trails Highway - extends through Oro Grande, into Victorville and continues up 7th Street to what is now known as Interstate 15.

Barstow, California
(Population: 25,000)

Barstow represents the first "turning" from the Route 66/I-40 Westward course since Oklahoma City. Barstow is 134 miles east of Los Angeles . . . another "High Desert" (2,142 feet above sea level) community. Not very high compared to the mountains surrounding the area, but high compared to the Mojave.

In 1853 Congress voted to build a railroad to connect the Mississippi to the Pacific Ocean. In 1888 a depot, hotel and eating establishment was constructed "where the train tracks left the Mojave River and headed for the Pacific Ocean." The depot and area came to be known as Barstow after the 10th President of the Santa Fe Railroad, William Barstow Strong. Barstow incorporated as a city on September 30, 1947. Originally located north of the railroad tracks, Barstow moved south and uphill in the mid-1920's as the Santa Fe railroad repeatedly expanded its facilities. Area businessmen pressured officials to locate the intersection of **Route 66 and 58 near First Street**, the result being a tremendous overpass above the Santa Fe rail yards.

The rich gold and silver mining companies of the surrounding area plus the availability of land for industrial expansion led to Barstow's prosperous growth. The Barstow Chamber of Commerce bills the area as a "mini-metropolis" of 60,000.

Calico, a Ghost Town and San Bernardino County Regional Park at Yermo, CA (10 miles north of Barstow off Interstate 15) is open all year long, except Christmas from 7AM to dusk.

Calico Ghost Town Gunfighter

There are camping sites there in shaded canyons with hookups available by calling 619-254-2122. A by-gone age lives on at Calico. You can relive the dreams of long ago prospectors as you roam the tunnels of Maggie's Mine or climb aboard a railroad car destined for old workings to the north. Along the wooden sidewalks of Main Street, there are shops and attractions of every type. At each stop, you'll find anything from a ten-gallon hat to a three-course meal. **Did Wyatt Earp once walk the streets of Calico?** The brochure says "Yes." A few miles further on from Calico will bring you to the **Early Man Site** where artifacts dating back 50,000 years are carefully preserved

Los Angeles, California

Ken & Carole Davenport at the end of Route 66 *Picture courtesy of the Davenports*

(Population: 9,000,000)
As a visitor to Los Angeles, you first have to decide **which** Los Angeles you want to see. The top tourist attractions **in the world** are here in the Los Angeles Basin. Hollywood, Universal Studios, Disneyland,

The Beaches, Beverly Hills, Sunset Blvd, . . . etc.

The "official" end of Route 66 is Santa Monica Blvd & Ocean Blvd. The Bellevue Restaurant - at the NE corner of the intersection - has been doing business there since 1937. Across the street is the Will Rogers plaque (his ranch was in the hills above the sea when he came West to make motion pictures) and just to the South is the Santa Monica Pier. The Pier is the starting point for the Eastbound riders in the annual Mother Road Ride/Rally©.

Palisades Park - Beautiful end to Route 66

Purists among the Eastbound riders will take Santa Monica Blvd east through the city, others take I-10 to more quickly escape the city.

Peterson Automotive Museum

The history of Los Angeles is the history of the automobile. The Peterson, with over 300,000 square feet of display space, is a monument to the automobile in it's many permutations. It showcases over 200 vehicles at any one time **including the third floor which chronicles the history of Harley-Davidson motorcycles.**

For riders on the "surface" streets that wend through Santa Monica, Pasadena and the towns north of I-10, California's most historic roads and trails converge at the Thomas Winery Plaza . . . home of California's oldest winery. Free admission. Gift shop carries a full range of Route 66 merchandise plus mementos of the Thomas Winery and the South Coast Wine District.3

Motorcycle Laws Along the Mother Road

To read this table: Get information from the pertinent square, then read information from the **Legend**. The ● means that there **is a law on the books**. The law may be modified by a note from the legend. Example: Daytime use of the headlight. It is **required** in Illinois **and** a modulating headlight is permitted. In Missouri there is no law on the books regarding daytime use of the headlight and a modulating headlight is permitted. In Kansas, there is a law on the books about daytime use of the headlight: It is required for vehicles manufactured after 1980. If the square is blank, there is no law or other stipulation.

State	Helmet	Eye Wear	Head Light (Day)	MC License	Pass Seat	Pass Footrst	Radar Detect	Helmet Speaker	Mirrors L=Left R=Right	Safety Sticker
Illinois		●	●-4	●	●	●			●	
Missouri	●		4	●						●
Kansas	●-2	●-3	●-5	●	●	●			●(L)	●-7
Oklahoma	●-2	●-3	●-4	●	●	●			●	●
Texas	●		●-4	●					●	●
N.Mexico	●-1,2	●-3	4	?	●	●			●	●-7
Arizona	●-2	●-3	4	?	●	●			●	●-8
California	●		●-4,5	?	●	●		6	●	●-7

Legend

1. Reflectorization required
2. Required under age 18
3. Required unless equipped with windscreen.
4. Modulating headlight permitted.
5. Required for vehicles made in 1978 or after.
6. Single earphone only.
7. Random
8. Annual emissions, some areas.

And if your interest is solely about **helmets**, here is our best information: *(Source: http://www.usff.com)*

Illinois=No law; **Missouri**=Mandatory, all riders; **Kansas**=Mandatory, Under 18; **Oklahoma**=Mandatory, Under 18; **Texas**=Mandatory, Under 18, over 18 must be able to demonstrate $10,000 in health insurance; **New Mexico**=Mandatory, Under 18; **Arizona**=Mandatory, Under 18; **California**=Mandatory, All Riders.

Motorcycle Guide to Route 66

Riding Safe Along the Mother Road

There are also a lot of theories about riding in heavy freeway traffic. There seems to be a consensus about some concepts:

#1. Keep up with or be slightly faster than the general flow of traffic. This - in light traffic conditions - can position your bike in a "dwell" between "packs" of cars . . . that is a very nice place to be, try to stay there.

#2. The inside, "fast," lane is arguably the safest lane. **All the lanes will likely be moving above the speed limit** and being inside means you have fewer entering and exiting vehicles to contend with. You usually will have a small shoulder to escape to as well. **If someone starts blinking their lights at you, move over to the shoulder and slow down enough to let them pass.** You **won't** be able to go fast enough to satisfy these jerks and you **don't** want to "fight" with them - their ton or two of cold rolled steel means it won't be a fair contest.

#3. Don't look into cars as you pass them . . . you might catch the attention of the driver and **people drive to where they look.** Not healthy for you.

#4. **Ride in the <u>center</u> of the lane.** Yes, that **is** a bad practice in urban areas because of the oil drips that can build up and make for very poor traction. However, on the Interstate that discoloration in the center of the lane is from wear, rather than drips. The center actually offers slightly **better** traction than the tracks where millions of tires have polished the pavement.

More importantly: By being in the center of the lane, you will discourage cars from "sharing" the lane with you. You will also have a larger buffer between you and other vehicles.

The cars behind you **will be much too close to stop in the distance a motorcycle can stop in.** Try to maintain room ahead - the **full two seconds** - even though people will cut in. Think in terms of maneuvering rather than jamming on your brakes.

Group Riding: "Staggered" is the method of choice for groups of bikes traveling together. That is: You **don't** ride side by side. You ride two seconds behind the bike in front of you and one second behind the bike to your right or left. It never hurts to open up those distances as speed increases. You may also want to tighten up when moving through city traffic to avoid having four wheelers get between the bikes, although it is **not** a good idea to form up a solid block of twenty or thirty bikes.

A word about "lane splitting:" The laws are 'spotty' about whether it's legal or not. Few would argue that it isn't dangerous. A traffic jam is no problem for a motorcycle. That's why police departments in large cities maintain bike fleets. **BUT** running between cars **at speed** is for those pros. The Mother Road Ride/Rally© recommends plugging along in your lane, or, if you're ready for a patrolman's snarl, moving to the inside or outside shoulder to get around a jam.

Motorcycle Dealers Along the Mother Road

Illinois

Mr. James Lesko, Owner
SCOOTER'S WORLD
1534 S WESTERN AVE
CHICAGO, IL 60608-1824
Phone: 312/421-5383
Number of Employees: 1

Mr. Michael Heinberg, Manager
SOUTHSIDE MOTORCYCLE REPAIR
2347 S CALIFORNIA AVE
CHICAGO, IL 60608-3628
Phone: 312/847-5458
FAX Phone:
Number of Employees: 1

Mr. Edward Blake, Owner
SHAGG CYCLE SEATS
3315 S WOOD ST
CHICAGO, IL 60608-6811
Phone: 312/927-0487
FAX Phone:
Number of Employees: 1

Ms. Sales Manager
MOTORCYCLE FRAME UP LTD
845 W DAKIN ST
CHICAGO, IL 60613
Phone: 312/296-1199
FAX Phone:
Number of Employees: 4

Mr. Paul Wolf, Manager
CHAMPION CYCLE CTR
3625 N WESTERN AVE
CHICAGO, IL 60618-4779
Phone: 312/528-6500
Number of Employees: 4

Mr. Mike Kline, Owner
MOTORCYCLE ENTERPRISES
2311 W BELMONT AVE
CHICAGO, IL 60618-6422
Phone: 312/404-2345
FAX Phone: 312/404-6234
Number of Employees: 3

Mr. Jim Rashid, Owner
FOUR & SIX CYCLE INC
3110 N KEDZIE AVE
CHICAGO, IL 60618-6904
Phone: 312/539-4600
FAX Phone:
Number of Employees: 5

Mr. Charles Spinler, Owner
CYCLE ASSOCIATES
7811 S WESTERN AVE
CHICAGO, IL 60620-5823
Phone: 312/471-1300
FAX Phone:
Number of Employees: 4

Mr. Waldemar Hillstrand, President
CALCO PLATING INC
414 N WOOD ST
CHICAGO, IL 60622-6260
Phone: 312/337-6201
FAX Phone:
Number of Employees: 50

Mr. Philip Mc Caleb, President
SCOOTER WORKS USA
7117 N CLARK ST
CHICAGO, IL 60626-2407
Phone: 312/338-4242
FAX Phone:
Number of Employees: 1

Mr. Dick Flanagan, President
AIRPORT HONDA KAWASAKI
4520 W 63RD ST
CHICAGO, IL 60629-5591
Phone: 312/767-7280
FAX Phone:
Number of Employees: 4

Mr. Al Katz, Owner
LITTLE AL'S MOTORCYCLE
5353 N MILWAUKEE AVE
CHICAGO, IL 60630-1222
Phone: 312/763-5025
Number of Employees: 1

Mr. Eddie Tator, Manager
THROTTLE MASTERS MOTORCYCLE
3921 S ARCHER AVE
CHICAGO, IL 60632-1115
Phone: 312/247-5211
FAX Phone:
Number of Employees: 4

Mr. Bill Davis, Owner
RAY'S PLACE
5931 S ARCHER AVE
CHICAGO, IL 60638-2802
Phone: 312/735-0824
FAX Phone:
Number of Employees: 2

Mr. Jim Langer, Owner
LANGER PRODUCTS
2852 N CICERO AVE
CHICAGO, IL 60641-5129
Phone: 312/777-7741
FAX Phone:
Number of Employees: 1

Mr. Larry Nelson, Manager
CHICAGO CYCLE CTR
7320 N WESTERN AVE
CHICAGO, IL 60645-1814
Phone: 312/338-7320
FAX Phone:
Number of Employees: 21

Ms. Sales Manager
CHICAGO HARLEY DAVIDSON INC
6868 N WESTERN AVE
CHICAGO, IL 60645-4795
Phone: 312/338-6868
FAX Phone: 312/338-8868
Number of Employees: 4

Ms. Sales Manager
J P CUSTOM METAL PLATING INC
1750 N CAMPBELL AVE
CHICAGO, IL 60647-5206
Phone: 312/486-0466
FAX Phone:
Number of Employees: 8

Ms. E. Bookman, President
MUNICIPAL INDUSTRIES
1134 N KILBOURN AVE
CHICAGO, IL 60651-3316
Phone: 312/252-0231
FAX Phone:
Number of Employees: 6

Ms. Sales Manager
PURPLE HOG
612 N MAIN ST
BLOOMINGTON, IL 61701
Phone: 309/828-4032
FAX Phone:
Number of Employees: 2

Ms. Winnie Feken, Owner
CHUCK'S HARLEY DAVIDSON
2027 E IRELAND GROVE RD
BLOOMINGTON, IL 61704-7103
Phone: 309/662-1648
Number of Employees: 4

Mr. Steve Karsten, Manager
SPORTLAND HONDA YAMAHA
2045 E IRELAND GROVE RD
BLOOMINGTON, IL 61704-7103
Phone: 309/662-0508
FAX Phone:
Number of Employees: 12

Mr. John Capodice, Owner
CAPODICE SUZUKI KAWASAKI
2434 S MAIN ST
BLOOMINGTON, IL 61704-7335
Phone: 309/829-6383
FAX Phone:
Number of Employees: 4

Ms. Sales Manager
MOTORCYCLES & SUPPLIES
805 E LOCUST ST
FAIRBURY, IL 61739-1305
Phone: 815/692-3769
FAX Phone:
Number of Employees: 4

Mr. Fred Garrels, Owner
GARRELS HONDA
RR 116 E
PONTIAC, IL 61764
Phone: 815/842-3175
FAX Phone:
Number of Employees: 4

Mr. Fred Garrels, Owner
GARRELS HONDA
RR 116 E
PONTIAC, IL 61764
Phone: 815/842-3175
FAX Phone:
Number of Employees: 4

Mr. David Ayers, Owner
SPRINGFIELD CYCLE SPORTS LTD
2912 N GRAND AVE E
SPRINGFIELD, IL 62702
Phone: 217/528-5859
FAX Phone:
Number of Employees: 6

Mr. Charlie Roberts, Owner
YAMAHA-SUZUKI OF SPRINGFIELD
1701 N DIRKSEN PKY
SPRINGFIELD, IL 62702-2115
Phone: 217/544-0126
FAX Phone:
Number of Employees: 6

Mr. Bill Mc Carthy, Owner
MC CARTHY CO
1100 N PARK AVE
SPRINGFIELD, IL 62702-3639
Phone: 217/753-8627
FAX Phone:
Number of Employees: 14

Mr. Dean Huston, Owner
CYCLE CONCEPTS INC
300 S DIRKSEN PKY
SPRINGFIELD, IL 62703-2105
Phone: 217/528-1898
FAX Phone:
Number of Employees: 4

Mr. Stan Hall, Owner
HALL'S HARLEY DAVIDSON
3755 N DIRKSEN PKY
SPRINGFIELD, IL 62707-7612
Phone: 217/528-8356
FAX Phone:
Number of Employees: 9

Missouri

Mr. John Stdko, Manager
E & M MOTORCYCLE
2218 S JEFFERSON AVE
ST LOUIS, MO 63104-2212
Phone: 314/773-4900
FAX Phone:
Number of Employees: 20

Mr. Bill Heggarty, President
BMW MOTORRAD OF ST LOUIS INC
4011 FOREST PARK AVE
ST LOUIS, MO 63108-3213
Phone: 314/531-4010
FAX Phone:
Number of Employees: 12

Mr. Steve Shackman, Owner
HENDERSON MOTORCYCLE CO
4207 HUNT AVE REAR
ST LOUIS, MO 63110-3801
Phone: 314/535-3818
FAX Phone:
Number of Employees: 1

Ms. Sales Manager
PLR RACING
2328 N LINDBERGH BLVD
OVERLAND, MO 63114-1626
Phone: 314/426-6633
FAX Phone:
Number of Employees: 4

Mr. Bob Korn, Owner
KORN'S CYCLE SVC
9440 BRECKENRIDGE RD
OVERLAND, MO 63114-2935
Phone: 314/423-5455
FAX Phone:
Number of Employees: 3

Mr. John Lichtenberg, Manager
BOB SCHULTZ MOTORCYCLE MARKET
8966 SAINT CHARLES ROCK RD
OVERLAND, MO 63114-4238
Phone: 314/428-4440
FAX Phone:
Number of Employees: 7

Ms. Sales Manager
STREETS UNLIMITED
4215 W NATURAL BRIDGE AVE
ST LOUIS, MO 63115-2843
Phone: 314/535-7930
FAX Phone:
Number of Employees: 4

Mr. Ron Widman, Owner
WIDMAN HARLEY DAVIDSON SUZUKI
3628 S BROADWAY
ST LOUIS, MO 63118
Phone: 314/771-2531
FAX Phone:
Number of Employees: 10

Mr. Ralph Schneiderwind, Vice President
DOC'S HARLEY DAVIDSON SALES 930 S KIRKWOOD RD
ST LOUIS, MO 63122
Phone: 314/965-0166
Number of Employees: 5

Ms. Dave Larsen, Owner
DAVE MUNGENAST ST LOUIS HONDA
5935 S LINDBERGH BLVD
ST LOUIS, MO 63123
Phone: 314/894-9179
Number of Employees: 8

Mr. Richard Willey, Owner
CYCLE CITY ENGINEERING
9630 GRAVOIS RD
ST LOUIS, MO 63123-4345
Phone: 314/631-3914
FAX Phone:
Number of Employees: 3

Mr. Richard Kniest, Owner
RICH'S CYCLE CTR
9500 GRAVOIS RD
ST LOUIS, MO 63123-4532
Phone: 314/631-1300
FAX Phone:
Number of Employees: 3

Mr. Larry Whalen, Manager
DONELSON CYCLES INC
11334 CONCORD VILLAGE
AFFTON, MO 63123-6906
Phone: 314/849-1830
FAX Phone:
Number of Employees: 6

Ms. Patty Bianco, Owner
BIANCO OLDSMOBILE & LEASING
6201 S LINDBERGH BLVD
ST LOUIS, MO 63123-7801
Phone: 314/894-2311
FAX Phone:
Number of Employees: 55

Mr. James F. Brady Jr., Owner
WORLD CYCLE INC
611 EASTGATE AVE
ST LOUIS, MO 63130-4819
Phone: 314/727-6543
FAX Phone:
Number of Employees: 3

Mr. Mike Hance, Owner
ROADWORTHY MOTORCYCLES INC
7020 PAGE AVE
ST LOUIS, MO 63133-1518
Phone: 314/725-9203
FAX Phone: 314/862-2249
Number of Employees: 1

Mr. Gary Meyer, Owner
ARCHWAY INTERNATIONAL CYCLE
6300 DR MARTIN LUTHER KING DR
ST LOUIS, MO 63133-2421
Phone: 314/383-4644
FAX Phone:
Number of Employees: 4

Mr. Jim Palmer, Owner
MIDWEST KAWASAKI SUZUKI
235 S FLORISSANT RD
FERGUSON, MO 63135-2735
Phone: 314/524-3141
Number of Employees: 5

Ms. Sales Manager
WESTERN LOVE ANGELS MOTORCYCLE
5719 MARTIN LUTHER KING
ST LOUIS, MO 63140-1348
Phone: 314/383-2051
Number of Employees: 4

Oklahoma

Mr. Breck Cotter, Owner
DOUBLE D CUSTOM CYCLES
2021 EXCHANGE AVE
OKLAHOMA CITY, OK 73108-2623
Phone: 405/524-4294
FAX Phone:
Number of Employees: 3

Ms. Manager
HARLEY DAVIDSON WORLD
2823 S AGNEW AVE
OKLAHOMA CITY, OK 73108-6231
Phone: 405/631-8680
Number of Employees: 9

Mr. Dan Johnson, Owner
FREEDOM CYCLES
3119 S ROBINSON AVE
OKLAHOMA CITY, OK 73109-6517
Phone: 405/631-2065
Number of Employees: 9

Mr. Dan Maxey, Owner
MAXEY'S HONDA-YAMAHA
4112 NW 39TH ST
OKLAHOMA CITY, OK 73112-2921
Phone: 405/946-0558
Number of Employees: 15

Mr. Chuck Cantwell, Owner
OKLAHOMA HONDA
3400 S SUNNYLANE RD
OKLAHOMA CITY, OK 73115-3598
Phone: 405/672-1423
Number of Employees: 13

Mr. Bill Schramm, Manager
HOUSE OF KAWASAKI SUZUKI
7900 NW 10TH ST
OKLAHOMA CITY, OK 73127-4405
Phone: 405/787-7901
Number of Employees: 10

Mr. Phil Chalifoux, Owner
B & C ACCESSORIES & CYCLE SHOP
5604 S SHIELDS BLVD
OKLAHOMA CITY, OK 73129-3626
Phone: 405/632-7528
FAX Phone:
Number of Employees: 2

Mr. Charles Adkisson, Owner
A & A CYCLE SALES & SALVAGE
714 SE 15TH ST
OKLAHOMA CITY, OK 73129-4305
Phone: 405/634-4033
FAX Phone:
Number of Employees: 4

Ms. Manager
AJAX KAWASAKI
8417 S I 35 SERVICE RD
OKLAHOMA CITY, OK 73149
Phone: 405/634-8400
FAX Phone:
Number of Employees: 4

Mr. Roger Bryan, Owner
BRYAN HARLEY DAVIDSON
2624 N MOORE AVE
OKLAHOMA CITY, OK 73160-3329
Phone: 405/793-8877
FAX Phone:
Number of Employees: 11

Mr. Billy Parsley, Manager
YAMAHA OF OKLAHOMA
2210 S SERVICE RD
MOORE, OK 73160-5549
Phone: 405/793-8600
FAX Phone:
Number of Employees: 5

Ms. Bobby Smith, Owner
S & H CYCLE SALES
OLD HWY 66
ELK CITY, OK 73644
Phone: 405/225-3265
Number of Employees: 3

Mr. Roy Canard, Owner
KAWASAKI
625 N VAN BUREN AVE
ELK CITY, OK 73644-3425
Phone: 405/225-6043
Number of Employees: 8

Ms. Reba Mc Clanahan, Owner
MYERS-DUREN HARLEY DAVIDSON
800 S UTICA AVE
TULSA, OK 74104-3613
Phone: 918/583-4440
FAX Phone:
Number of Employees: 9

Mr. Carl Wilson, Owner
CARL'S MOTORCYCLE SVC
2510 E ARCHER ST
TULSA, OK 74110-5334
Phone: 918/838-1677
FAX Phone:
Number of Employees: 4

Mr. Orvel Sawvel, Owner
ORVEL'S CYCLE SHOP
851 S HARVARD AVE
TULSA, OK 74112-3835
Phone: 918/834-1555
FAX Phone:
Number of Employees: 1

Mr. Ken Johnson, Owner
ATLAS CYCLES
6708 E 11TH ST
TULSA, OK 74112-4620
Phone: 918/835-9959
FAX Phone:
Number of Employees: 1

Mr. Ray Nichols, Owner
YAMAHA OF TULSA
7302 E 11TH ST
TULSA, OK 74112-5704
Phone: 918/832-7091
FAX Phone:
Number of Employees: 6

Mr. Bobby Donnell, Owner
HONDA
4926 E 21ST ST
TULSA, OK 74114-2202
Phone: 918/744-5551
FAX Phone:
Number of Employees: 15

Ms. Sales Manager
TULSA CYCLE SUPPLY & SALES
5268 E PINE ST
TULSA, OK 74115-5328
Phone: 918/834-0367
FAX Phone:
Number of Employees: 4

Mr. Ron Parham, Owner
RON'S CYCLE LAND
6710 E PINE ST
TULSA, OK 74115-5653
Phone: 918/835-8215
FAX Phone:
Number of Employees: 1

Mr. Marshall Farr, Owner
FARR'S CYCLES INC
7465 E ADMIRAL PL
TULSA, OK 74115-7912
Phone: 918/834-2622
FAX Phone:
Number of Employees: 11

Mr. Ken Barnett, Owner
KEN'S CUSTOM CYCLES
8534 E ADMIRAL PL
TULSA, OK 74115-8101
Phone: 918/834-6922
FAX Phone:
Number of Employees: 1

Mr. John Knox, Owner
PRECISION MOTORCYCLE WORKS
4941 E ADMIRAL PL
TULSA, OK 74115-8405
Phone: 918/834-7228
FAX Phone:
Number of Employees: 3

Ms. La NELLE. Meyer, Owner
JACK'S MOTORCYCLE SVC
5041 E ADMIRAL PL
TULSA, OK 74115-8407
Phone: 918/838-3100
FAX Phone:
Number of Employees: 2

Mr. Tony Mills, Owner
AMERICAN MOTORCYCLE BUYER
15300 E PINE ST
TULSA, OK 74116-2423
Phone: 918/835-9292
FAX Phone:
Number of Employees: 1

Mr. Cliff Cook, Owner
C & C HARLEY DAVIDSON
2134 S GARNETT RD
TULSA, OK 74129-5106
Phone: 918/437-0131
FAX Phone:
Number of Employees: 5

Mr. Norm Mc Donald, Owner
K & N MOTORCYCLES PAWN & GUN
6105 NEW SAPULPA RD
TULSA, OK 74131-2648
Phone: 918/446-6657
FAX Phone:
Number of Employees: 7

Texas

Mr. Alvin Sharp, Owner
SHARP'S HONDA SEA-DOO
4413 E INTERSTATE 40
AMARILLO, TX 79104-4235
Phone: 806/373-3051
FAX Phone:
Number of Employees: 8

Mr. Don Gould, Owner
S & S CYCLE
816 E AMARILLO BLVD
AMARILLO, TX 79107-5401
Phone: 806/374-8760
FAX Phone:
Number of Employees: 2

Mr. Darrell Dreasher, Owner
AMARILLO HOBBY HOUSE
4127 W 34TH AVE
AMARILLO, TX 79109-4435
Phone: 806/355-2921
FAX Phone:
Number of Employees: 3

Mr. David Brown, Owner
DAVID BROWN SPORT CTR
4203 CANYON DR
AMARILLO, TX 79110-1105
Phone: 806/358-4572
Number of Employees: 3

Mr. Terry Tripp, Owner
TRIPP'S HARLEY DAVIDSON SALES
4241 S GEORGIA ST
AMARILLO, TX 79110-1719
Phone: 806/352-2021
Number of Employees: 6

Arizona

Ms. Sales Manager
NORTHLAND YAMAHA KAWASAKI
4401 N US HIGHWAY 89
FLAGSTAFF, AZ 86004-2407
Phone: 602/526-7959
FAX Phone:
Number of Employees: 4

Motorcycle Guide to Route 66

Mr. Joe Prosser, Owner
BIG JOE'S CYCLES
2800 N WEST ST
FLAGSTAFF, AZ 86004-3456
Phone: 602/774-4662
FAX Phone:
Number of Employees: 4

Mr. Chuck Crockatt, President
FLAGSTAFF HARLEY DAVIDSON INC
IH 40 EXIT 185
BELLEMONT, AZ 86015
Phone: 602/774-3896
FAX Phone:
Number of Employees: 4

Mr. Gawin Horrocks, Owner
PAGE HONDA
27 POPLAR ST
PAGE, AZ 86040
Phone: 602/645-3251
FAX Phone:
Number of Employees: 7

Mr. Jerry Bartlett, Owner
OUTDOOR SPORTS
861 VISTA AVE
PAGE, AZ 86040
Phone: 602/645-8141
FAX Phone:
Number of Employees: 3

Mr. Rick Van Cleve, Owner
KINGMAN CYCLE
4085 STOCKTON HILL RD
KINGMAN, AZ 86401-2476
Phone: 602/757-1166
FAX Phone:
Number of Employees: 5

Mr. David Bein, Manager
KAWASAKI SUZUKI
2365 NORTHERN AVE
KINGMAN, AZ 86401-2502
Phone: 602/757-2480
Number of Employees: 3

Ms. Sales Manager
ARIZONA PERFORMANCE CYCLE
208 W ANDY DEVINE AVE
KINGMAN, AZ 86401-5848
Phone: 602/753-4115
FAX Phone:
Number of Employees: 4

Mr. Bob Kruse, Owner
TUTTLE'S MOTOR SPORTS
1600 ACOMA BLVD W # 17
LAKE HAVASU CITY, AZ 86403-2812
Phone: 602/855-8106
FAX Phone:
Number of Employees: 1

Ms. Sales Manager
HAVASU CYCLE & WATERCRAFT
790 LAKE HAVASU AVE N
LAKE HAVASU CITY, AZ 86403-2963
Phone: 602/680-6622
Number of Employees: 4

Mr. Walt Beck, Owner
WALT'S KAWASAKI YAMAHA PLUS
1551 PALO VERDE BLVD S
LAKE HAVASU CITY, AZ 86403-4635
Phone: 602/855-5019
Number of Employees: 10

Mr. Steve Henline, Owner
HAVASU WHEELS
1665 MESQUITE AVE
LAKE HAVASU CITY, AZ 86403-5694
Phone: 602/855-3119
Number of Employees: 8

Ms. Sales Manager
TWO WHEELS MOTORCYCLE REPAIR
1086 HIGHWAY 95
BULLHEAD CITY, AZ 86442
Phone: 602/754-6700
Number of Employees: 4

Mr. Gordon Schmid, Owner
BULLHEAD BIKE CTR
2140 S HIGHWAY 95
BULLHEAD CITY, AZ 86442
Phone: 602/758-3200
Number of Employees: 6

New Mexico

Mr. Bud Cowan, Owner
NEW MEXICO MOTORCYCLE
4123 BROADWAY BLVD SE
ALBUQUERQUE, NM 87105
Phone: 505/877-4003
FAX Phone:
Number of Employees: 3

Mr. Carl Neiderman, Owner
SOUTHWEST MOTORCYCLE SALVAGE
1656 BRIDGE BLVD SW
ALBUQUERQUE, NM 87105
Phone: 505/242-9498
FAX Phone:
Number of Employees: 3

Ms. Barbara Rose, Owner
ROSE-DALE ENTERPRISES
6626 4TH ST NW
ALBUQUERQUE, NM 87107-6144
Phone: 505/345-7195
Number of Employees: 6

Mr. Chick Hancock, Owner
CHICK'S HARLEY DAVIDSON INC
8207 CENTRAL AVE NE
ALBUQUERQUE, NM 87108-2407
Phone: 505/266-6777
Number of Employees: 12

Ms. Edith Bodwell, Owner
HONDA BMW SUZUKI
6919 MONTGOMERY BLVD NE
ALBUQUERQUE, NM 87109-1420
Phone: 505/884-9000
Number of Employees: 15

Mr. Bob Rowland, Owner
B R MOTORS
3600 OSUNA RD NE # 303
ALBUQUERQUE, NM 87109-4427
Phone: 505/345-8109
Number of Employees: 1

Mr. Robert Johnson, Owner
BOBBY J'S YAMAHA INC
4724 MENAUL BLVD NE
ALBUQUERQUE, NM 87110
Phone: 505/884-3013
Number of Employees: 12

Mr. Jim Bewley, Owner
ALBUQUERQUE YAMAHA
3305 JUAN TABO BLVD NE
ALBUQUERQUE, NM 87111-5130
Phone: 505/292-8011
Number of Employees: 12

Mr. Jim Chung, Owner
RISING SUN CYCLES
2450 JUAN TABO BLVD NE
ALBUQUERQUE, NM 87112-1818
Phone: 505/275-0002
Number of Employees: 7

Motorcycle Guide to Route 66

Ms. Ozie Mc Casland, Owner
M & M HONDA MOTO GUZZI
1425 WYOMING BLVD NE
ALBUQUERQUE, NM 87112-3849
Phone: 505/293-1860
Number of Employees: 15

Mr. Rick Alcon, Owner
R & S KAWASAKI
9601 LOMAS BLVD NE
ALBUQUERQUE, NM 87112-5269
Phone: 505/292-6692
Number of Employees: 15

Mr. Robert Cresto, Owner
DESERT CYCLE
N US HIGHWAY 666
GALLUP, NM 87301
Phone: 505/722-3821
FAX Phone: 505/863-2555
Number of Employees: 5

California

Mr. James Bearup, President
LOS ANGELES MOTORCYCLE SALVAGE
425 E 58TH ST
LOS ANGELES, CA 90011-5319
Phone: 213/233-8792
FAX Phone:
Number of Employees: 3

Mr. Gary Hull, Owner
MOTORCYCLE MAMA
1324 S FIGUEROA ST
LOS ANGELES, CA 90015-2800
Phone: 213/746-7465
FAX Phone:
Number of Employees: 1

Mr. Marco Dippilotto, Owner
SCOOTER TECH ACCESSORIES
10967 WEYBURN AVE # B
LOS ANGELES, CA 90024-2811
Phone: 310/470-4745
FAX Phone:
Number of Employees: 1

Mr. Juno Kim, Owner
HANMI MOTOR SCOOTERS
1785 WESTWOOD BLVD
LOS ANGELES, CA 90024-5607
Phone: 310/473-5644
FAX Phone:
Number of Employees: 3

Mr. Jack Sneh, Owner
HOLLYWOOD MOTORCYCLES
1339 N HIGHLAND AVE
LOS ANGELES, CA 90028-7608
Phone: 213/962-5522
FAX Phone: 213/962-1610
Number of Employees: 8

Mr. Richard Klune, Owner
AMERICAN MOTORCYCLE OWNER'S
1344 N HIGHLAND AVE
LOS ANGELES, CA 90028-7609
Phone: 213/465-2409
FAX Phone:
Number of Employees: 2

Mr. Mike Copeland, Owner
T & M CYCLE SPECIALTIES
6108 VENICE BLVD
LOS ANGELES, CA 90034-2218
Phone: 213/938-6048
FAX Phone:
Number of Employees: 1

Mr. Ram Gilboa, Owner
L A KAWASAKI
1535 S LA CIENEGA BLVD
LOS ANGELES, CA 90035-3714
Phone: 310/854-7788
FAX Phone:
Number of Employees: 1

Mr. Bill Robertson, Owner
HONDA-BMW-KAWASAKI OF HOLLYWD
6525 SANTA MONICA BLVD
LOS ANGELES, CA 90038-1450
Phone: 213/466-7191
FAX Phone:
Number of Employees: 130

Mr. Bill Barlow, Owner
CYCLE PRODUCTS WEST
11900 W PICO BLVD
LOS ANGELES, CA 90064-1392
Phone: 310/477-0997
FAX Phone:
Number of Employees: 2

Mr. Gary Sulkin, Owner
MARINA SUZUKI
12973 W WASHINGTON BLVD
LOS ANGELES, CA 90066-5128
Phone: 310/306-8595
FAX Phone:
Number of Employees: 8

Mr. Ted Evans, Owner
TED EVANS MOTORCYCLE SALES
13347 W WASHINGTON BLVD
LOS ANGELES, CA 90066-5185
Phone: 310/306-7906
FAX Phone: 310/306-6122
Number of Employees: 6

Mr. Mike Isenburg, Owner
THUNDER ROAD MOTORCYCLES
8363 W SUNSET BLVD
WEST HOLLYWOOD, CA 90069-1515
Phone: 213/650-6011
FAX Phone:
Number of Employees: 5

Campgrounds Along The Mother Road[21]

All have tent sites - call for more detailed information on facilities

Illinois

Chicago
Hide-A-Way-Lakes
8045 Van Emmon Rd
Yorkville, IL 60560
708-553-6323

Hi-Tide Recreation
4611 E 22nd Rd
Leland, Il 60531
815-495-9032

Mendota Hills Campground
642 US Rte 52
Amboy, IL 61310
815-849-5930

Springfield
Holiday Trave-L Park & RV Center
Exit I-55 @ Exit 83 (Northbound), Exit 88 (Southbound), on West side of Interstate.
217-483-9998

Mr. Lincoln's Campground
Exit I-55 @ Exit 94, go 1 mile West on Stevenson Drive.
1-800-657-1414

---

[21] We are indebted to *Woodall's Plan-it • Pack-It • GO* for the information in this section. The publication ($12.95 @ Woodall Publications, 28167 N Keith Drive, Lake Forest, IL 60045, 708-362-6700) is generally available in most large book stores. It focuses on places to tent and fun things to do and is a treasure for the serious tent camper. In addition to the "commercial" operators, the guide also includes state parks with camping facilities that often are terrific bargains.

Missouri

Rolla
Lane Spring Campground
Mark Twain National Forest
From Hwy 72 & US 63 Junction go 12 miles South on US 63.
314-364-4501

Joplin
KOA
I-44 & Hwy 43 (Seneca exit 4) go 1/8 of a mile South on Hwy43.
417-623-2246

Oklahoma

Oklahoma City
Tinker AFB FAMCAMP *Only open to active or retired military*
405-732-7321

Lake Hepburn
13 miles South of Salpula, OK on State Route 66.

Rockwall RV Park
West on I-40 three miles from the join with I-44. Exit 143
405-787-5992

KOA
Exit I-40 @ Exit 166. Go North
6200 S Choctaw Rd
Choctaw, OK 73020
405-391-5000

New Mexico

Tucumcari
Conchas Lake State Park
Go 34 miles Northwest Hwy 104
505-868-2270

Albuquerque
Kirtland AFB FAMCAMP *Only open to active duty or retired military.*
505-846-2059

American RV Park
Exit I-40 @ Central Ave, 1/2 mile West on South frontage road.
800-282-8885

Sandia National Forest
Exit I-40 at Tijeras/Sandia Crest exit. Ranger Station and maps are available south of the Interstate.

Albuquerque West RV Park
4 1/2 miles West on I-40 from the I-40 / I-25 join. Exit @ Exit 155 then 1/4 North on Coors Road
505-831-1912

Arizona

Holbrook
KOA
Exit 289 off I-40
102 Hermosa Dr
Holbrook, AZ 86025
520-524-6689

Flagstaff
Woody Mountain Campground
2727 W Route 66
Flagstaff, AZ 86001
800-732-7986

Bonita Campground
Coconino National Forest
Exit I-40 @ #201 and go 14 miles north on US 89, then east 2 miles on FR 545.
520-527-7042

California

We are indebted to Elaine Downing, Bureau of Land Management, Needles, CA for the following listing.

Moabi Regional Park
(San Bernardino County)
Park Moabi Rd
Needles, Ca.
(760) 326-3831

River Road Resort & Motel
3396 River Rd.
Needles, Ca.
(760) 326-3423

Rainbow Beach Resort
Route 4, Box 139
River Road
Needles, Ca.
(760) 326-3101

KOA Kampgrounds of America
5400 National Old Trails Highway,
Needles, Ca.
(760) 326-4207

Public Lands - Bureau of Land Management
Needles to Ludlow Section
Needles Field Office
101 Spikes Rd.
Needles, CA 92363
(760)326-7000 or Visitor Center
Tues - Sun (760) 326-6322

Public Lands - Bureau of Land Management
Ludlow to Victorville Section
Barstow Field Office
2601 Barstow Rd
Barstow, CA 92311
(760) 252-6000

Calico Ghost Town (San Bernardino County)
P.O. Box 638
Yermo, Ca. (Daggget texit from I-40, I-15 or National Trails.)
(760) 254-2047

Barstow Calico KOA
Outer Highway 15 North
Yermo, Ca.
(760) 254-2311 or 254-3318

Rainbow Basin Natural Area/Owl Canyon Campground (BLM)
Irwin Rd.
Barstow, Ca.

Shady Oasis Victorville KOA
16530 Stoddard Wells Rd.,
Victorville, Ca.
(760) 245-6867

Mojave Narrows Regional Park
(San Bernardino County)
18000 Yates Rd.
Victorville, Ca.
(760) 245-2226

Silverwood Lake State Recreational Area (State of California)
San Bernardino County
(760) 389-2281 or 389-2303

San Bernardino KOA
1707 Cable Canyon Rd.
San Bernardino, Ca.
(909) 8874098 or
(800) 562-4155

San Bernardino National Forest
(U.S. Dept. of Agriculture)
1824 South Commercenter Circle,
San Bernardino, Ca.

(909) 383-5588

Camping on BLM public lands is limited to 14 days in one location within any 28 day period (free). Of course, the traditional tables, stoves, litter pickup, and restrooms are not provided on the undeveloped portions of the public lands. Some things to remember: Park your vehicle no more than 300 feet from a vehicle route when camping or stopping, unless posted otherwise. Try to use existing campsites rather than making new ones. Practice "Leave No Trace" principals. You may find more information about Leave No Trace at: http://www.lnt.org/.

Los Angeles
Malibu Beach RV Park
Go 3 miles NW on Highway 1 from the junction of CR-N1 (Malibu Canyon Road) & Hwy 1. Entry sign will be on your right, go up the hill. Tent space is available.
310-456-6052

Leo Carrillo State Beach
From Malibu go 5 miles NW on Highway 1.
818-706-1310

Route 66 Organizations

ROUTE 66 ASSOCIATION OF MISSOURI
PO BOX 8117
ST LOUIS MO 63156

NATIONAL ROUTE 66 FAN CLUB
PO BOX 66
MANCHESTER MI 48158

GEORGE RIMINI, COORDINATOR
ROUTE 66 MOTORCYCLE ASSOCIATION
RR 2   BOX 16
GIRARD IL 62640

HISTORIC ROUTE 66 ASSOCIATION
2127 FOOTHILL BLVD. #66
LA VERNE CA 91750

HISTORICAL ROUTE 66 ASSOCIATION
PO BOX 66
KINGMAN AZ 86402

HISTORIC ROUTE 66 ASSOCIATION
PO BOX 169
RIVERTON KS 66770

HISTORICAL ROUTE 66 ASSOCIATION
PO BOX 8117
ST LOUIS MO 63146

HISTORIC ROUTE 66 ASSOCIATION
1415 CENTRAL NE
ALBUQUERQUE NM 87106

HISTORICAL ROUTE 66 ASSOCIATION
901 MANUEL AVE
CHANDLER OK 74834

HISTORIC ROUTE 66 ASSOCIATION
PO BOX 66
MCLEAN TX 79057

HISTORICAL ROUTE 66 ASSOCIATION
PO BOX 8262
ROLLING MEADOWS IL 60008

ROUTE 66 ASSOCIATION OF ILLINOIS
2743 VETERANS PARKWAY, #166
SPRINGFIELD, IL 62704

Essential Extras for the Touring Motorcyclist

Seasoned long distance tourers pack a few extras that can save time and trouble.

First Aid Kit - With particular attention to treatment for the painful burn(s) one can pick up from hot pipes.

Handheld CB Radio - Uniden, Midland and Cobra dominate the quality hand-held CB market. They are kinda interesting to listen to the truckers and **invaluable** for staying in touch with other people you are riding with. **IMPORTANT:** Before you buy one **be sure** to sit on your bike with it and **start your engine**. Inexpensive CB's will not be shielded from ignition/spark plug noise and the racket will make the radio useless. Mother Road Ride/Rally® participants found such bike to bike communications very helpful (using Channel 5). It is truly amazing how quickly bikes can become separated - particularly in metropolitan areas.

Tire Repair Kit - Ok, so this **is** in **your** saddle bag, but a lot of 'round towners' don't pack one and on some stretches of The Mother Road the wait for help can be long and lonely. Some kits include CO^2 cartridges represented as being capable of re-inflating a tire.

If your tire repair kit doesn't include an equalizing tube (can connect a full tire with a flat one . . . won't completely inflate a flat tire but will transfer enough to make a **slow** roll to the next compressor) then you will want to add that to your tire repair kit as well.

Siphon Tube - And a 'catch' container as well. It **is** dumb to run out of gas, but if you have 8 feet of 1/4 - 1/2 inch plastic tubing any good Samaritan can get you out of a tight spot. The catch container will mean you can avoid getting a mouth full of gas in the process. **Electrical Tape** - To temporarily mend broken reflectors and light covers. Actually, it's handy for a lot of other short term hold downs. A sports car owner told us that you can practically rebuild fiberglass panels with **duct tape.**

Tire Pressure Gauge - A **good** one. And you should check the pressure of both tires every morning. Long Distance touring builds up terrific heat inside the tires which can keep them inflated during the day's run. When the tire is cooled down in the morning will give you an accurate reading. **A tire can be dangerously low in pressure and still look and kick ok.**

Flashlight(s) - One of those that incorporates a head band is *super* when trying to effect repairs at night or for setting up/taking down your tent in the dark. **Road Flares** can be worth the space if you break down at night. *Be sure* to position them wwwwaaaaayyyy back from where you are stopped. **At least** 100 yards, 200 is better . . . further if there is a crest of a hill between oncoming traffic and you.

Prescriptions - medication **and** eyeglasses. Actually, an extra pair of eyeglasses could easily be the difference between a "busted" trip and a minor inconvenience. Given the attitude of some law enforcement agencies towards motorcyclists, it might not be a bad idea to carry a copy of your doctor's prescription if your medications include narcotics or "dangerous" medications. That's particularly true if your **full name** doesn't appear on the prescription container.

Tow Rope - Worst case solution to getting to the next town. You'll want 10 feet of 1/2 inch line. **And be careful where you attach it.** The front **frame** is the stoutest part of the front of your bike and the same is true of the back if you are the towing vehicle. **This is no place for granny knots.** Looping around your frame and then, rather than tying off, bringing the free end up to your right hand is safest. You'll be able to disconnect from the towing vehicle whenever you want to. **Keep slack out of the tow line** with your brakes to avoid damaging snap loads.

Tool Kit - Some large touring bikes include these. But in any event **a vice grip** wrench is one of the finer inventions of mankind. Good for a **lot** of tasks. You'll also want a knife. Those big Swiss Army models are practically a tool kit within themselves.

Plastic Garbage Bags - The short wastebasket model is the most useful . . . for lots of stuff.

Joe Miller, Dayton, Ohio, Rides the Mother Road!

©Copyright 1998 Joseph M. S. Miller. All Rights Reserved

Editor's Note: Joe Miller participated in the 4th Annual Mother Road Ride/Rally« in June, 1998. He writes with wit and insight about his experiences on America's most famous highway. His Journal is reproduced here with his permission.

It's already fall here in Dayton but I promised both myself, Kirk [Woodward], and some other friends that I would write a description of my trip on Route 66 this past June. It was a wonderful trip and even though I had few expectations, they turn out to have been much too low. As with any trip of mine it twisted and turned in many different ways, not the least being the people I met. A true Route 66 trip. Since I kept a road journal, I am going to follow that format with side trips (although maybe all of this is a side trip.)

Pre-Day. Miles 0-256
I took off from Dayton on Friday afternoon for Chicago. I wanted to get there in time for dinner with Kirk and thus had made room reservations at the Essex. I took my time across Indiana on IN38 to I65 and was still astonished at the amount of water left in the fields yet from the spring rains. In one scene I saw two young boys up to their waists in a pond in a corn field. But I didn't see any rain till some place south of Chicago where I felt hail!! The Harleys were out in force going north for the 95th celebration in Milwaukee. After the usual Chicago transportation delays and dysfunction I made it to the Essex around 5PM and checked in with all the other tourists. The bikes of Kirk and Richard [Datko] were already there in the parking garage so I was in the right place.

Somehow I got a Lake view room on the 9th floor which I discovered was a big advantage later in the evening. I went down at 7:00 to group up for dinner and after a few non-chalant strolls through the lounge met up with Ken and Carole Davenport. Richard Datko showed up a few moments later. We waited for Kirk, whom none of us had met personally. Eventually Kirk made it and asked the age old question of the locals (Ken and Carole) Where is the best place to eat for us roadies to remember Chicago by? Carole came to our rescue and suggested Berghof, the famous German restaurant on Adams street. That was several blocks north of the Essex but near the old Route 66 start sign.

The sign was gone but the food was fine and we thoroughly enjoyed the setting. It seemed a classic Chicago evening, a summer's warmth with lake breezes cooling it down. I went back to my room, opened up my curtains toward the lake and was welcomed to a laser light show on the Field Museum building on my right(looking east). But it didn't stop there! A full blown fireworks commenced and from the 9th floor it was pretty impressive. I never did get the full scoop on the shows but it was a nice end to the evening.

I should add that walking back from the restaurant we spotted a motorcycle and rider at the end Route 66 sign on Jackson (it is one-way so the start is on Adams) Billy Lane had ridden the old road from LA to Chicago and was now headed to Milwaukee and the 95th Harley celebration. I was curious how his cycle, a venerable Honda 750, was going to be accepted at a Harley fest but he looked like he would do fine.

Day One, June 13, Saturday. Miles 0-400
Chicago to Diamond MO
I should add here that Kirk was filming his famous Illinois Route 66 video so all along the way, starting here in Chicago, we were 'video extras'. Saturday dawned cool and hazy in the canyons of downtown Chicago but we were ready to roll. At the appointed place and hour there were about 15 people ready to ride west on Rte 66 with one particular couple having started earlier in the morning in Green Bay, Wisconsin (Steve and Mary Jane). We started our engines! Roared away! And stopped around the corner. Kirk wanted to video all of us taking off so we

Ready to Roll from Downtown Chicago

agreed to stop after taking off and get everyone back together. That was the closest we were for the entire trip and even so some had very itchy throttle hands. Finally we were on our way down Rte 66 er..I55! The interstate was deserted at that time of day, and it was basically a pleasant ride to our exit north of Joliet.

After getting off at the exit we had our first official briefing from Kirk about the Road! The rest of the day was a pleasant mix of old road, tourist site and freeway. The stops were frequent and noteworthy places from the old road such as the Spaceman [Gemini Giant] at Launching Pad [Drive Inn] in Wilmington. He was actually in good, well painted condition! The Dixie truck stop of McLean was lunch for us, plus gas and the museum amongst the building renovation. The starting group from Chicago was already breaking up with some wanting the slower old alignments and others joining us since Chicago. In any case the day was beautiful, and the road beckoned for all in what ever manner.

To roll along the highway was a magnetic and magical effect on all. With video camera rolling we cycled into [Abraham] Lincoln's Springfield for a stop and look around. Next was Niehaus Motorcycles with a welcome mat and souvenir caps. One last gas stop and the St Louis Arch awaited our arrival. We arrived and couldn't find a place to park!!! So after stopping along the busy quay some of us voted to continue on and find a spot for the night. Ken and Carole stayed in St Louis but we still had the couple from Green Bay Steve and Mary. Kirk and some others intended to camp for the evening, but not I, I intended to follow along and meet up in the morning. Well, even though we were close to the longest daylight of the year it was beginning to run out by the time we discovered that the campground we headed to was only a daycamp. So, ok it's a motel for everyone.

We were near a string of motels by Six Flags amusement park but could not find one that had room for all of us. So on the road again! It was now completely dark, so the next Holiday Inn had room for our Green Bay Trailer couple Steve and Mary. They took it. Kirk, Mike, Richard and I kept on and found a Best Western at the next exit. We tried to contact Steve and Mary but could not. In fact I did not see them or the Davenports the rest of the trip although I heard about them along the way. I sought out a roadside diner that seemed to look good at first with people around but the food was pretty bad in spite of the recommendations.

Day 2 June 14 Sunday mileage 400-694 Diamond, MO to Miami, OK

There was some rain at night, but we woke up in the morning to the clouds breaking and

University of Missouri's Stonehenge reproduction at Rolla, MO (14th & Bishop)

another beautiful day. Discovered that Ken Lato and the Harley couple Jeff and Sherry Toeller, who went on the older alignment in Illinois after the Dixie truck stop, also stayed at the Best Western that night. This unexpected meeting seemed to be a normal reoccurrence on the trip in spite of the fact we often seemed to be going at much different paces and with different motivations. Kirk, Mike, Richard and I got on the freeway again while the others kept to the old Route 66 paralleling the freeway very closely.

The next major stop was the Stonehenge at the U of M in Rolla. This was also a meet up point so we stayed a bit longer. Although one half scale to the real thing, the engineering feat is still very impressive. We took pictures, talked, and moved on! This time it was just Kirk and I with Mike and Richard wanting more time on the old alignment with Ken and Jeff and Sherry. Kirk and I exited off of the I44 to find Devils's Elbow, an infamous curve on Route 66, but first we got lost finding the old alignment because it is marked only with county road numbers in many places. Then I completely missed seeing it since the curve had been straighten somewhat from its original bad shape. We stopped for lunch at a roadside diner with cars, and the food was good without tourist pretensions. Next stop for Kirk and me was a puzzle store (again which I completely missed seeing although Kirk and I talked about it). Out in the country, with an old corrugated building, we parked the cycles in the grass observing the 'no parking' signs and 'don't drive on the grass' signs all the while parking on a slope.

The real Stonehenge is TWICE as large!

But inside was a puzzle dreamers delight with row upon row of puzzles. Kirk, good roadie that he is, couldn't pass up a chance to buy one from such a source. The next stop was the Route 66 raceway on the west side of Joplin which was another join up point. By now it was quite hot, and I was looking forward to some ice cream from a concession stand. But our racetrack was quite a bit less than that. It had certainly seen better days, and all that was available was from a vending machine. Now it was mainly a go-kart track which can be nice but this was a pretty run down place. Kirk and I sat in the shade and drank some soda before heading on.

It was now Kansas, a very small portion of the overall length of Route 66 but none the less had some important stops. We motored through Galena and on to Riverton where we stopped at the quint essential Route 66 mom and pop store [Eisler Brothers General Store]. Here was our ice cream as well as Sasprillia. In a back part of the store was a Route 66 tourist store, but of the real old kind. However that was not the find here. Rather one of the young high school kids made sure we knew about the old 'rainbow' bridge that had been fixed up on old Route 66. I don't know if this is the one mentioned in the guide books, but from Riverton there are no signs for it. You just have to know where to turn off! Kirk and I turned off and took off down the road with nothing in sight except Kansas grassland.

Just when I thought it wasn't there, there it was! Bright and white and clean. Kirk and I took the requisite pictures. We followed the old route back to KS69 which brought us into Baxter Springs. Here there was a sign for the old route to the bridge. As we came up to a stop light here where none other than Mike and Richard. They had gotten separated from Ken, Jeff and Sherry back at Devil's elbow and had gotten this far. They joined us for the motel in Miami. We were now on the old route with the interstate beside us although it was not too far away. Kirk's wife had stayed at 'Miiammme' one time and so we stayed as well.

We had a fine meal and discussed getting up early for a good morning start. Richard begged off at this point arguing that he needed a new rear tire on the cycle and not wanting to be under the influence of others which was fine by us!!

Day 3 June 15 mileage 694-990 Miami to Clinton, OK

So early in the morning after a continental breakfast (which is not near enough for me) Kirk, Mike and I took off. West out of Miami there is an old stretch that is a single lane of Route 66 called the ribbon road. So narrow that it's hard to turn a bike around on it. Kirk had visited it last year for some photo opps, so we drove west to stop and see it. However when we stopped they were tearing it up and we could not see far enough to judge whether any of it was left.

Understandably this part was now an old county road that needed rebuilding. We did not go back into Miami to see if there was a part of it left. We took off! In the next town (Afton or Vinita) [Editor: Afton] we saw some bikes outside a Route 66 restaurant, so stopped and had a proper breakfast. This was another meet-up with Ken, Jeff and Sherry. After a good breakfast Kirk, Mike and I kept on going on the old route which is a well maintained and used road since the I44 is tollway from the Kansas border to Oklahoma City. Mike wanted to see the memorial in Oklahoma City. Kirk was going to finish the day by driving home to Grapevine. I wanted to get to Clinton for the Route 66 museum plus OK BBQ was on the menu for lunch. Pretty stretched out goals, but they fit in quite fine on a road trip that's open to anything.

The next stop was the Will Rogers Memorial in Claremore which is very large and very good. Kirk wanted to show us the Blue Whale which is near Catoosa. The Blue Whale, Catoosa, Oklahoma It is hidden enough that it is easy to drive past but we got stopped in

I ponder the deeper meaning of The Blue Whale (if any) at Catoosa, Oklahoma

time. With the requisite pictures we headed on. Tulsa was city, and so we drove around it and started looking for a BBQ. I was in the lead and just coming off the freeway there was such a restaurant but I was past before I could safely turn in. I also thought there would be plenty more in the small towns along the way. Wrong I was. Although we had a great lunch I wouldn't call it a BBQ place.

We were on our way to Oklahoma City with a stop at the house built like a Phillips 66 gas station (see it in the video) and the round barn at Arcadia (it was closed). Kirk led us to the Federal building, and we parked to walk around. It's hard to imagine the violence of the blast with so many buildings close by, even though many of them had been taken down due to structural damage. There were a lot of people there with many flowers and remembrances of loved ones along the fence.

From here Kirk headed south to home. Mike and I fueled up and headed west for Clinton. We were in the plains now with hot wind and long views. The rolling hills of eastern Oklahoma were behind us. We made the museum with plenty of time to spare and so had a leisurely tour. In fact I bought some shirts to remember it by. The museum is well done in a fifties neon style. Its focus is The Road. We stayed at the Best Western [Tradewinds Motel] across the way, but did not opt for Elvis's room. By the time we went out for supper I had forgotten Jiggs Smokehouse (for that OK BBQ) and ended up at Pop Hicks restaurant. A very eclectic restaurant with good history, melmac plates and glasses and so-so food, but we enjoyed it.

Day 4 June 16 mileage 990-1454 Clinton, OK to Albuquerque, NM

Now it was just Mike and I. So we took off early in the morning intending to put some mileage under our bikes. And that we did. (Note the mileage above for the day, 464 miles) Our first stop was in Shamrock TX for breakfast. But the U-Drop-Inn was boarded up and dusty so we went across the road which was fine. As I spoke of above, we were now in the Great Plains or Prairies. The wind was strong and the heat increasing by the minute. Our bikes were strong but it was a chore to hold on. We may be getting the miles but it was an effort. To see the horizon disappear because of distance, not hills or trees and to feel the wind all that distance is pretty overwhelming. Add the heat, and it's not hard to experience an extreme aloneness.

The buried Cadillacs are over my left shoulder.

We stopped at the Cadillac Ranch on the west side of Amarillo. Rumor was that it was gone but it had only moved to exit 60 and was still there in all its glory!! We finally stopped for lunch at the Half-way cafe in Adrian TX. As is often the case when one is engulfed by the landscape we stumbled upon the restaurant. It was perfect for the moment, air-conditioned and a quint essential road cafe. After eating and resting we took off with thoughts more of can we make it' because the bikes had the horsepower and stamina to carry on. We stopped once for gas but not for a rest until about 50 miles east of Albuquerque where there was a trading post and modern gas station.

We got off the bikes and were immediately struck by how much cooler it was than just a few miles ago. It felt like 20 degrees cooler. Altitude really makes a difference, especially in hot weather. The landscape is so level that there is almost no perception of altitude gain as one travels (Clinton is at 3800ft. and Albuquerque 6300ft). We went into the gift shop trading post but resisted buying anything. A great thing about cycles is the room makes you think before you buy. We took the freeway into Albuquerque. I wanted to stay at an old Rt. 66 motel I had stayed at earlier but was a bit unsure as to how to get to it directly. So we were wandering around a bit with the sun and heat in our eyes but we found it, the Monterey Motel.

It's on the edge of Old town and a really great place. Mike and I agreed that to this point in the trip this was one of the nicest older motels we had found with wonderful wood doorways and trim though out the rooms. A quick stroll across Route 66 and we were in Old town. This was Tuesday night and so there were not a lot of people around. It felt like we were now truly in the Southwest with the Spanish town squares. As the sun set cooling, but pleasant breezes touched us. Mike and I went to one of the Spanish restaurants on the square. I think it was in the old administrators building. My previous experience was that Albuquerque was much more authentic and interesting than Santa Fe and again I was not disappointed.

Day 5 June 17 Wednesday mileage 1454-1881 Albuquerque, NM to Elk City, OK

Well, this is where Mike and I parted ways. I headed back and Mike continued on. I had not expected to get this far at all but was very glad I did. We got up early, took the photos and said goodbye. This time I simply followed Route 66 through town enjoying the old buildings and sights and stayed on it to Moriarty. Filled up with gas and got on the freeway but not before somebody described the Dutch bikers through there the previous day on Route 66. But I had to again put on some miles to make it back home in reasonable time. It's great to stop and wander but also great to just go!

I stopped at the Half-way cafe in Adrian TX and the Texas Christian Cross someplace east of Amarillo [Groom, TX] Like the Cadillac Ranch, the bizarre with the surreal in an unending landscape. It was nice to have the wind at my back but the heat was even worse than the day before. Seems to me were about at the limit of daytime travel across the Southwest. On a whim I took the Elk City exit and wandered into town. I had wanted to make Clinton again but remembered that Elk City had a Route 66 Museum as well and wanted to see it. It was closed by the time I got to it and so I drove down to the next motel in the line. Got my room, turned on the air-conditioner and took a shower. Upon coming out to check something on the bike there was none other than Ken Lato's bike parked beside mine.

He was as astonished to see me as I was to see him. He was really tired so we rested awhile before going to the restaurant next door to hear each others' stories and catch up. They had stayed much more on the old two lane route but had put in some really long days. Where as on Monday Mike and I only made Clinton, Ken, Jeff and Sherry had made it to Tucumcari and stayed at the Blue Swallow Motel. They also took the old route which is now Rt104 from Tucumcari to Las Vegas. Even more that morning Ken had breakfast with the Davenports in Tucumcari . So Ken and I talked for a long time oblivious to most of the conversation around us being in Spanish.

Day 6 June 18 Thursday mileage 1881-2410 Elk City, OK to Clinton, AR

I took a bit of time to wander around the grounds of the Elk City museum, but this time I was too early to get in. From what I saw it was more an 1890's build up. Very nice and interesting but very, very different from the Route 66 Museum in Clinton. Which is fine, but they are not competitors as it may be made out to be. Just very different eras represented. Today I left Route 66 as a traveling road heading east toward Nashville across Arkansas and then home to Ohio. Join us next year on a new Route 66 trip west and I hope to see you there.

 Joe.Miller@udayton.edu
 University of Dayton
 937/229-4526
 BMW '91 K75SA (the Eggplant)
 Honda '84 Sabre(VF700S)
 Suzuki '76 GT500,GT380

Lew Bellinger Taught His Motorcycle to Type . . . and what a story Babe tells

Hello I would like to introduce myself, I'm called babe, I was born in 1982 and was given the name of Goldwing, but I guess Lew, my rider, prefers Babe. A few weeks ago he wouldn't have let me say that, but since Laura Brengelman admitted patting the tank on the Drifter, he's ok with it. I currently have 170,000 miles to my credit and as I said, am ridden by Lew. He also has a few years on him like 60 to be exact and looks like he has a like number of miles on him. So why am I writing to you? I would like to share our experiences on RT 66 with you.

Babe - The Motorcycle that learned to type.
Pictures courtesy of Lew Bellinger unless otherwise noted.

To begin with, Lew received many questionable stares from other riders when he first mentioned taking the trip on me. Most felt like I was way beyond my useful years for any serious riding. It's been said that "To be friends and trusted, one not only has to have shared in laughter but that folks must have cried together before their friends". Well, Lew and I have done that. You see a few years ago Lew got a little too free with my throttle and we took a little side trip while negotiating a turn into a ditch and up on the road again. Then, for reasons neither of us are quite

Lew Bellinger
Picture from video "The Millennium Run"

sure of, we did the high side thing. Well we both lay there within a few feet of one another until he was picked up by an ambulance and me with the tow truck. Amazing, as it is, a couple of months later we were both ready for the road again, so you see, we trust one another.

It's during that period of time that old Lew played on the Internet too much and came across the WEB site called the "Mother Road Rally" **www.hhjm.com/rally** hosted by Kirk Woodward and the boyhood idea of riding Route 66 returned to the fore front of his mind. He simply substituted motorcycle for car. Well it took a lot of planning to be on vacation for nearly three weeks and all that goes along with that. In December of '99 it all looked good to go, so full scale planning when into action. For me that included a stay with Mike at Casey Honda of Newport News, Lew's trusted mechanic, for a complete physical and new rubber. Considering the amount of time that Mike has had his hands on me over the years, I really think we are married or at least engaged; whatever, he really is a great mechanic. During the next few months Lew continually filled and emptied all of my cavities with various pieces of equipment and clothing to see what would fit and what wouldn't. June 6th, we were ready.

June 10, what can I say, the first full day on the "Mother Road"! We rode into Chicago and stopped at the beginning of RT 66, would you believe we parked on the sidewalk? We then rode the original road out of Chicago and believe me it's not a road you would want to be on by yourself. We passed through towns like Joliet, Elwood, Braidwood, Odell, and on and on. Visits to the Lunching Pad, Dixie Truckers

Home, Cozy Dog Drive Inn, Soulsby's Service Station, etc. I cannot put my feelings into words, I think it's something you have to experience. It looked like we were about to really get wet, but Jerry Mitchell said, "those are wind clouds." We did beat the rain but those "wind clouds" got us wet the on the 11th. We stopped for the night in St. Louis Missouri. Something worth mentioning here, as we were trying to find the road into the motel, a local police officer spotted us and turned on his lights stopping traffic so we could make an uninterrupted left turn. How about that and thanks whoever you are.

June 11, we rode through Missouri, Kansas, and stopped just inside Oklahoma in a little town by the name of Miami. We visited the small version of Stonehenge in Rolla, Missouri and Eisler Brothers Grocery, in Riverton, Kansas. Great 66 stuff at good prices. To actually see and ride the Devils Elbow in Missouri and cross over the Rainbow Bridge west of Riverton, Kansas was delightful. To see towns that are nearly ghost towns because the interstate bypassed them is a little heart breaking. We rode through a storm today west of Springfield, Missouri that contained an unbelievable amount of Jerry's wind but we all really got wet from it, strange kind of wind

June 12, We traveled down a piece of RT 66 today that is only 8ft or so wide I believed its called the Rainbow Road west and south of Miami, OK, [*Editor: Ribbon Road]* visited the Will Rogers Memorial in Claremore, OK and what a beautiful place. We stopped at the Blue Whale in Catoosa, OK and the Round Barn in Arcadia, OK.

Then a stop by the Cowboy Hall of Fame, in Oklahoma City then off to visit with Lucille who manages the Hydro Gas Station established in 1941. She is 85 and a wonderful person. The station was closed but we knocked on her door as the sign in the window said to, and she opened it up for us. We sat her on one of the bikes and took pictures; you should have seen her face. These were the highlights of the day but certainly not the only things that brought delight. We are spending the night in Clinton Oklahoma, at the Best Western where Elvis is said to have spent the night on several occasions. Across the street was the Route 66 Museum.

June 13 left Oklahoma through Texas and stopped for the night in San Rosa New Mexico. Lots of the old road available and we rode it, passed through far too many towns that are dead because of I-40. In one little place the only living thing we saw was an old hound that decided bikers would be good sport for the day. Seen the leaning water tower in Groom, TX and the U Drop Inn Café [Shamrock, TX], eat at the famous Big Texan Steak House [Amarillo, TX], visited the Cadillac Ranch, played around a one room jail house probably used for speeders at one time [Texola, OK], visited the Devil's Rope Museum [McLean, TX], etc. I could go on and on what a beautiful day. The countryside is just unbelievable, vast, and beautiful. The wind today across the open lands kept one busy, guess I will wear down the ride sidewalls on the return trip. We passed the RT 66 half way point in Adrian, Texas. The waitress at the Midpoint Café was just outstanding.

June 14, traveled across New Mexico and spending the night in Gallup NM. We took

Riders watch Ray change a tire. Looks like a Government Job.

a side trip today to ride Sandia Crest. We climbed to 10,678 feet on roads full of switchbacks and curves. In fact the only time we seemed to be level was the instant that I rolled from right to left or left to right. The view is something a camera cannot do justice to. The ride back down was even better then the ride up. Ray Ussery was pulling a travel trailer and as luck would have it, a tire gave up the ghost. We all stopped of course to assist, only to find out that Ray's jack wasn't available. So, they got the tire ready and everyone gathered around the trailer and they lifted it, so he could change the tire. Everyone has a camera and no one thought to take a picture. They had lunch at a great place called what else "Route 66 Dinner" in Albuquerque. One hundred percent 50's. Stopped at a RT 66 memorial in Grants and at the Continental Divide. Another great day! Along RT 66.

June 15, left New Mexico and into Arizona, spending the night in Kingman, AZ. I now know what heat in the desert feels like and I think it's only sane to ride those routes in the early morning :-) We took a ride through the Petrified Forest and Painted Desert not sure of the mileage but something like 30 miles or so. Lew was taken back by the beauty of it and said that he wished he could express his feelings better with words, so that all would know the beauty of this country that we been given the privilege to live in. Saw the Wigwam Motel [Holbrook, AZ], had lunch at a 50's dinner in Williams, AZ called "Twisters" what a neat place and visited Delgadillo's Snow Cap Café [Seligman, AZ]. Mostly we just rode the old road. Remember Ray? The guy that had the flat? Well, the other side gave up the ghost today and they did get pictures this time.

June 16 left Kingman AZ, spending the night in Fontana, CA. Made it to CA!!! We rode to Oatman this morning using the old road, I believe its called the Gold Road, and what a ride. We spend some time in Oatman. Lew and the others just walked around and drank coffee in one of the shops. Left there and crossed the desert to Barstow making several stops for water. Visited the Roy Rogers/Dale Evans Museum in Victorville. It was a great day but somewhat on the down side since we all realized this was the last full day of riding together. Tomorrow morning we will go into LA and complete the ride, then each going their separate ways.

June 17, we completed the ride this morning, departing Fontana at 5:25 am and driving the 66 miles or so to Palisades Park in Santa Monica. They parked us with our rear tires

Pat Evans (left) and Lew Bellinger

to the curb, and took tons of pictures, walked around a bit, had some coffee, and then had to face the inevitable, saying goodbye. A lot of hugs later Lew and I departed to Barstow for the remainder of the day and to rest for the trip home. I know Lew has many mixed emotions concerning the trip. Would he do it again, you bet, would we do things different, only to the extent of reading up on desert riding, the heat really got to Lew and some others from the east. We will not bore you with our trip home. Lew thanked the Lord for giving him the strength to make the trip and for permitting him to fulfill his boyhood dream, I'm thankful for being a part of it and we thank Kirk for organizing it. Patrick Evans said it best as we prepared to leave for the ride into Santa Monica; he read the following from his trip journal:

"I awake from a night of restless sleep-anticipating the arrival at our destination-but not the end of the ride. We are a group that started at the beginning bonded by the adventure of riding the 'Mother Road Rally". Now the journey together and friendships that have developed along the way bond us. There is something there in riding the old road that is lost on the inter-states; a closeness to the people still in many of the little towns, our country, and the pace of another time."

I've included a picture of Lew at the Will Rogers Route 66 plaque to denote the end of route 66 in Palisades Park in Santa Monica, a picture of myself in front of Ann's Restaurant at the beginning of the trip, The tire fixers, Chicago departure, and one of Lew and Pat. See you on RT 66, yes Lew's decided to ride it again next year so on the second Saturday of June you'll find us in Chicago again. Check out the WEB page given earlier, its rather interesting.

Lew Bellinger at end of Route 66

Babe and Lewis Bellinger

TRIP INFORMATION

START/START .... Mileage .. Rode
Home 63,472.0
Chicago .... 64,355.9 .. 883.9
Santa Monica .... 66,715.3 . 2,359.4
Home .... 69,482.5 . 2,767.2
Total 6,010.5
16 days and 15 nights on the road
Number of gals of fuel used - 133.4 gals
Miles per Gal - 45.1
Average Price per Gal - $1.77
Number of fuel stops - 55
Shortest Ride Day - 145.1 miles
Longest ride day - 639.8 miles
Fuel Cost - $ 235.74
Food Cost - $ 321.84
Motel Cost - $ 588.26
Tolls $ 20.65
Total Cost - $1,166.49

Best Meal - The Big Texan Restaurant, Amarillo
Most nostalgia - Route 66 Dinner, Albuquerque
Best Hamburger & Malt - Twisters, Williams, AZ.
Worst Meal - Loretta Lynn Country Kitchen, TENN.
Most value for the dollar - Smaldino's, Lima, OH.

Roger & Jane Take Their Act On The [Route 66] Road[22]

*(And The Mother Road will **never** be the same!)*

Roger & Jane Holm, Apple Valley, MN

Best Breakfast: Clanton Cafe, Vinita, OK.
Best Lunch: Norma's Cafe[23], Sapulpa, OK
Best Dinner: Ranch Kitchen, Gallup, NM

Least Loved as a Biker: Tradewinds Motel, Clinton, OK. Elvis may be welcomed there, but bikers aren't!

---

[22] Roger & Jane Holm, of Apple Valley, Minnesota. Their schedule required that they leave before the "main body" of people participating in The 2nd Annual Mother Road Ride/Rally® in June of 1996. We are indebted to them for their colorful and witty "diary" of their run down each and every mile of Historic Route 66. Their pictures are throughout this Guide . . . with many thanks!

[23] Norma also made the Holm's list of *Neatest People* as did Mr. Clanton at The Clanton Cafe in Vinita, OK.

Most Disappointing 66 Icon: Pop Hicks Restaurant, Clinton, OK. Food was plentiful, service was friendly, but the restaurant was really dirty. **Did have some neat 66 stuff.**

Neatest People:

Lillian Redmond at the Blue Swallow Motel, Tucumcari, NM. She is no longer young - wheelchair bound - did her "66 Routine" by memory.

The Waldmires: Buzz at the Cozy Dog in Springfield, IL and **Bob** at the Old Route 66 Visitor's Center in Hackberry, AZ.

The Funks: Any generation in Funks Grove, IL. Five generations there now and counting . . . excellent syrup, or as they spell it: sirup. *(When you've been there since 1846, you get to do that sort of thing.)*

Illinois: Funk's Grove. Dixie Trucker's Home -- known for its broasted chicken which is really incredible.

Missouri: Watch where you're going! Directions are terrible.

Kansas: Note the Route 66 painted on the road. Eisler Brothers Grocery, Riverton, KS. Great 66 stuff to buy -- the best prices we found on the whole route. Best selection of many items. In some cases it was the only time we saw some items. Scott will welcome you and help you in any way he can.

Oklahoma: Truly the Route 66 state, especially from the Kansas border to Oklahoma City. The Will Rogers Memorial in Claremore, OK is wonderful. The Blue Whale is such a neat example of what this road portrayed.

Texas: McLean is a **must.** Wow. We got into town early, before 9AM. In Amarillo folks everywhere were friendly. Nice place. Ghost Towns abound in Texas.

New Mexico: Tucumcari may advertise over 2,000 rooms but it must be remembered that those signs are very, very old. Most of the rooms are now closed, which probably is a blessing. If you want a true sense of 66 in the old days, stay at the Blue Swallow. Or drive on, as we did, to Santa Rosa. The trip up to Sandia Peak east of Albuquerque was beautiful. It's on the original route to Santa Fe.

Arizona: "Don't forget Winona?" Well, do. The Museum Club, Flagstaff, AZ is an old-time roadhouse. We stopped, thinking it was a restaurant. It isn't, but had a taco bar for happy hour which worked as dinner. Terrific local flavor with real cowboys and great atmosphere. Be sure to look through the scrapbooks they have there of the past.

California: As soon as we crossed the border, things changed. Gas went form $1.47 a gallon to $1.98 a gallon. People were rude. We were definitely done with the charm of 66. But, so were the Joads[24] by this part of their journey. Californians seemed just as cold, uncaring and self-centered as they must have been in the 1930's when they turned away the Okies at will. We watched for the old, defunct agricultural station out in the desert that turned away all of those people in the 30's and found it.

Route 66, at best, is a thinly disguised remnant of the past. The desert from Needles to Barstow was beautiful. It was 5AM, cold and wonderful as the sun rose and warmed us. We had the "Music for the All American Highway - 66" playing all the way across the desert. The one song talks about the "Children of 66" as all people who have ridden the road. We joined the ranks that day!.

The trip from Barstow to the Santa Monica pier was a nightmare. I really think that folks doing the trip should be made aware of what they are in for -- six lanes in either direction, speed limit now 75MPH and kamikaze drivers.

The trip was fantastic! We were lucky with weather. Our concern was Tornado Alley through Oklahoma and yet we hardly got our faces wet. We did suffer with the hot 60MPH+ cross-winds in both Texas and New Mexico. We had snow in Flagstaff

---

24

Fictional family of John Steinbeck's "Grapes of Wrath." They traveled from the dust bowl of the 30's to the "promised land" of California . . . much of it along Route 66. The movie shot many scenes along the route.

and again on our way home in Utah and Colorado. We put on every item of clothes we had with us and were still cold. But . . . all part of the adventure.

The memories will last a lifetime!!

Excerpts from the Holm's Diary.

Saturday, May 18, 1996 - 6AM - Odometer Reads: 22,529

Got off Lake Shore Drive to find Grant Park and the start of Route 66 . . . just happened to find the Start of Route 66 sign. *(150 feet west of Michigan Avenue on Adams, it is a sometime thing in that Route 66 signs get ripped off quite often and there is only one "Begin Route 66" sign.)* Drove out of Chicago on Adams, through the southwest part of Chicago on Ogden Avenue to Cicero and Berwyn. Not a great part of town although the Route is well marked. Had to get on the Interstate for a few miles until the exit for Joliet and Highway 53.

We found a section of the old 66 to ride that paralleled Highway 53 outside of Braidwood for a short time. It's not driven often, lots of grass growing through the concrete.

Braidwood and Godley are old mining towns. Godley once had 21 mines within 1.5 miles but all were shut down by 1906. Quiet, small towns today.

In **Dwight, IL** there is a Marathon Gas Station from 1927. Considered to be a Route 66 relic as is the nice old coot who was running it. The old road is visible here but not driveable. Old Route 66 cuts off from Highway 53 at times but every turn is marked by signs.

By 10AM we reached **Funks Grove, IL**. The Funk family has sold maple syrup here since 1825. The 5th generation is now running the "store," which is a small building out behind their house. We had a sample (they spell it `sirup') and bought our first Route 66 souvenirs.

At little before 11AM we got to **The Dixie Trucker's Home** in McLean, IL, which has been open on Route 66 since 1928. Fourth generation Walters are running it 365 days a year . . . back in 1965 they did close for a single day due to a fire.

In Litchfield, IL we stopped at **Niehaus Honda**. They were running their Customer Appreciation Days and there were bikes everywhere. We talked with Brad Niehaus because we had sent him pictures of last year's open house. Across the street is the 66 Motel from the 1920's.

The old road disappears a few miles south of Litchfield, so we hopped on the Interstate at Hamel, IL. It is now 101 degrees. It was still 100 degrees when we crossed over the Mississippi river into Missouri and St. Louis. We took Interstate 55/44 through the city then went south on Watson Road to Chippewa Street and the **Ted Drewes Custard Stand.** It was a welcome stop and we met Travis Dillion, the current manager and son-in-law of Ted . . . third generation on Route 66. Watson Road has mile after mile of old filling stations and "tourist courts." Some are abandoned but many still are in business . . . and many have carports or garages for each unit.

Stanton, MO . . . **Meramec Caverns.** Ads in 10 states, on 58 barns, 48 billboards. Like Wall Drug, the billboards are every few feet as you get closer to the caverns. We're there too early in the day - not open yet.

Doolittle, MO. Here we took the advice of the owner of the Mule Trading Post outside St James, MO and found ourselves on a back road going . . . nowhere. The road was a beautiful road for biking -- hilly, nice curves, very scenic. We kept going, and going and going . . . we saw an occasional house, the road got bumpier, the dips in the road got lower, signs syndicating the road floods appeared, signs in the woods such as "Fred is watching YOU" and "You're not wanted here!" We kept hoping for a town but instead got a sign that said "Pavement Ends" - and it did. We backtracked quickly to the Interstate. We even had a six foot black snake slither in front of the bike. Ick!

State Line Bar & Grill. (Just west of Joplin, MO, at the Kansas state line). In doing a U turn for one of Jane's many picture stops, the bike's foot shifter falls off. We get off the bike and search the ground. We find all three pieces of the shifter. Two "good ole boys" are watching us with great interest. We decide to stop in the bar to cool off and quench the thirst. Interesting place. Then we're back on the bike for the 13.2 miles of Route 66 in Kansas. The Route 66 shield is painted on the roadway in Kansas - nice touch.

After spending the night in Baxter Springs, KS (one mile from the Oklahoma line) we hit the state where Route 66 was born: **Oklahoma.** John Steinbeck in *Grapes of Wrath* called it The Road of Desperation. Home of the "Okies." A car with three mattresses on top meant rich Okies, two mattresses meant mediocre wealth and one mattress meant dirt poor. Three hundred thousand Okies fled the dust bowl of the 30's. **Commerce, OK**'s main street is Mickey Mantle Boulevard . . . it's where "The Mick" was born and raised.

In Vinita, OK we mine a genuine Route 66 treasure: **The Clanton Cafe.** In addition to the great breakfast, (two eggs, over medium, hash browns, biscuit & gravy *for $1.90)* we meet Mr. Clanton and **all** the staff. We're asked to sign his guestbook and we take pictures. The walls are covered with old pictures of Route 66 as well as a current picture of the Governor Illinois - Mrs. Clanton's cousin.

Clanton tells us about his history with Route 66. His grandfather started the restaurant 70 years ago. His father was a puller. He stood behind the horses to make Route 66. Clanton's college roommate is now the Chief of the Miami Tribe "up the road a bit." His mother in law is now 100 years old and came to Vinita by train as a young girl. Will Rogers went to school in Vinita. We listened to his stories for an hour and hated to leave.

At Catoosa, OK (Cherokee meaning "Here live the people of the light") we ponder **The Blue Whale**, now permanently beached and looking a bit worse for wear. *(Editor's note:* Rumor has it that this tattered remnant of Route 66 has earned a **Federal Grant** to be restored to it's original "splendor.")

In **Stroud, OK** we stopped at the Rock Cafe. It is said that the original owner paid $5.00 for all of the building's stone. It had been excavated from the Route 66 construction and the contractor was delighted to be rid of it. Everyone there when we stopped was riding the Route. A couple from Austria and a man from Washington state.

At the **Cadillac Ranch**[25], west of Amarillo, TX we caught up with some German names we had seen in the Guest Books we'd been signing as we moved west. Early in the trip they were two days ahead of us, then one day, then same day. On two of the seven spoke any English at all. We criss-crossed with them the rest of the "Cadillac Ranch" day, then moved out in front for the rest of the trip.

In Vega, TX, **within a few miles of half way between Chicago and Los Angeles**, we stopped at the Neon Cafe & Route 66 Museum. We pulled in along with the seven German bikers. We noticed a VW van out front and - lo and behold - it was Bob Waldmire. We had been watching for him since talking with his brother, Buzz, in Springfield, IL. Here he was. Painting a mural on the outside of the restaurant. He invited us to visit his visitor's center in Hackberry, AZ.

The museum sells everything imaginable regarding Route 66 - from new souvenirs to old, original signs. It **was the best display we saw on the trip.**

In **Glenrio, TX** (a ghost town that straddles the state lines of Texas and New Mexico) we found the motel made famous by Route 66 - now in a shambles. On the **west side** of the motel the sign says *First Motel In Texas* on the **east side**: *Last Motel in Texas.* Apparently this clever bit of marketing did not cause the motel to prosper.

Endee, NM was known for its brawls. There were so many Sunday morning burials after the Saturday night shoot-outs that a trench was dug each Saturday at the edge of town to save time. It's a **lot** sleepier now. We stayed the night in **Santa Rosa, NM** where we met David and Lynn, a couple from Tulsa traveling on their motorcycle. We had supper with them and swapped bike stories. Nice. One of the icons of Route 66, **Club Cafe**, was closed but plans to re-open in 1997.

Tijeras Canyon is just east of Albuquerque. We pulled into the Ranger's station for information and walked a bit of a trail to old Pueblo ruins[26]. The sign there says "Stay on the trail so you see the snakes before they see you." Yikes. We followed the road up the mountain -- the first part of

---

[25]

Ten Cadillacs buried nose down in the ground. We parked by the side of the road and walked to the cars. We added our names to the graffiti already on the cars. Evidently they are repainted every few years and the graffiti artists start over.

---

[26]

This - and for many miles in all directions - is Anasazi country.

the road is the original Route 66 on its way to Santa Fe. We turned off to climb the mountain. Beautiful, twisting road. The elevation at the Canyon is 6,300 feet. We then climbed to 10,378 at Sandia Crest. The view is 15,000 square miles -- a 100 mile radius. We looked down over the city of Albuquerque.[27]

In the city of Albuquerque we stop at the **Route 66 Diner**, a renovated Phillips 66 gas station.. All of the servers have taken on the persona of cartoon characters -- from their nicknames to their haircuts. Lots of neon and 50's music. We continued on, crossed the Rio Grande and headed out of the city. At the western edge of the city is Nine Mile Hill. To the west old 66 becomes a frontage road and then disappears. A roadrunner runs in front of the bike. After Albuquerque, the land changes again. The road passes through ancient black lava flows -- considered to be the New Mexico Badlands. Quite a sight.

Six miles west of Thoreau we cross the **Continental Divide** -- elevation: 7,275 feet -- the highest point on Route 66. We are totally worn out from battling a 40 mph cross wind. The higher gusts try to throw the bike off the highway and throw sand in our faces. **Gallup, NM** is only 31 miles away and it seems like an eternity to get there. Gallup is considered to be the leading Indian trading center of the Southwest. Zuni, Hopi and Navajo art and goods are plentiful. There is a trading center on every block.

We drove old 66 in Gallup. Passed the El Rancho Hotel. Guest register there includes Tracy, Hepburn, Kirk Douglas, Alan Ladd, Bogart, Jack Benny and more. Erroll Flynn is said to have ridden his horse into the bar. We chose Super 8. They had their own Indian trading post in the motel and we bought some delightful jewelry.

We realize we are truly in desert country when the Weather Channel back at the motel tells us that (at 10:30PM) the temperature has dropped from the 90 degrees of the afternoon to 65 degrees. By 5AM it is 50 and when we leave the motel at 6:15AM there is no wind. We're in turtle necks and sweatshirts with long johns. At 6:45AM we cross into Arizona and switch to Mountain Daylight Time. We stop in **Holbrook, AZ** for breakfast at The Plainsman . . . eggs, toast and coffee for both of us comes to just $4.00! Just off old Route 66 (beyond Winona, AZ) is **Meteor Crater**. We toured the museum and walked part of the rim of the crater. At noon we are in **Flagstaff, AZ** with beautiful pine trees and mountains -- a pleasant change from the desert.

We checked in to the Super 8 in Flagstaff and noticed **lots** of motorcycles. We spoke with a German couple on their rented Harley who were riding the route. Also spoke with a group of 'Wingers from California who were on their way home from

---

27

Editor's Note: On the east side of the Sandia Crest you can do as the Holm's did and "bike" up to the top. West of Albuquerque you can ride to the foot of the Peak and take a dramatic tramway ride up to the top.

the Black Hills and Mt. Rushmore. The **Museum Club** at Flagstaff is listed in all of the books and was only a few blocks from the hotel. It sounded like a great place for dinner. When we got there we realized it was a bar and not a restaurant, but they had a taco bar, so we stayed. Had tacos and a beer for supper. It is a wonderful place. It's an old road house, complete with stage and dance floor . The other bikers were there, too and we had great fun.

On Saturday, **May 25,** 1996, we wake up to rain and 36 (!) degrees. We figured that if we went back to sleep for an hour it might be better. At 6:30AM there is no rain but it is **31 degrees.** We left Flagstaff at 7AM in bright sun and 32 degrees. We were on the road about 15 minutes when the rain clouds started building in front of us. We stopped along the road to put on rainsuits. They helped as much with the cold as the wet air. There was **snow** accumulated along the road and **snow showers.**

By 8AM we had made **Seligman, AZ** and stopped for breakfast at the Copper Cart. Seligman is home to the **Delgadilo brothers.** Angel is the town barber[28] and brother Juan runs the Snowcap Drive In -- home of the dead chicken dinner. Seligman is the starting point for a large loop of original Route 66 that was cut off by construction of the Interstate. **Hackberry, AZ** is on that loop and Hackberry's Route 66 Visitor's Center may be the only buildings still standing in Hackberry. It used to be the Old Hackberry General Store and is the province of **Bob Waldmire**, who has made all the Route 66 books, maps and videos.

After **Kingman, AZ** we hit Sitgreave's Pass . . . the Back Country Byway of the Black Mountains. It is said that 'flatlanders' (Okies) were so petrified of this pass that they paid the locals to drive their cars across it. The cars and trucks of that era had a gravity feed system so they were driven backwards up the mountain. **Oatman, AZ** is the liveliest 'ghost town' one is likely to visit. Route 66 is the Main Street . . . the only street in town. Steep mountain cliffs surround the town on all sides. The area, including the town itself, is known for the wild burros. This was a mining area until the mines were shut down in 1909. The miners left town and left their burros behind. The burros are known to eat helmet liners and bike seats so we only stopped long enough for a couple pictures. The **Oatman Hotel** was where Clark Gable and Carole Lombard spent their honeymoon.

The **road from Oatman down the mountain to Topock, AZ** is beautiful. Lots of twisties. Some of the turns said 15 miles per hour. Roger said they were miss marked and should read 5 MPH. At 3:30PM **we cross into California.** This was the place where the Okies, thinking that they had made it to the promised land, got out of their trucks and waded into the Colorado River. They didn't realize they still had to cross a desert and two mountain ranges before completing their journey.

When we reached **Needles, CA,** it was 70 degrees and sunny. Wonderful!

---

[28] And President Emeritus of the Arizona Route 66 Historical Association.

We had supper at the Hungry Bear Restaurant with a terrific homemade strawberry pie. After supper it was such a beautiful night we biked through the town of Needles. Saw the Route 66 stops. We rode down to the Colorado River with a rainbow over the Black Mountains we had just crossed. We also had the chance to talk with firefighters who were on call in the southwest due to the large number of forest fires.

If you've ever wondered about the cost of gas: We topped up our tank in Needles proper for $1.66 a gallon. Two blocks away -- on the freeway -- it was $1.96. Just another reason to get off the Interstate and take a look at the original Route 66.

We had been warned to cross the Mojave Desert very early in the morning due to the extreme heat. We headed out at 5:10AM. Sunrise in the Desert was beautiful . . . and cold. Very cold. In **Victorville, CA** at 8:30AM it is 63 degrees and not a cloud in the sky. Our goal this morning is to get to the Santa Monica Pier as quickly as possible to avoid traffic in Los Angeles.

Beginning in **Barstow, CA,** the freeway is four lanes wide in each direction. The speed limit is 75 and most people are doing 90. The road is crowded, the expansion joints of the road don't follow the lanes[29] so Roger is continually bracing over bumps.

At 9:10AM we gas up in **Ontario, CA** and then get back on the freeway and continue to play dodge 'em with kamikaze drivers. We can hardly wait for this to be over . . . and . . . at 10:15AM it is! We reach the **Santa Monica Pier, the End of Route 66!!** where it is sunny and 72 degrees.

We parked the bike on the pier; tried to ignore the guy eating food out of the garbage can next to us and congratulated ourselves on our journey. The Pier includes the wonderful carousel from the movie *The Sting*. We had a shrimp lunch while "people watching." Then it was time to head out again.

In Barstow, CA, we cross our "inbound track" and church bells are ringing with the sun low in the sky. **Our Route 66 adventure is complete.** Now it's time to head home. And **that** odyssey must be the subject of a separate diary!

A Harley on The Mother Road[30]

Graeme Ware, in September 1995, rode a 1979 Harley Davidson FLH80 from Chi-

---

[29] Virtually all freeways in the Los Angeles Basin have been "re-laned." That is: by use of new lane stripes they have created an additional lane (or two!). The original expansion seams lined up with the lanes but that is no longer the case.

[30] Reprinted with the permission of the author, Graeme J. Ware E-Mail: 101655.1370@compuserve.com

cago, Illinois, all the way to Santa Monica, California. He found well over 80% still drivable (or ridable), more if you include the dead-end sections and parallel routes caused by various re-alignments over the years. His "diary" of the ride gives us terrific insights into riding the route on two wheels . . . particularly if you've been feeling you will need a brand new bike for such an ambitious ride of 2,400+ miles.

It was mid-morning as I rode down Lakeshore drive towards Downtown Chicago. A brief stop at the birthplace of my two-wheeled steed the day before had meant an overnight stay near Milwaukee, Wisconsin, home of Miller and many other breweries, but most notably the home of Harley Davidson. With the factory now behind me, I was almost there. The start of a lifetime's ambition. Route 66 on a Harley.

The unmistakable twin spires atop the Sears Tower, the focal point of the Chicago skyline. I remembered it from my visits in 1990 when I vowed I would return, not really believing that just five years later I would fulfil my dream. The bright morning sunshine and cool breeze from Lake Michigan coupled to the deep throb of the V-twin beneath me gave a sense of apprehension, delight and ecstasy all at once. The feeling a child has at Christmas when that long awaited day arrives and all the presents lay in front of him. Contrary to popular myth, the 66 never did go 'shore-to-shore' but a quick photo session at the lakeshore was an essential point of the trip. Then on to the real start.

Having located the junction of Jackson Blvd and Michigan Ave to take the necessary photographs, the journey proper started. Unfortunately, Jackson is one way, in the wrong direction. Therefore a quick lap of the block was necessary to ensure that I rode as much of the original route as possible. Another slight detour to Lou Mitchell's for brunch meant that I was well behind schedule. I had spent too long prior to starting the trip and now had less than three weeks including my return ride from L.A. to Tennessee. The bike had run like a dream coming up from Tennessee on the previous two days. Only one bolt had shaken loose (the one holding the gas tank !) and that was easily replaced. I followed the route markings through Chicago's South-Side, thinking to myself that this was going to be easy if the route was all marked.

I hadn't expected route markings and had therefore attached my guide and route map to the top of the tank, with bungy cord, for easy reference. Just as I was thinking what a great start I'd had, I heard a 'thunk' and couldn't hear myself think any more. I throttled back, indicated, pulled-over and put the bike onto the side-stand in one action. The cause was obvious at once. The front exhaust manifold bolt had totally fallen out, leaving the exhaust hanging some distance away from the cylinder. I had no option but to ride on until I could find a workshop or garage.

Riding 5 miles (8km) with a Harley on open-headers is something that I won't forget in a hurry (nor will most of Chicago !).A speed-shop spotted on the side of the road assisted, once the motor had cooled down, by supplying a bolt and assorted washers to 'shorten' it. Off I went again, content in the knowledge that the problem was fixed, in the direction of Joliet. An essential stop was the old prison; but where was it ? Having ridden through the town twice, I stopped at what appeared to be a Police Dept. It was in fact the workshop for the 'black-&-whites'. Needless to say the mechanics came out to have a good look at the bike when I arrived. A more helpful bunch you couldn't meet. Armed with directions, I set off to the start of the Movie (The Blues Brothers, for anyone not following so far !) Well there it is, just like in the movie. But wait. Where are the gates ? Can this really be the place ? I rode up to the visitors entrance, removed my crash helmet as instructed by the sign on the door, and tried to go in. It was locked. After a few minutes I heard the operation of a solenoid lock, pushed the door and went in.

The guard assured me 'yes Sir, it sure is' in answer to my question. But where is the gate ? He pointed it out to me, and yes, although changed now, I was in the right place. Seeing the camera around my neck he cautioned that no photos were allowed. I went away somewhat disappointed, but stopped briefly a little way up the road to take photos anyway, then roared off into the distance, waiting for the wail of sirens.

Getting back onto the old Route 66 proved to be a slight problem, but seeing a friendly looking State Trooper outside the Joliet Police Dept. I thought I'd take a chance that an APB had [not] been put out about an English Harley rider taking photos, and ask directions."Down to the lights, take a right. At the next lights go straight over and keep going. If anyone troubles you at the second lights just keep on going right through". Interesting, I thought, the area didn't look so bad!

I continued down the old 66, which at this point is well signed. Thought it was about time to get a Mc D's, so stopped in Pontiac. The manager wanted to know all about the Harley. Seems a lot of people want to know what year it was made ("Hey bud, what years that Shovel?" or "Sure like your scoot. What year is she?"). Overnight stop was taken somewhere between Pontiac and Bloomington (after Chenoa but, I think, before Lexington - I don't remember exactly where). Much of the last 10 miles I took the original 66 which says 'Road Closed'. Presumably it was decided to maintain only one two lane carriageway of the old road, since the I55 runs parallel to it now. The second carriageway is on the west side (i.e. between the I55 and the 66) and is now fairly broken up, and has grass growing through it. Did that stop me? No!

An early start (6.45am) was made the following day, due to my poor choice of camping place, having been rudely awakened at half past midnight and again at 4.30am by freight trains rumbling through. I had ridden until darkness and had been unable to find a camp-ground easily. I therefore found a small road and followed it, then a few yards down I took a dirt track around a corn field, then parked up. I rolled out my sleeping bag on a large plastic survival bag and had fallen asleep. What I hadn't noticed was that it was only 10 yards from the railway tracks! At 12.30, I heard a loud engine noise and thinking that it was an off-road vehicle coming down the track that I was sleeping on, I rolled into the hedge to protect myself. The noise got louder and louder, as did my heart-beat! When the train finally sounded the horn it sure woke me up!

Fine sunny weather and a good morning chill made riding a real pleasure. Little traffic and the rumble of the Harley to allow a gentle relaxed cruise. However, just before Bloomington the fog cut safe speed to 25mph and visor/glasses became totally covered with water after a few hundred yards. Fog cleared at around Funk's Grove, the famous Maple Syrup (which they seem unable to spell correctly) production area. From there on, a fine ride was had down to the 'Dixie Truckers' Home' (est. 1926) at McLean. Here, besides obtaining a hearty breakfast cheaply ($6 for full cooked breakfast and coffee), there is a Route 66 display and Hall of Fame, together with a souvenir shop selling lots of Route 66 goodies and the best selection of books on the subject that I came across along the Route. The next port of call was Williamsville, a quaint quiet little town with an excellent museum. Then on through Springfield, and Mitchell.

'Chain of Rocks Bridge', just beyond Mitchell is worth a detour. It is signposted and mentioned in most of the books on the 66. It became famous because of John Carpenter's 1981 film 'Escape from New York'. Shortly before this, I had my first 'disagreement' with the Harley Davidson. Luckily I took to the grass and little damage was done to me or the bike. After a brief rest at the Chain of Rocks, a superb sight at sunset, I crossed over the Mississippi and into Missouri.

St. Louis at approaching night-fall seemed a bad idea, so a note was made to visit again on another trip. So a quick detour to say that I'd visited, and I was back on the old road (as best I could here, as there are many alignments bypassing downtown). Over the years there have been many variations in the official route of the 66, and it is sometimes possible to find several 'alignments' running parallel to each-other. Each has just as much right to call itself the Route 66 as the next one has! Through Kirkwood, where both the railroad depot and the National Museum of Transport are worth a visit. Little of the original alignment exists from here to Gray Summit, most being under the I44, so the later Manchester Road (SR199) was taken. The road is a superbly scenic drive, especially on a bike. Camping over-night at a site near Six Flags, another interesting parallel route was noted.

With the morning sun just struggling over the horizon, the Harley was fired-up and I headed back the way I'd come, to check out another alignment. An hour and a half of marvelous open roads later, I was back at Pacific then followed along to visit the Red Cedar Inn. This landmark opened back in 1934, and still has the 'old route' feel, although unfortunately closed when I visited. Locals said that the owner is a lovely lady who is glad to explain the history to any passing travellers on the Route 66. The community seems extremely proud of their past; and so they should be! On through St. Clair, Stanton. Wait! Stanton, ahhhh, home of Meramec Caverns. Signed on billboards from the start of the road in Illinois, perhaps the biggest tourist trap on the 'Main Street of America'! Opened in 1935, it has been an attraction since. I decided to press on without visiting, and left Jesse James and Kate Smith in peace.

Sullivan, Bourbon (no, wine country, not the hard stuff!) where the main street is still a piece of the past, with signs painted on the shop walls and old gas stations. On towards St. James the open road was dotted with stalls selling fresh grapes and locally produced wine and produce. A quick halt to buy grapes and have a chat with the owner of one such stall, then on towards the 'Big Piney River'. In Cuba you can't miss the 'Wagon Wheel Motel', which I'm told is a great place to stay whilst travelling through (ample parking for bikes and cars). On from St. James, through Rolla, Doolittle and nearly into Arlington. The old, old road can be followed here. Best to plan this for a warm sunny afternoon. There is an original steel-truss bridge, complete with cobble paved deck, and shortly after the 'Devils Elbow'. The memory of this will stay with me not just because of the fantastic river bluff scenery.

The right exhaust-pipe, which had held on since Chicago, now decided to part company from the engine. Shattering the peace, I pulled up to let everything cool down and carry out the necessary repair. With such amazing scenery there are worse places to break down! All bolted back together and off I went through St. Robert to Waynesville. Onto Lebanon and then Springfield, via a long stretch of original road. Time to find a campsite, which following a brief visit to the airport (where there are airports there are taxis, and taxi drivers must know the campsites). Arriving late into the campsite, after stopping for a good meal, I noticed another tent pitched at the far side of a large grass area. A Chevy pick-up was parked close to the tent and two people were sitting by a large camp-fire. Got chatting to the couple, who were from Illinois. Chris and Kristy were heading down to Tulsa, OK, having just spent time at a rodeo. We drank a few beers together, chatted for a while, then they headed off to check out a couple of country and western clubs. I remained, sorting out the bike for the next morning and keeping warm by the fire, accompanied by the dog 'Thunder'.

Now it is 7:30am and we were cooking hotdogs over the remains of last-night's fire. First stop was the Shrine Mosque in Springfield. This was a mini 'Grand Ole Opry' at one time. This is 'Wild Bill Hickok' country, with all the tourist hype that goes with it! Take the stories with a very large pinch of salt! Heading west again, Halltown is full of 'antique' shops and is worth a browse. Along this section several old sections of road can still be seen and many can still be driven. Albatros, Phelps, Rescue and other marvelously named places struggle for their survival, some have perished already. Between Carthage and Centerville a bridge was being rebuilt, meaning that I couldn't get through at all, but by doing a large loop and coming back to the other side of where the bridge had been, I ensured that none of the 66 was missed. The road-builders that I questioned must have thought I was mad when I asked if it was possible to get through on a motorbike (I didn't know that the bridge was totally out at the time, which explained why they had a good laugh!).

Continuing on through Joplin, it started to rain. West of Joplin a quick jog right results in the opportunity to follow a very old stretch. It is signed, but it is easy to drive past seeing it only when it is too late (as I did). The sign reads 'Old Route 66 Next Right'; watch out for it!

Just before Galena, Kansas starts. Motorbike paradise. Kept in use by the locals and fully supported by them. Galena seemed to have very little to make me stop, and since the weather was less than wonderful (slight drizzling rain), I continued on through to Riverton. Riverton is a sleepy little place; nobody seems to have told it that the 66 isn't a major route anymore! West of Riverton, the Brush Creek March Arch Bridge, complete with graffiti, has been restored (structurally, but not optically!) by the local Route 66 association. A plaque proudly proclaims this achievement. Baxter Springs was passed in a flash, and that was the end of Kansas! Of all the States visited, I think Kansas had tried to keep the 66 alive as much as any. Streamers and billboards with 66 events all over the place. Shops with Route 66 collectibles in the windows. Perhaps because they only have a few miles, there is less for the enthusiasts to take care of.

West by CB750 on Route 66[31]

---

[31] Mitch Boehm writing in *Cycle World* May, 1993, page 92. *Cycle World* has the largest circulation - by a **lot** - of any motorcycle magazine. A worthwhile addition to anyone's library.

THE CYLINDER HEAD CAME OFF with a minor yank. "There's your problem," said Jerry Post, the baby-faced mechanic at Farr's Kawasaki/Suzuki shop who had pulled the engine from my sick CB750 just minutes before, "that piston is about to come apart." He was right. Besides several cracks, an ugly sinkhole had developed in the crowned center of the engine's number-four piston. Along with the blown head gasket, it wasn't hard to figure out why the motor had made such a nasty racket as we rode into Tulsa, Oklahoma, the day before.

"I'm amazed the thing ran," Post added, as he, myself and Editor David Edwards considered the crippled engine lying on the workbench, "there's no way this bike would've made it to California." At that point, I realized we would be staying in Tulsa a lot longer than the one-night stopover originally planned. The weird chain of events that led us to that dealership aboard a pair of mostly original 1969 Honda CB750 Kos-"K-Zeroes" in collector-speak-began about a month earlier as I thumbed through a copy of Walneck's Classic Cycle Trader, a monthly paper dealing primarily in classic motorcycles. On the next-to-last page, just below a grainy black-and-white photo of a pair of bikes sitting in a field, I spied an ad that read: (2) 1969 Honda CB750. I red, I blue. Both original and nice. Trades or offers."

I had always dreamed of owning a first-year CB750, even back in the early '70s in northern Ohio, where I spent the majority of my youth tearing up the fields behind our house aboard my very first motorcycle, a fire-engine-red Honda SL70. A guy who lived at the end of our street had an aqua-blue 750 Honda, and every day he would roar past our house on his way to and from work, the crisp, almost magical wail of those four exhaust pipes ricocheting through the neighborhood. The image of that bike and the sounds it made were powerful stuff for a 10-year-old just discovering motorcycling, and they had stayed with me since.

The ad had been placed by a Mr. Thomas L. Smith, who made his home in southeastern Illinois, about 90 miles north of St. Louis. I remember thinking that Illinois was a long way to go to buy any motorcycle, let alone a sight-unseen one, but after all, this was a pair of honest-to-goodness '69 CB750s in supposedly good shape, an intriguing find. So I yelled into the next office. "Hey David," I said, "you wanna buy a '69 Honda 750?" Now, Edwards can't get enough old, neat motorcycles, but since he's already got a half-dozen or so classics cluttering up the Cycle World garage, I expected little interest from him.

Big surprise. Sixty seconds later we're hunched over his desk, scheming away like a couple of 12-year-olds in a tree fort. "Here's what we'll do," he said, "we'll fly back there, buy the bikes, and ride 'em home on Route 66. It'll make a good story: I'll shoot the photos and you can write it." After some dickering, Smith said he would take $4000 for the bikes, a lot of money for a couple of unproven 23-year-old Hondas, especially considering the state of my bank account, but the plan-foolish and irresponsible as it was-had its appeals.

After all, this wasn't simply a chance to traverse Route 66, the most renowned two-laner in America, the road John Steinbeck called "the mother road, the road of flight" in his epic novel The Grapes of Wrath; here was a chance to secure for my garage the very machine that helped ignite my lifelong attraction to motorcycling, a bike I'd lusted after since I was a kid. Heck, this was perhaps the most important Japanese motorcycle ever made. And there was more. Unlike a typical cross-country trek, this excursion would give us the chance to tour The Way Folks Used To Tour, back in the days before full fairings, air suspension and four-speaker audio systems. Financial chaos or not, I was all for it. David would get the aqua-blue bike; I'd get the red one, which would go perfectly with my candy-red 1979 CBX Six.

Three weeks later, cash in our pockets and an absolute minimum of riding gear in our Rev Pak bags, we boarded a Boeing 757 bound for the St. Louis, Missouri, airport, where Smith had agreed to pick us up. Somewhere over eastern New Mexico, I wondered for the 20th time what condition the bikes would actually be in: Would they be as mechanically sound as their owner thought they were? Or were they actually worn-out heaps that would strand us in the middle of the Texas Panhandle, which, from my vantage point at 35,000 feet, looked mighty desolate.

When we got both bikes running later that day in Smith's garage, I felt better about the whole deal, though it was clear to me that we weren't dealing with particularly well-maintained machinery here. Besides needing a healthy amount of coaxing before it would fire, my candy-red 750 sounded noisy and loose, as if it had twice as many miles as the 24,000 showing on its clock. It had also been repainted, which did little for my disposition, since I'd been told that its paint was original. David's aqua-blue 750, with about half as many miles, sounded much tighter and looked significantly better, though neither machine appeared eager to deal with a journey of the magnitude we had planned, even after mounting the new tires and seats we had sent ahead from California.

After saddling up the bikes, we waved goodbye to the Smith family and headed south toward St. Louis and the point where we'd pick up 66. Our goal that chilly evening was to ride the 90 miles to St. Louis, find rooms, and pray for good weather and reliable motorcycles the following day, when we planned to get as far as Tulsa, Oklahoma, roughly 400 miles to the west. As we headed through the endless cornfields of southern Illinois, I felt what must have been the same mixture of excitement and apprehension the members of Steinbeck's Joad family must have felt as they embarked on their westward journey from the Oklahoma dust bowl of the 1930s. Our prayers for clear weather and trouble-free mounts obviously went unanswered, because we were greeted with foul weather and flawed motorcycles the following day.

The steady rain and 40-degree temperatures weren't so terrible-we'd brought electric vests and rain-gear-though the oil pumping from the breather systems of both engines was. Within a hundred miles, oil had covered our luggage and the rear tires of both bikes. Add that to the pouring rain, he frigid temperatures and the growing metal-to-metal clatter coming from my bike's engine, and you get a pretty good idea what our 10-hour ride to Tulsa on Day One was like.

Our luck changed the following morning, however, through a chance encounter with a gentleman named Jerry Burnell, who we met at a gas station and who led us to the only dealership within 200 miles that was open on Mondays, a Suzuki/Kawasaki shop owned by Funnybike drag-racer Marshall Farr and his wife Vicky. Burrell told us that the folks at Farr's were not only good people, but good with the wrenches, too. He wasn't kidding. Especially young Jerry Post, who turned out to be a veritable CB750 wizard who had rebuilt dozens of single-cam 750s as a teenager.

As it turned out, David's bike had wrongly routed oil-breather lines-a-relatively easy fix for Post. He even routed additional lengths of breather hose out past the rear fender, old-Triumph style, just in case the oiling problem came back. My bike, however, was far more seriously flawed. A previous owner had done a particularly miserable job of installing a big-bore kit; pressure was blowing past the rings, pressurizing the crankcase and pumping oil out of the breather tubes. The bike's top end was a mess, and only after scouring the Tulsa area for a new cylinder and a set of pistons and rings were we able to finally get my bike running right. After two-and-a-half days, we were on our way. Again.

Up to that point, we'd seen little of legendary 66. But as we rode westward from

Tulsa, through small towns with names like Sapulpa and Chandler, the 66 I'd read about and imagined began to come alive. These were small, country hamlets, each, it seemed, with a filling station, a church and a Main Street lined with cafes and antique shops. At one point, we rode past a deserted high-school football field with faded wooden bleachers and tall light poles surrounding the field. I closed my eyes and could picture the scene on a Friday night: The packed grandstands, the brisk night air filled with the sound of cheering and the smell of hot dogs and freshly mowed grass. Just like back home in Ohio.

Like the towns it cut through, the road itself radiated character and history. As we rode along, the bikes now running smoothly and crisply, and dripping only a bit of oil, we noted older, original sections of 66 branching off from the main route. These were usually short loops the woods, or sections that parallel to the newer route, with weeds growing though the cracks. Not all of these sections were asphalt; some were concrete, laid down in sections like rows of dominoes. Over the years, the climate and traffic had broken the surface, which made both bikes, with their worn, underdamped legs, bounce around a lot. What must it have been like to travel this road back in the '30s and '40s?

Buddy Marion, an older gentleman who is a fixture at Faff's shop, recalled his travels on 66 as a kid in the '30s. "Back then," he said, "66 was the only way to get to Oklahoma City, or anywhere else west. Going to OK[32] City roughly 100 miles away was a big deal back then. My dad would spend a whole day checking over the car, a '38 Ford, I think it was."

We stopped for lunch at the Sweets'n Eats Cafe in Stroud, Oklahoma, which featured a recently restored, vintage Coke sign painted on the side of the 88-year-old building. Elmer and Peggy Williams owned the place; Peggy cooked, and, if you were willing to listen, Elmer told stories. "Back then, the road was mostly sand and gravel," he told me. "I went west on 66 in 1936; musta had 40 flats on that trip, and we broke an axle somewhere in Texas."

Despite the cozy towns and the neighborly people along the old route these days, it was tough to ignore the decay that had taken place along its path over the years, especially as we drove westward into the flat, dry desert of Texas. In towns like Texola and Shamrock, homes and businesses were boarded up by the dozens. It was eerie; each of these abandoned filling stations, tourist courts and cafes were once-thriving businesses, healthy enterprises that represented someone's hard work and dreams, a future for their family. Now, they were no more than faded, crumbling ruins, homes for rats and birds and drifters.

People we talked to along the route were bitter about the decline. These folks missed the Old Days, when business and life in

---

[32] The "locals" pronounce it: "Oak City."

general along 66 was better. In Grants, New Mexico, a uranium-mining boom town that flourished until Reagan-era deregulation cut the guts out of the U.S. uranium business, we met up with Pete Chandis, the son of Greek immigrants, who had come to Grants back in '55 and operated a cafe called the Western Host Restaurant. In those days, Chandis, now 71, was open 19 hours a day, employed a dozen people, and had a line of people waiting impatiently at the door when he'd open up every morning. Now it was just him: host, waiter, cook and cashier.

"Those were the good old days," he said, as David and I ate the breakfast Chandis had just cooked for us, "I was open 5 a.m. to midnight every day." I asked him what had happened. "The interstate killed us," he said, looking at the dusty tables cluttering the dining room, "the day I-40 opened, it was like an atomic bomb hit this town." One of Chandis' few regular customers, Colonel Bill Loughnane, a sharp, West Point grad in his 70s who had flown P-47 Thunderbolts in WWII, F-86 Sabres in Korea and F-4 Phantoms in Vietnam, agreed. "Eisenhower's buddies didn't make enough on the war," he said, "so he had them build the interstates."

Breakfast finished, we gave Chandis a big tip, thanked him and the Colonel for the conversation, and walked to the bikes. As we saddled up, I couldn't help but smile at the sign in front of the cafe. It said: "Yoo-hoo ... Eat here, or we both starve. 34 years. Breakfast always." Like the road he lived his life on, Pete Chandis was a survivor. In a way, our bikes were survivors, too. Like 66, the golden years of the mighty CB750 have been decades past, but these first-year bikes had stood up pretty well over time despite the mechanical gremlins we had uncovered. Just as Pete still made a pretty good bacon-and-egg breakfast, these bikes could still get you from point A to point B in comfort and style, and do so with enough power and handling ability to keep things interesting. They weren't overly fast, they had flimsy brakes and a loose, distinctly "old bike" feel, but considering their age and the low-maintenance life they'd led, they worked surprisingly well.

Heading west, though, we couldn't quite steer clear of mischief Just out of Santa Fe, New Mexico,[33] we stopped at the Santo Domingo Trading Post, a neat little mercantile that had attracted the likes of John F. Kennedy and the editors of Life magazine to its doors in the early 60s. The bikes looked particularly brilliant basking in the golden, afternoon sun, so we rolled them onto the train tracks just in front of the trading post to take a photo or two.

Out of nowhere, an Amtrak train came barreling around a bend in the tracks at about 80 mph. Caught completely off guard by both the appearance and speed of the train, we sprinted the 30 or 40 feet to the bikes, pushed them off their centerstands and rolled them off the tracks. We got them out of harm's way maybe five or six seconds before the train thundered by, and the adrenaline that flooded my gut damn near made me throw up.

---

[33] Santa Fe - the capital of New Mexico - was on one of the earlier "alignments" of Route 66. Even before the Interstate, the route was changed to run directly west to Albuquerque.

We ran into more bum luck just out of Oatman, Arizona, an old mining town that once housed Clark Gable and Carol Lombard for the night on their honeymoon. On a steep, switchback grade, David's drive threw its masterlink, which allowed the chain to wad up against the engine case and knock out a hole large enough to give a clear view of the transmission gears-not an uncommon occurrence with early Honda 750s. We temporarily fixed the hole later that evening after limping back to Kingman, using a scrap of aluminum and some amazing metal epoxy called JB Weld.

The wildest part of the Oatman breakdown was the appearance of Cajun and Wanda-a beer-drinking, outlaw couple who rode up on a Harley Softail and stopped to help. Attached to a buckle on his right boot, Cajun just happened to have a correctly sized master link, which he agreed to sell us. As Wanda pulled a Budweiser from one of the Harley's leather bags, Cajun grabbed the $10 bill from David's hand and drawled, "You guys are lucky; we usually don't stop for Jap bikes."

Ironically, we'd brought extra master links for just such an emergency, though they had been machined incorrectly and didn't fit. Two days later, after crossing the California desert through Needles, Amboy, Barstow and Victorville, we started down the Cajon Pass, which would funnel us into the Los Angeles basin. Heading down the grade, we rode a neat old section of original 66, which paralleled the freeway yet rarely saw traffic. Then, just before it dumped us into smoggy San Bernardino, Route 66 suddenly dead-ended.

David and I stopped, killed the engines, and just sat there, staring off past the barricade. The original path of old 66 went another 75 miles, all the way to Santa Monica and the Pacific Ocean. Very little is left today, and neither of us had much enthusiasm for finding it. For us the real end of 66-The Mother Road-was here; ending this inspiring trek on the crowded and dirty streets of L.A. would be somehow sacrilegious.

As I sat there, replaying the last 10 days in my mind, two things came clear to me.

One was that Route 66 and the CB750 I was sitting on were somehow linked in history: Both had been the only game in town at one point; the best and most popular in their respective fields. Both had gotten old, decayed, and been forgotten. And now, both were experiencing a renewal, a sort of rebirth. This blending of old road and old motorcycles was a good thing, for going backwards in time and reliving a slice of the past gave me a perspective on motorcycling and on life that I hadn't had before.

The second was that I'd do this trip again in a heartbeat. Just like Bobby Troup's hit song says: Won't you take this timely tip/When you make that California trip/Get your kicks on Route 66. Yeah, kicks, even on an old Honda 750. Preferably one without a big-bore kit installed.

Route 66 Resources

We're often asked about **other** sources of information on Route 66. We assembled the following from myriad sources.

Books

Woodward, Kirk G. **Motorcycle Guide to Route 66.** ISBN: 1-929954-06-9. Trade Paper $19.95. Published by: HHJM, Inc., 2024 Heatherbrook Drive, Grapevine, TX 76051-3048. 1-800-553-5883. Published by the organizers of The Annual Mother Road Ride/Rally®, this book draws heavily on the experiences of motorcyclists who have travelled Route 66. It includes one of the few West to East (Los Angeles toward Chicago) route guides. Most guides are written for the Westbound (Chicago toward Los Angeles) traveler. There is also a summary of the laws regarding motorcycles in the eight states Route 66 passed through and a listing of motorcycle dealers along the route.

Riding Route 66 - Kirk Woodward's diary - with pictures - of riding two wheels down Route 66 in 1997. One of the newest 66 books. It includes the new "icon" at the Convention Center in Tucumcari. $9.95 Order at: 817-488-4940.

Rittenhouse, Jack D. **A Guide Book to Highway 66.** ISBN: 0-8263-1148-2. Trade Paper $7.95. Published by: University of New Mexico Press, Albuquerque, NM. This is an exact facsimile of the first guidebook of its kind for the full length of the famous Route 66 from Chicago to Los Angeles. It was first published in 1946, less than a year after the end of World War II. You can use it to retrace the Mother Road as it was at its peak.

Clark, Marian. **The Route 66 Cookbook.** [Illustrated]. ISBN: 1-57178-020-3. Trade Paper ($17.95 (Ingram Price), $17.95 (Retail Price)). Published by: Council Oak Books.

Wallis, Michael. Wallis, Suzanne. **Route 66 Postcards: Greetings from the Mother Road.** [Illustrated]. ISBN 0-312-09904-5. Trade Paper ($8.95 (Ingram Price), $8.95 (Retail Price)). Published by: St Martin.

Witzel, Michael K. **Route 66 Remembered.** [Illustrated]. ISBN: 0-7603-0114-X. Trade Cloth ($29.95 (Ingram Price), $29.95 (Retail Price)). Published by: Motorbooks Intl.

Wilde, David. Gunderson-Montoya, Ida L (Illustrator). **Route '66: The Five Year Diary of a Journey Across America.** [Illustrated]. ISBN: 0-9625472-3-9. Trade Paper ($12.95 (Retail Price)). Published by: Wilde Pub.

Smith, Jay L. **The Boy; Okie Passage on Route 66.** ISBN 1-881972-07-0. Trade Paper ($8.95 (Retail Price)). Published by: Tall Cotton Pr.

Mahnke, Dan. **Antique Roads of America: Bicycle Guide for Route 66.** [Illustrated]. ISBN 0-9633853-0-5. If you're traveling Route 66, this mileage guide will help you with all the proper turns you'll need to take. In 1992, being the 66th anniversary of Route 66, this guide was put together primarily for bicyclists, but it is set up for all vehicles to follow: travelers, memorabilia collectors, geography enthusiasts, & senior citizens with memories of the old route. The guide starts in Santa Monica & ends in Chicago, 2482 miles later. Best for bicyclists to traveleastwards, it is also laid out to travel west. Each chapter covers each of the eight states which Route 66 passes through, along with a brief introduction to the state. One hundred photos of old buildings, new buildings, city streets, old highway 66, & one of a Space Shuttle Astronaut statue are included. With all the necessities that come with traveling, there are notations in the guide of: gas stations, eating places, motels & campsites, water stops, rest areas, & some bike shops. The guide was mentioned in the July 1992 newsletter of the Kansas Route 66 Association & in the upcoming Fall 1992 New Mexico Route 66 Association newsletter..

Trade Paper ($9.95 (Retail Price)) Published by: D Mahnke (the author).

Other books on Route 66[34]

Route 66 : The Mother Road by Michael Wallis. Wire bound, full color, segmented according to states.

Route 66 : The Highway and its People. Photographic essay by Quinta Scott, text by Susan Croce Kelly.

Searching for 66 by Tom Teague.

Route 66 by Patrick Sautelet, Serge Labrune, Jean-Luc Moreau and Philippe Fauconnier [in French!].

Route 66 by Willy Francois [in Dutch!].

Route 66 : A Guidebook to the Mother Road by Bob Moore and Patrick Grauwels.

Route 66 Across New Mexico : A Wanderer's Guide by Jill Schneider.

Guide to Historic Route 66 in California Vivian Davies and Darin Kuna of the California Historic Route 66 Association.

Streckenpilot Route 66, entlang der Traumstrasse Amerikas [in German][35]

---

[34] No ISBN numbers are available for these books. A helpful clerk or librarian may be able to do some "detective" work for you in locating the titles with this information.

[35] There is a great deal of interest in Route 66 in Western Europe. Associations have formed in France and The Netherlands. A group of German motorcyclists "ran" Route 66 in 1994.

Route 66 Remembered by Michael Karl Witzel.

Magazines on Route 66

Route 66 Magazine

Out West has a regular section on Route 66

Roadside

Heartland Highways

The Route 66 World News

The Heart of Route 66

The Slow Lane Journal

Yesterday's Highways

Lost Highways Quarterly

Maps of Route 66

Here it is! Route 66, The Map Series by Jerry McClanahan and Jim Ross. A separate map for each of the 8 states Route 66 passed through. $14.95, available from HHJM, Inc., 2024 Heatherbrook Drive, Grapevine, TX 76051, 1-800-553-5883.

Road Map of Historic Route 66 by Dave York

Historic Route 66 : auto tour prepared by Forest Service, Kaibab National Forest.

Historic Route 66 : mountain bike tour prepared by Forest Service, Kaibab National Forest.

Historic Route 66 Williams to Flagstaff auto tour prepared by Forest Service, Kaibab National Forest.

Books with parts on Route 66

The magic bus-An American odyssey, by Douglas Brinkley

Videos on Route 66

Route 66 - Texas
Route 66 - Illinois
Route 66 - Arizona
Route 66 - New Mexico
Route 66 - California
(Video series produced by HHJM Video, 2024 Heatherbrook Drive, Grapevine, TX 76051 - 817-488-4940)

Route 66; An American Odyssey video directed by John Paget

A journey down Route 66 by Michael Wallis

Cruising' Oklahoma 66

Route 66 Rendezvous by Paul Petersen

The Signs & Rhythms of Burma Shave

The Spirit of 66

Radio programs on Route 66

Route 66 by The Kitchen Sisters

CD-ROM on Route 66

Drivin' Route 66 by Cambridge Digital Media and Creative Multimedia

Route 66 related music

Route 66 by David Williams

The Songs Of Route 66: Music From The All-American Highway

Miscellaneous.

1996 "Route 66" CAR CULTURE Calendar by Lucinda Lewis

The Route 66 Commemorative Watch by Rich Company

HHJM, Inc., 2024 Heatherbrook Drive, Grapevine, TX 76051 has a catalog of Route 66 merchandise: T-Shirts, caps, maps, lapel pins, etc.

The Annual Mother Road Rally[SM]. A "motorcycles only" annual event (2nd Saturday of June). Participants leave from Chicago, Santa Monica Pier or any of the "join up points" along Route 66. Participants also receive a commemorative pin and maps. Event merchandise includes: T-Shirts, cups, caps and a monthly newsletter. HHJM, Inc., 2024 Heatherbrook Drive, Grapevine, TX 76051. 1-800-553-5883.

("Highway of Dreams" was originally published by the American Motorcyclist Association in their magazine: American Motorcyclist. It is reprinted here by permission. The Association is a good investment for all motorcyclists)

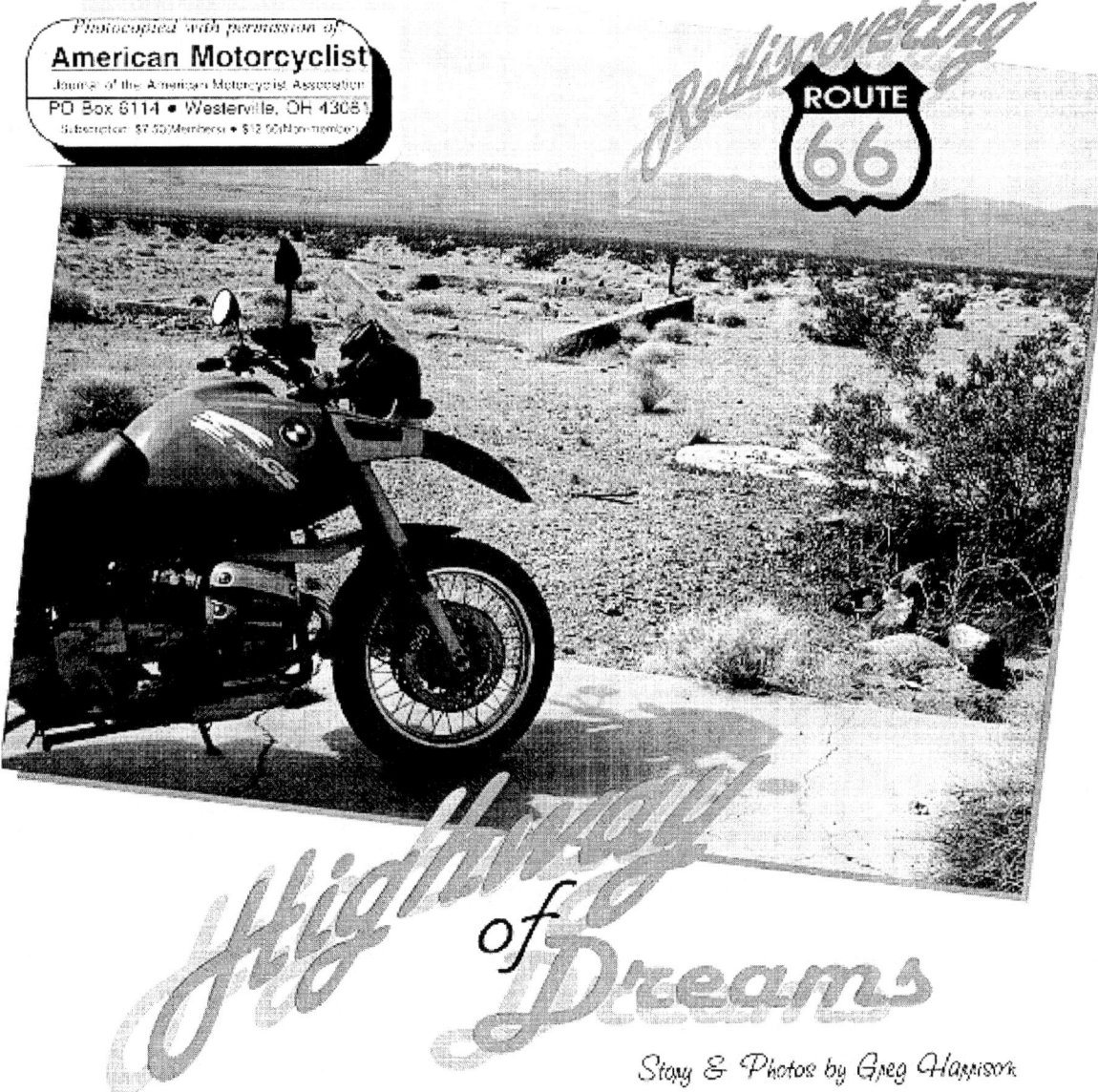

Rediscovering Route 66
Highway of Dreams

Story & Photos by Greg Harrison

It's eerie how quiet a place can be when the sound disappeared decades ago.

The BMW's engine was still ticking and popping as it cooled in the desert air. But beyond that the only noise was the scraping of my riding boots as I walked across the sandy ground.

I'd stopped because my fingers were freezing in the early morning cold and I needed to get my heavier gloves out of the saddlebag. But I'd stopped at this particular spot, just east of Barstow in the California desert, because I'd spotted the faint outline of a foundation next to the pavement.

Sunrise softly illuminated the old road, which aimed straight east, like an arrow poised to impale the new day. I could trace its course all the way to the horizon where I was headed. There wasn't another vehicle in sight.

Looking around, I began to pick out details that identified my rest stop as a combination diner, gas station and tourist court from a half-century ago. A driveway led from the road to a crumbling concrete pad where two gas pumps once stood. The foundation of the diner itself, now covered with sand and sagebrush, was right behind the pumps.

Another driveway veered off to the south, leading toward the remains of a half-dozen tourist cabins. The drive was bounded by rows of rocks, some of them still showing touches of red, white and blue paint.

The cabins would have faced east, toward the dawn, meaning that the travelers who stayed in them might have enjoyed the same awesome sunrise spectacle I was witnessing. Just above the horizon, the clear sky was already a warm yellow. But higher up, it ranged through orange and rosy red into deep blue.

Beneath that sky was open desert -- humbling to those of used to the neat, orderly patchwork of farms and towns back East. Aside from a low mountain range in the distance and the steel highway of the Union Pacific paralleling the road, there was nothing but pucker bushes and rocks as far as the eye could see.

I imagined the place as it must have looked in the '50's. I saw an oasis for an anxious Midwestern family that had traveled a little too far into the blackness of night on their long-awaited vacation trip west. I saw a welcome and familiar rest stop for a trucker piloting a Diamond Reo full of California vegetables to Tulsa, St. Louis or maybe all the way to Chicago.

Out here, in the middle of nowhere, this little tourist court must have been a neon-lit outpost, ready to welcome travelers:

"Fill 'er up, mister? High test or regular?" the attendant would ask over the buzzing of the pink neon "EAT" sign on the restaurant. I could almost hear the juke box offering up snatches of a Dorsey Brothers tune each time the door swung open. Inside, under the harsh fluorescent lights, the grill would be sizzling, silverware would be clinking, and a smiling waitress would be waiting with a pencil to scratch your order onto her green pad.

A small lizard scampered across the broken concrete, reminding me that I was in the 1990s, far removed from the era of tourist courts, the Dorsey Brothers, Diamond Reos . . . and for that matter, this old highway.

•

John Steinbeck called it "the mother road." It was the escape route, "the road of flight," for the Joad family in "The Grapes of Wrath" and for thousands of others they represented -- people who traded the barren dust bowl of Oklahoma for the lush promised land of California.

But Route 66 was much more than that. Whether you were headed west for a better life, for a family vacation or just for the experience of traveling, Route 66 was a part of the American dream. It represented freedom and adventure. Truckers, motorcyclists and even a couple of guys in a Corvette convertible on TV took "the highway that's the best" and got their "kicks on Route 66."

The road covered more than 2,400 miles from the shores of Lake Michigan in Chicago to a Pacific Ocean beach in Santa Monica. Along the way, it traversed Illinois, Missouri, Kansas, Oklahoma, Texas, New Mexico, Arizona and California, linking hundreds of small and large towns along the way. In many cases, Route 66 created those towns, nurtured their growth and presided over their death.

The concept of the mother road was born in 1926. It was a vision of a paved highway that would connect the Midwest to the Pacific coast, replacing a network of roads that ranged from hard-surface two-lane routes to dirt paths.

The paving project took more than a decade, but when the final concrete was poured in 1937, Route 66 became the main street of America. Previously, a car or motorcycle trip to the West Coast had been an expedition. Now, it was within reach of almost anyone.

However, the seeds of Route 66's demise were planted only a few years after the road was completed. When Gen. Dwight Eisenhower got his first glimpse of the German Autobahn, he quickly realized the military significance of a limited-access highway system. When he was elected president in the

'50s, Ike turned that idea into reality with a federal highway bill that fueled a nationwide freeway-building craze.

As sections of the interstate system were completed, Route 66 died a piece at a time. In 1977, when Interstate 55 was completed from Chicago to St. Louis, workmen removed the "End of Route 66" sign from the shores of Lake Michigan. The final death knell was sounded in October 1984, when the last section of Interstate 40 around Williams, Arizona opened. The mother road had been replaced by the superslab.

Like a lot of people, I was under the impression that most, if not all, of Route 66 simply doesn't exist anymore -- that it had been torn up or paved over or chopped into pieces too small to recognize.

As I found out, those rumors are wrong. Route 66 is still out there, if you know where to look. And so are the dreams it represented.

•

Tales of the mother road's dangerous parts were an integral part of the highway's folklore -- repeated and exaggerated by nearly everyone who traveled Route 66. But topping all the rest was the stretch between the California border and Kingman, Arizona, where old 66 crossed Sitgreaves Pass in the Black Mountains.

Back in the road's heyday, terrified flatlanders used to pay tow truck drivers to haul them and their cars over the pass while they covered their eyes and prayed. The story was that Route 66 didn't just double back on itself on the way to the Sitgreaves crest, it tripled and even quadrupled back on itself.

Guess what? It still does.

I ignored the advice I'd heard from a waitress at a coffee stop in Barstow ("That road's a mess -- you'd beat yourself to death"), and headed straight for this legendary stretch of road, which begins near Topock, Arizona. I didn't know exactly what to expect, but I figured that any road capable striking fear in the hearts of Dodge drivers in the 1950's might be just about perfect on a modern motorcycle.

It turned out even better than I hoped. Recently, this part of old Route 66 has been designated a Back Country Byway by the federal government, and it's been freshly paved. Of course, anyone who really wants to get from Topock to Kingman takes Interstate 40 today, so the GS and I had the brand-new asphalt to ourselves as we climbed toward Oatman, an old mining boom town that somehow manages to hang on despite two near-fatal busts.

Oatman was founded as a gold-mining settlement around the turn of the century, growing from a tent camp into a city of 15,000 people in the roaring '20s as miners dug millions of dollars worth of the precious metal from the surrounding hills.

But by 1940, the rich gold veins had begun to dry up, and with the outbreak of World War II, the federal government closed the mines as "non-essential to the war effort." Miners left in droves, freeing hundreds of burros which had been used to haul mining cars. Their descendants still roam what's left of the old town today, looking for handouts from tourists (and nibbling on the salty liners of helmets left by unsuspecting motorcyclists).

What kept Oatman alive through the war years was Route 66, which ran right down the main (these days the only) street in town. But then came the second blow, when the state relocated the road in the 1950's. An account in the Kingman, Arizona, Daily Miner newspaper notes: "One afternoon in 1951, traffic was coming steadily over Sitgreaves Pass -- then it was silent. Someone rushed to Oatman with the news that they had cut the ribbon the new section of U.S. 66 between Kingman and Topock. Six of the seven service station families started to leave the town the following day, and other businesses quickly followed."

Today, Oatman survives as an eccentric little town with an old-west flavor, attracting tourists who are willing to travel pretty far off the beaten path. Getting there from the California border is great. Heading from Oatman over Sitgreaves Pass to Kingman is even better. And today, you don't even have to contented with a bunch of families in Dodges being hauled behind tow trucks.

•

When I told J. B. Norris, our eastern advertising manager, that I was going to take a ride in search of Route 66, I could hear the jealousy in his voice. J. B. lives in Springfield, Illinois, and was born practically within sight of the mother road, so it made sense to give him a call and ask if he had any information that would be useful to me.

I remember him muttering something about "cozy dogs" before promising to get back to me with "something hot."

The next morning, I received a packet of bizarre postcards and maps, all drawn by some guy named Bob Waldmire. And I got a return phone call from J. B.

"I gotta' do this too," he said. "I've been dreaming about it for years. Besides, I just bought the new Beemer and this ride would be perfect for it."

"But I'm flying to California tomorrow to get the bike," I said. "I'll be headed back east the day after that."

"The way I've got it figured," he answered quickly, "if I leave tonight and blast a little bit, I can meet you in, uh, let's see . . . " I could hear maps rustling the background. " . . . How about Kingman, Arizona? I'll see you there Saturday night."

As many an advertiser has found out over the past several years, J. B. is a difficult man to say no to.

"OK," I said, not sure how he planned to cover nearly 1,900 miles in that time span, "but dinner is on you."

J. B. rolled into Kingman about an hour after I did, with his new BMW Paris-to-Dakar thoroughly broken in. We had enchiladas at a great little Mexican restaurant, and my wallet never left my pocket.

•

The soulful sound of a Santa Fe freight train woke us up early the next morning. By the time the sun was fully above the horizon, we were on our way, headed east under a crystal-clear sky.

Arizona boasts the longest surviving section of Route 66, a 160 mile stretch running from the California border all the way to Ash

Now retired from the road, Bob Waldmire still lives his Route 66 dreams every day. A second-generation legend of the mother road, Waldmire has big plans for his visitors center in Hackberry, Arizona.

Fork, about 50 miles west of Flagstaff. Along this part of the road, you'll find some of the best scenery the highway has to offer, and some of its most interesting characters, too.

Following the old road is easy in western Arizona. It's officially designated state Route 66, and the signposts even call it Old Route 66 in places. As a result, this area makes a good training ground for 66 hunters.

The road was nearly deserted and J. B. was used to covering miles, so we left Kingman behind us pretty quickly. The open highway gave us a chance to explore the capabilities of J. B.'s R100GS and its descendant, the loaner R1100GS I was riding. In fact, we got so wrapped up in that pursuit that we nearly missed one of the great visionaries along Route 66 today. But as we approached a wide spot in the road known as Hackberry, Arizona, J. B. suddenly braked and pulled into a gravel parking lot.

•

Bob Waldmire must have been sound asleep when J. B. began beating on the door of the 1930s-era gas station and general store that he calls home.

"Come on, J. B.," I implored after his second attempt to rouse somebody. "He isn't here. Let's go."

"There's his VW bus," J. B. pointed out, "so he's got to be here. Don't worry, I know him -- sort of."

Did I mention that J. B. is hard to say no to?

On the third series of knocks on the door of a building that looked like it might not be up to many more, a thin, bearded and very sleepy man appeared in the doorway. He was barefoot, wrapped in a blanket and didn't look all that pleased to discover strangers arriving very early on a Sunday morning.

"Yeah," he said, squinting into the sunlight.

"I'm here for a cozy dog," J. B. responded.

The squint turned into a crooked smile. "Well, you're a couple thousand miles off-base, but come in and I'll make some coffee instead."

Waldmire opened the door a little wider, then said over his shoulder, "And try to generate some body heat while you're at it."

Waldmire padded around the chilly interior of his old store, digging out the coffee pot and fixing us the first of several batches. Then he sat down, and over the next two hours, he told us about his dream.

Bob and his older brother, Buzz, are the sons of the late Ed Waldmire, who qualifies as a true Route 66 legend. You see, Ed invented the corn dog back in the 1940s in Springfield, Illinois.

That might not rank right up there with the work of daVinci or Edison, but it was a true breakthrough in the field of driving while eating, and that invention charted the course of the Waldmire family's future.

Ed's wife, Ginny, named his invention a "Cozy Dog," and the Waldmires opened the Cozy Dog Restaurant right on Route 66 in Springfield in the early 1950s. Buzz and Bob worked in the restaurant from the time they were kids.

"Dad instilled in us a sense of business right from the start," Bob said. "He used to pay us two cents for each fly we killed. We learned pretty quick. If business got a little slow, Buzz would prop open the screen door when Dad wasn't looking."

The Waldmire boys also inherited their father's love of Route 66, the famous road that brought people from faraway places to their doorstep. Buzz continued to work at the Cozy Dog, and when Ed passed away recently, he became the owner and operator. Bob, on the other hand, had a different path to follow.

"I was in and out of college back in the '60s," he told us, "until I finally dropped out for the last time about 1969. I was always pretty good at art, so I decided I'd be an artist. Yeah, that sounded good. Besides, it was that or get a real job."

Bob bought a school bus to live in and began to travel, drawing and selling his works along the way. Usually, that "way" was Route 66. Eventually, he became the road's unofficial artist, and a recognized highway historian. Traveling in that school bus and its successor, a VW micro-bus, he created a number of bird's-eye view posters and postcards (including several that J. B. had purchased back home at the Cozy Dog) that qualify as works of art as well as informative guides to the route.

But the road, the bus and maybe even Bob eventually got a little old, so he decided it was time to retire his traveling show and find a place where his customers could come to him. With the help of his dad, Waldmire settled down in the old general store early in 1993.

"My dad took a train out here, looked around and said, `Everywhere I look I see work,'" Bob recalled, "I said, `Yeah, but I've got the rest of my life.'

"You know, though," he added, "his words echo a lot today. I've accomplished a lot since I got here. It probably doesn't look like I've done that much, but I've started a hundred projects and I've finished, oh, four or five. I have a whole bunch more in my mind."

Bob took us outside to show us what he meant. Out by the road is a sign reading, "Old Route 66 Visitors Center -- International and Bioregional Study Center." The debris piled up against the front the structure, he noted, is actually a "lean-to solar greenhouse that I'm working on. It's made completely from recycled materials." Well recycled, I might add.

Bob's VW, covered with a map of Route 66, sits in front of what appears to be a ramshackle abandoned house. Eventually, he said, that will be his "self-serve bed and breakfast hostel." And the dusty path leading into the scrub growth beyond? Bob calls it an "interpretive hiking trail."

"That first part is already wheelchair accessible," he pointed out, "and I'm going to build interpretive displays and maps and everything.

"Over here," he said, directing our attention to the area behind the store, "I want to build an International Peace Village, with replicas of native structures like a urt, teepees, hogans. And over there will be the tent-camping area.

"I can see it all," he added, his voice rising in excitement. "I can see it all."

For now, Bob sells the occasional Route 66 map, a jar or two of vegetarian chili and, from time to time, a piece of his artwork. In between, he busies himself with a paintbrush, a hammer and his dreams.

As we started the bikes and pulled back onto the highway, I thought about Waldmire's lonely outpost along the mother road. It struck me that a lot of us from his generation started out to be Bob Waldmire, and today still fancy the idea that a part of us is. The difference is, Bob's never been anything else.

•

From Waldmire's Route 66 Visitors Center, the road leads northeast, into the vast high country of the Hualapai Indian Reservation. Then it drops down into Seligman, Arizona, home of Angel and Juan Delgadillo, two more people who got Route 66 in their blood at an early age and never left it behind.

These two brothers almost joined the migration to California back in the '30s when local jobs were scarce and their father's combination barber shop/pool hall closed. But they didn't leave then, and they haven't left over the long decades since.

Today, Angel cuts hair and dispenses his knowledge of Route 66 from his late father's old shop on Main Street, while just up the road, Juan operates the incredible Snowcap Drive-In ("Home of the Dead Chicken" dinner), where the calendar might just as easily say 1954 as 1994.

What is it about this road that attracted so many dreamers decades ago, and continues to hold them today, long after the rest of the world has passed Route 66 by? I couldn't be sure but it was becoming apparent that if you lined up all the fascinating characters you can meet on Route 66, they' stretch from L. A. to Chicago. And probably back again.

•

We were forced off the old pavement near Ash Fork, where Interstate 40 was constructed right over the top of the existing road. From there past the snow-capped peaks around Flagstaff, we were able to find only short stretches of old 66, and we wouldn't have located those without a lot of help from our guidebooks.

Well east of Flagstaff, precisely in the middle of nowhere, the Beemer's low-fuel warning light came on. The only civilization in sight was a lone gas station at a remote exit marked "Two Guns." It was there, far enough from the nearest town to make 911 a toll call, that we stumbled across treachery, murder, the abuse of a corpse, as well as Robert the mountain man and his dog Gypsy. All that, plus a descent into a remote cave with a guide who was carrying a long knife and a .38 pistol on his belt, and appeared to be looking for a good place to hide some bodies . . . perhaps ours!

But that will have to wait until next month. ■

(The series appeared over a three month period)

Highway of Dreams
Part 2

Story & Photos by Greg Harrison. Reprinted from the *American Motorcyclist* magazine.

Seeing the cloud of dust being kicked up by the ATV making a beeline toward us across the Arizona desert gave me a sick feeling in my gut. It reminded me of the times as a kid when I'd been caught someplace I wasn't supposed to be.

Admittedly, J. B. and I had strayed a bit. We'd pulled off Interstate 40 at an exit marked "Two Guns" because it looked like it might be the only place to get gas for miles. But after we'd topped off the bikes at a gas station occupying the sole building at the Two Guns exist, we'd taken a short detour.

From the highway, we'd seen an abandoned two-lane bridge a few hundred yards from the exit. It could only be a relic of Route 66. And since we were attempting to follow the old road from California to its ending point in Chicago, we needed to investigate.

Father west, it had been easy to follow the former Main Street of America. It's even called Arizona state Route 66 these days. But as we approached Flagstaff, traces of 66 had grown scarce. Most evidence of the old road was obliterated when the interstate was completed in the '70s. So when we saw the fenced-off highway bridge standing there in the desert, unconnected to any road, we'd ridden our BMWs across a bit of scrub land to the edge of a cliff to get a better look.

It didn't seem like a big deal, but the guy on the ATV seemed hell-bent on reaching us in a hurry. I was sure he was about to inform us that we were in a heap of trouble.

The ATV rider raced up, spun the bike in a half-circle and jumped off in one fluid movement. I quickly noticed a couple of things: First he had a big Buck knife strapped to one hip. And second, he had a pearl-handled .38 strapped to the other. When he told us to leave, I wasn't going to argue.

Instead, though, he wiped his right hand on his well-worn jeans and extended it to me. "Name's Robert. And this here's Gypsy," he said, pointing over his shoulder where, on cue, a dog came galloping up. "I'm kind of the caretaker of this place. You boys want a tour?"

A $5 bill started Robert talking, and he didn't stop for 90 minutes. During that hour-and-a-half, he told us tales of vengeance, murder, corpse abuse and much more -- all part of the legend of Two Guns, Arizona.

They area's checkered history began in 1878, Robert told us, when Apache Indians used nearby Diablo Canyon as an escape route after raiding Navajo encampments.

"The Apaches would raid the camps, steal horses and some of the women, and escape through the canyon," Robert said. "The Navajos would ride out after them, hoping to cut them off when the came out of the canyon. Only the Apaches would -*poof* -- disappear."

As we talked, Robert led us toward the rock strewn gully that was the Apache escape route. Eventually, he said, Navajo scouts discovered a large cave in the canyon, and they heard voices inside -- Apache voices.

In spite of the fact that a number of their women were held captive inside, the Navajos took drastic action. They gathered a huge pile of sagebrush and wood, built a fire, and then pushed the burning mass into the cave.

According to the legend, the Apaches threw what little water they had on the fire. Eventually, they even killed their horses and tried to quell the flames with their blood. But it wasn't enough. When the fire burned out the next day, the Navajos discovered 42 badly charred bodies inside.

Pointing in the direction of the cavern, located just a stone's throw from the Two Guns gas station, Robert told us the site has been known as the Apache Death Cave ever since. Anyone who disturbs it, he said, runs the risk of being cursed by evil spirits.

The area's violent history didn't end there. In 1905, two outlaws, Bill Evans and John Shaw, had their luck run out in Two Guns.

In September of that year, Evans and Shaw bellied up to the bar at the Wigwam Saloon in nearby Winslow, Arizona, for a drink. But as the bartender poured whiskey into their glasses, the two noticed a nearby dice table sagging under the weight of some 600 silver dollars that were being wagered. Shaw and Evans stared at the money, then reached for their guns instead of the whiskey. They relieved the dice players of their stakes, then made tracks for points west.

The two got as far as Two Guns before a posse ran them down. In the ensuing gunfight Shaw was shot dead and Evans was wounded. Evans recovered, but Shaw was buried where he fell.

When word of the gunfight reached the boys who had remained behind, drinking whiskey at the Wigwam Saloon, a short, drunken moment of silence fell over the place. Then somebody piped up that although it wasn't very neighborly of the two to rob the place, it seemed a shame that poor old John Shaw never got that last shot of whiskey he'd left on the bar.

A plan was quickly hatched. Somebody rounded up a bottle of whiskey (and several others to keep it company) and the saloon keeper provided a shovel. The gang of well-lubricated mourners hopped a freight train and jumped off at Two Guns. There, they exhumed Shaw's bullet-riddled corpse, stood him up and poured a shot of whiskey between his blue lips. One of the men even took pictures.

Robert's version of this particular tale closely agreed with other accounts I've read. In fact, I even ran across a photo of Shaw's final drink. I'm told that the original photo hung in the Wigwam until the place was torn down in the '40s. From the looks of it, Shaw didn't much enjoy having one for the road delivered to his gravesite. It was kind of like giving a stiff one to a stiff one, if you ask me.

Chain-smoking and talking all the way, Robert led us over unstable piles of boulders ("earthquake did that"), crumbled buildings ("watch for nails, busted glass and snakes"), and rotting wooden bridges over deep chasms. He told us these ruins represented another phase in the history of Two Guns.

In the late '20s, he said, when Route 66 was in its infancy, an entrepreneur named Henry Miller (a.k.a. "Two Guns Miller" and "Chief Crazy Thunder") opened a gas station, wild animal zoo and Apache Death Cave exhibition. Miller had a partner, Earl Cundiff, when he started the project. But whether you chalk it up to the Indian curse or some other cause, their association didn't last long.

Robert pointed with his knife to a dilapidated building. "That there," he said, "is where Miller shot and killed Earl Cundiff in '26. Shot him over some woman . . . got off scot-free, too."

Finally, Robert led us down a treacherous pile of rubble left behind by an avalanche and stopped inside the mouth of the Apache Death Cave. Then he lit an old lantern, held it up to his face and croaked, "Follow me."

Up until then, I'd been thinking of Robert as a friendly eccentric, a self-proclaimed mountain man who lived in the middle of nowhere by choice and sometimes liked to "sit in the ruins late at night and watch for stuff."

But a few minutes later, when he walked us deep into the cave, then extinguished the lantern to show us how dark it was, I began to have other thoughts. My mind wandered to things like Robert's knife, my wallet, his gun and my life. When he re-lit the lantern, I noticed J. B. apparently shared my apprehensions. He had inched a good 20 feet back toward the mouth of the cave, banging his head on the low ceiling in the process.

Our experience in the Apache Death Cave was similar to the tours Two Guns Miller offered tourists back in the '30s and '40s, except that Miller, the man who blew out the lantern on them, really had killed a man there!

In spite of the scare he threw into us, Robert was careful to make sure we got back to our bikes safely. And along the way, he explained how Two Guns was going to be rebuilt just like it was by a rich investor "real soon now."

As for the curse, Robert Says it still exists. How else can you explain the fact that the motel and gas station at Two Guns survived for decades in this remote location, then burned to the ground on the very day Interstate 40 opened and Route 66 was bypassed? It had to be the curse -- or perhaps that mysterious form of spontaneous combustion that can occur when a deed rubs up against an insurance policy.

●

The next morning, New Mexico greeted us with an endless blue sky. Sunshine warmed the air and illuminated distant buttes and mesas. It was a perfect day for riding.

We'd spent the night at one of the most interesting surviving attractions of the Route 66 era, the Wigwam Motel in Holbrook, Arizona. Back in 1950, Chester E. Lewis built the Wigwam from blueprints he'd purchased through a company that had designed other wigwam villages across the country. Lewis was sure that Americans traveling from coast to coast would want to stay in an Indian teepee. Decades later, a few of us still do. In fact, two other teepees were rented that night to a group of Harley-riding AMA members.

As we loaded up the bikes outside our teepee in the morning, J. B. reminded me of one of his goals for the trip: Finding the ultimate example of that rarest of desert animals, the American jackalope.

Skeptics might suggest that the jackalopes sold in tourist traps across the Southwest are nothing more than stuffed rabbits with fake antelope antlers stuck on top, but J. B. knows better. He's made a detailed study of the species and plans to write a short monograph on the subject someday.

In the meantime, he was searching for a perfect specimen of the breed to display back home in Illinois. We compared dozens at various shops until he found a beautiful seven-point buck, stuffed and mounted, in a great two-story teepee-style store near Gallup.

His eyes gleamed as he carried his purchase up to the cashier.

"Will ya' look at the rack on that boy?" he said proudly.

"That there's a nice one," the cashier responded with a straight face. "You don't see many of them that nice runnin' around."

She had us there.

●

In parts of New Mexico, following old Route 66 is easy. It's clearly marked in some places, but even without the signs you can often identify it was the only major east-west highway off the interstate.

Elsewhere, Route 66 can be as elusive as a wild jackalope. With days of experience behind us, though, we were developing a knack for tracking the old highway.

In a few areas, 66 simply doesn't exist anymore -- the interstate has been built right on top of the old roadbed. But as you travel the limited-access roads that replaced it -- Interstates 10, 15, 40, 44 and 55 -- you'll often find chunks of Route 66 paralleling the newer road. In a cruel twist of fate, some parts of old 66 even serve as access roads for the interstates.

There are several guidebooks that can help you find major remaining sections of the route, but to a great extent you're on your own in piecing together the more isolated chunks. That just adds to the experience, though. Discovering an obscure section of the highway is part of what makes riding the road such a challenging and rewarding adventure.

You can discover old Route 66 on any street motorcycle. But we learned that big dual-purpose bikes like J. B.'s Paris-Dakar Beemer and my loaner R1100GS were ideal for the job. Parts of the road have been abandoned and have fallen into disrepair, but they're still navigable by dual-sport machines. In fact, some of the most incredible sections we rode aren't even mentioned in the guidebooks because they present serious obstacles to ordinary vehicles. But we were able to find and ride them simply by following some common sense guidelines:

First, we learned to watch for old telephone/telegraph lines. If the road we were on went straight while the poles veered left or right along a lesser traveled path, we followed the poles, and usually found evidence of Route 66 along the way.

A second rule for following old 66 is to remember that where the railroad goes, so (usually) goes the road. Highway builders weren't trying to be imaginative when they laid out Route 66. Often, they stuck to the route already laid out for the iron horse.

Armed with those rules and several guidebooks we picked up along the way, J. B. and I still managed to get ourselves seriously lost on several occasions. But we also found places like a beautiful two-lane section of old Route 66 outside Santa Rosa, New Mexico. It wasn't listed in our guidebooks, but it should have been.

The road stretched as far as the eye could see across the open landscape. We raced a roadrunner, watched hawks soar on the updrafts, and traveled for nearly an hour before we saw another human being.

There's still a lot of magic left in the old road.

●

The Texas panhandle is so flat that you can see two days ahead of you, or so the local saying goes. And when the wind blows, you better have something big to hold on to -- like a BMW R1100GS.

We were blown out of New Mexico and into Glenrio, Texas, by a strong west wind that chased us along an old stretch of 66. In the heyday of Route 66, this border town was a major stopping point for travelers.

Homer Ehresman was among those who saw the opportunities the road presented here. He built the First/Last Motel in Texas (depending on which side of the sign you read) in 1950, and his tall sign joined others beckoning travelers to stop at the town's tourist courts, gas stations and cafes.

The interstate hasn't been kind to places like Glenrio. The town still merits an exit on the interstate, but its lifeblood -- the traffic that once crowded its main street -- is long gone. As we rode down that street, a once-vital link in the nation's transportation system now reduced to a weed-choked path, a couple of mangy black dogs made a half-hearted effort to chase us.

Time and the incessant wind have taken a toll on the town. Today, Ehresman's sign reads: "M O E L: FIR IN TEXAS -- CAFE." I-40 roars by just out of sight, but even the noise of the interstate is reduced to a background hum. And over it, we could hear the "rreeee, rrreeee" of a tin sign swaying in the wind above the door of the boarded-up hotel. The sign read: "Homer Ehresman, proprietor."

It looked like a fine place in its day.

●

Back in 1934, John Nunn told builder J. M. Tindall that he wanted to create a combination gas station and cafe that would be so beautiful it would stop traffic along Route 66 in Shamrock, Texas. Nunn pulled a nail out of his pocket and traced what he had in mind in the dirt. Tindall looked at the rough design and agreed to build it.

On April 1, 1936, Nunn's outrageous art deco Tower Station and U Drop Inn opened for business. Nearly 50 years later, it's still open, and still capable of stopping travelers in their tracks. At least it worked on us.

The U Drop Inn is one of those places that instantly feels as comfortable and familiar as your easy chair back home. We arrived in time for breakfast, and as we scanned the menu, we listened in on a five-man card game at the table behind us.

"Whatcha' holdin' there, bud?" asked a guy in a plaid shirt.

"That's for me to know and you to find out . . . maybe," laughed an older fellow in bib overalls.

It looked like the game had been going on since the Nixon administration. And it didn't show any signs of ending soon.

The only other patrons in the "U" that sunny morning were a woman named Cathy and a young boy with her. In between kibitzing with the card players, she seemed genuinely interested in finding out about our trip.

"So you're goin' all the way east," she said. "And you started where? L.A.? Now that's travelin'! You know, a lot of people around here have never been farther than Amarillo."

"Where you from?" she asked J. B. "Illinois? I went to visit my in-laws once in Indiana. Me and my husband went to a bar there one night and -- now don't think I'm stupid or nothin' -- but they were playin' country music on the juke box there. I couldn't believe it. I didn't think they *had* country music there."

When one of the card players snickered she shot back, "Shut up, Lonnie! You've never been nowhere, so you don't know sickem' either."

Breakfast was great, but looking at a sign in the window, I started wishing we'd hit town on Sunday afternoon.. The sign advertised "Sunday Buffet: Chicken, Dressing, Chicken Fried Steak, Roast Beef, Soup and Salad, Mashed Potatoes, Green Beans, Corn, Fried Squash, Peach Cobbler, Homemade Hot Rolls, $4.95."

As we got up to leave, Cathy said, "Y'all stayin' around this evenin'?"

"No," I answered. "We've got a long way to go."

"Well, you should stay," she said.

"Why?" I asked, thinking that perhaps there was something special going on in Shamrock that night.

She thought a minute, then smiled and said, "It took you a long time to get here. It seems like a shame that you're leavin' so soon."

•

Making time on the interstate means covering a lot of miles without stopping. But that term takes on a whole new meaning when you're riding Route 66, where you want to make time to get to know the people and places along the road.

That's why we traveled a solid 60 seconds from the U Drop Inn before stopping again, this time at Clay Motors, an Edsel dealership.

OK, it's not an Edsel dealership anymore. But you couldn't tell that by looking at the place. In fact, we found J. D. Clay Jr. hard at work under the hood of a rare 1960 Edsel convertible.

There's only about 15 of these convertibles left," Clay told us. "Edsel didn't build too many, since they were already in trouble back then."

Like the Edsel, Route 66 belongs to a different era. Fortunately though, there are people like Clay who remember.

"When I was in high school," he said, "they called it the mother road, and buddy, Route 66 was a busy sumbitch.

"There was motels with flashy neon all around. There was 18 restaurants here alone, and about 23 filling stations. It reminded me of Las Vegas with all those lights all lit up at night.

"There was something like 15,000 cars a day that went through here in the '60s. Man, I can remember when it would take five or six minutes 'fore you could find a break in the traffic to run across the street."

He gestured with the back of his hand toward the street that used to be Route 66. An old red pickup rumbled by, dragging its muffler.

I asked him what living and working on Route 66 is like today.

"You'd be surprised who comes through here," he said. "We had a club the other week from Norway. They shipped their cars to California, and they were headed to Chicago.

"It's nothin' like it was, though."

No, it isn't. But talking to people like J. D. in Texas or Robert in Arizona, and seeing places lie the U Drop Inn or the Wigwam Motel, you get a sense of what it must have been like when Route 66 was the Main Street of America.

•

We'd been on the road, rediscovering Route 66, for four days. Ahead of us lay Oklahoma, with some great old concrete sections of the mother road; deadman's curve in Missouri; the Route 66 Hall of Fame in Illinois; along with Lucille Hammond, Pig Hip sandwiches and Cozy Dogs.

In other words, part three of this story. Look for it in the May issue.■

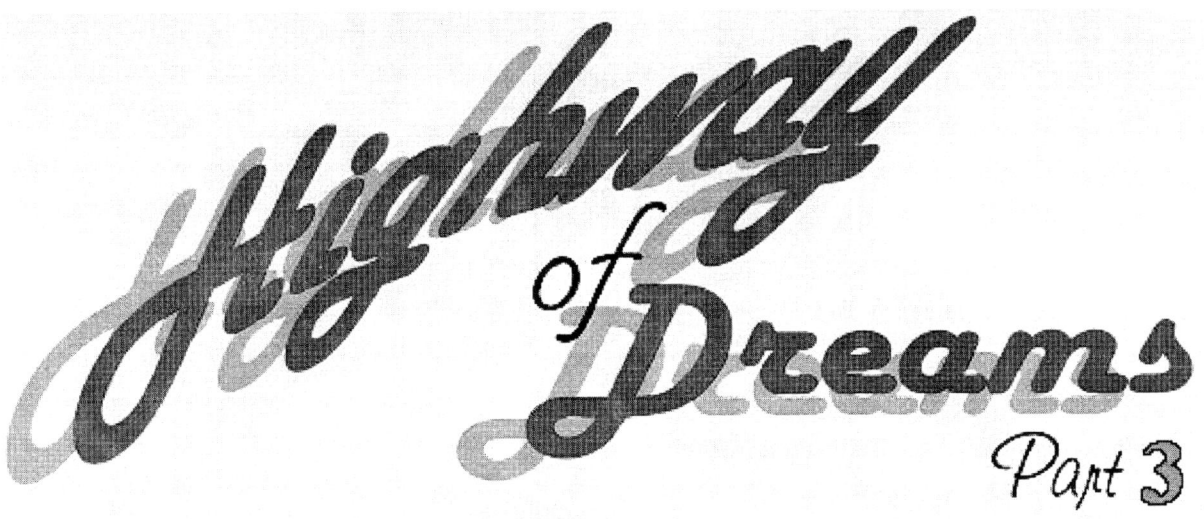

Highway of Dreams Part 3

Story & Photos by Greg Harrison. Reprinted from *American Motorcyclist* magazine.

Somewhere just east of the Oklahoma/Texas state line, the West kind of peters out and you realize you've entered the Midwest.

The last actual canyon you see along old Route 66 is just a few miles west of the border town of Texola. From there, the grassy plains of eastern Texas give way pretty quickly to trees, low hills, fields of crops and armies of migrant workers tending them.

In the 1930s, this was the Dust Bowl, the place where the wind literally blew the topsoil away over years of severe drought, leaving thousands of farmers and farm workers stranded. That experience, documented in John Steinbeck's novel, "The Grapes of Wrath," was responsible for much of the mystique associated with Route 66, which was the road of escape for Okies fleeing the Dust Bowl.

Water conservation programs in Oklahoma today supposedly give the state more surface water per square mile than lake-covered Minnesota. What you see from the road, though, still looks dry and dusty -- at least it did when we entered Oklahoma on a May afternoon. But the storm clouds building in the west looked ready to change all that. Oh well, the farmers would be happy.

We'd been on the road a week, riding through the wide-open beauty of the American West. With the scenery changing, the weather closing in and home still days away, it would have been easy to jump on the interstate and skip over Oklahoma. But it also would have been a big mistake.

For anyone interested in the history of Route 66, Oklahoma is a gold mine. The Mother Road stretched nearly 400 miles across the state, roughly following Interstate 40 from the Texas line to Oklahoma City, then paralleling Interstate 44 northeast to Tulsa and Joplin, Missouri. And if you're persistent, you'll find nearly every mile of the old road is still out there, waiting to be ridden.

We were persistent, which meant we got lost a lot. But it also meant we were able to find places like Lucille Hamons' Historic Highway grocery store/carryout/ex-tourist court and gas station in Hydro, Oklahoma, about 60 miles west of Oklahoma City.

You can see Lucille's place from the freeway, but you can't get to it unless you take the old highway, located just north of the interstate. And you'd better not call the road you take to her front door an access road. That's Route 66, Buster.

One more thing. Don't interrupt this charming lady if you've caught her in a talkative mood, or you might miss something.

"This place was built in 1926," she said as she set a couple of cups of coffee for us on the well-used kitchen table in the back of the store. "My husband and I came out here in 1941 and bought it. And now these people want to make it a historic place -- can you imagine?

"When I first came out here," she added, "the country was just getting over the Dust Bowl days and the Depression, and all these people from eastern Oklahoma and Arkansas were still headed to California, where they thought they'd get jobs.

"They had their kids and their cats and dogs with 'em and they were all just about flat broke, with mattresses on the roofs of their cars -- You boys want cream or sugar -- We used to say that you could tell a rich Okie back then because they was the ones with *two* mattresses on the roof. That made them a little richer than the Arkies, and that's the God's truth.

"There weren't a lot of motels then; just little places like mine, and by the time they got here, whole families of them, sometimes they were so broke . . .

"I can't tell you how many times I give people some gas just so they could get on down the road. I've fed people. I've kept them in my cabins. I used to have a whole yard full of old jalopy cars and trucks that broke down here that I'd buy so they could keep gettin' on down the road.

"Who knows if they ever got jobs, or even made it to California. We just did what we could to help 'em out. Cabins were a dollar and a half a night, and I'll tell you, they were full about every night.

There was another motel across the street. It was a real pretty place, and the man who ran it always kept a real pretty yard, but the highway (Interstate 40) took all that back in 1966. Still, they paid him for his property when they did it, while they just left me high and dry.

"They didn't take my property, but they sure took my business. So my husband and several others went to Oklahoma City to talk to some of them big shots there about why they were taking our business away, and some man told them, 'That's what we're trying to do, get those little places off the highway.' Well sir, I stayed on -- if for nothing else just to spite him."

Lucille paused a second, then added: "I'm a survivor. I stayed open when a lot of other business closed. I had to start selling beer back in 1966 when I got cut off from the interstate. If it hadn't been for beer, I'd probably be closed up. Before that, we used to sell a lot of groceries and sandwiches and stuff, but with that new highway, I started selling beer to survive.

I'm here seven days a week, 10 till midnight. Now some people are trying to get back on board with Route 66 and make money off it, but I'll tell ya', I've had a terrible time makin' a livin'."

The bell above the front door rang: a customer. Lucille jumped up and went to see. "Turned out it was a false alarm. A man had run out of gas and just needed to use the pone.

He left, and Lucille returned to her chair.

"Now, where were we? You know, my daughter was born upstairs above the store. We used to live above this place, then a while ago, I had a house built out back -- I don't know why, because I'm just over there long enough to sleep each night. Once we had all the relatives over for a big dinner and I was tryin' to fix a big meal over there in the house and, you know, I just didn't know how to use the stove over there. I'm better off right here -- Want some more coffee? Are you boys hungry?

"Right now, things are slow because of the rain, but there's a lot of new interest in Route 66. I had a girl here yesterday from New York. I've been on TV in Germany, and I'm mentioned in this German book, too. I guess I've had about every TV station in Oklahoma City come out and film me over the years. And I've got more than 1,600 letters from people all over the country who've stopped in this place.

"I've been to New Mexico several times, and I've been all the way to California once, but I do most of my traveling right here. I don't even like goin' to stay with my girls -- right here is where I belong.

"See, people come to me with their memories -- it's a road of memories. One older couple stopped by a year or so back and told me they'd spent their honeymoon right here with me. Then I had a man come by wonderin' if this place was still here. He said he and some other guy was here back in 1944. He said they stopped cuz' they noticed on the pumps that the gas was 17.9 cents. They came in and had ham, eggs and coffee, and when they got ready to pay, it came to 15 cents apiece.

Lucille laughed. "Memories are what keeps me goin'," she said, "and that's the God's truth."

•

In the early days, most of Route 66 was a narrow two-lane strip of concrete with concrete curbs. The curbs were designed to keep cars from running off the road, and they worked, albeit a little too well.

If a driver got a little drowsy behind the wheel and lost control, instead of running off the road hitting a tree, he bounced off the curb and hit another car head-on.

That wasn't a very desirable quality in a road, so the curbs were taken out as the highway was improved over the years. As a result, you find few original sections of Route 66 left today. But Oklahoma has mile after mile of it, complete with curbs.

J. B. and I cruised along quiet, tree-lined sections of the old road, rolling up and down the gentle hills of central Oklahoma. The rain that had caught up with us in Hydro ended quickly, and our tires sang on the old concrete. The road took us past herds of cows peacefully grazing on what had become a beautiful spring day.

We stopped to take photos next to an antique iron bridge crossing a small creek. The field next to it was ablaze with yellow wildflowers. A path led from the road down to the creek, and it wasn't hard to imagine a family stopping at this spot a half-century ago, perhaps having a picnic lunch next to the water on the way west.

•

Northeast of Oklahoma City, you'll find Route 66 running alongside Interstate 44 on the way to Tulsa and Joplin, Missouri. The interstate is known as the Turner Turnpike through this stretch, and it's a toll road. As a result, this part of old 66 carries more traffic today than any other surviving section of the road. The locals don't call it the Mother Road anymore -- instead, it's known as the Free Road.

We slowed down in the small town of Chandler, about 35 miles from Oklahoma City, and stumbled across the state headquarters of the Oklahoma Route 66 Society. There, we met Tom, yet another 66 freak. He told us the Oklahoma Legislature had allocated $16 million to help promote the old road and erect signs marking it. It was a story we'd heard from Route 66 Society members in other states. Many people, it seems, are recognizing the tourism potential of the old road.

Unfortunately, we also found ample evidence that this rebirth is coming too late for most of the roadside attractions Route 66 one supported.

Take the Blue Whale amusement park just outside Tulsa, for instance. The trademark whale, once a diving platform in a pond, now lists to port, while a handful of buildings that housed the Dodg'em cars, the shooting galleries and the Skee Ball games are all in various stages of decay.

The Blue Whale looks like the kind of place that would have caught my attention as a kid in the '50s. I can picture myself bugging my parents to distraction as we approached, in an attempt to get them to stop the family car and let me ride the rides and play the games.

Back then, of course, we wouldn't have had the time to stop. And now that I had the time, it looked like I was too late. A faded sign on the ticket booth read: "Shotgun security. Have brains? Use them and get out."

•

Route 66 barely trespassed into southeastern Kansas in the old days, with no more than a dozen miles of roadway in the state. But the road zigs and zags so much in that short stretch that we spent an hour and a half trying to follow it.

Fortunately, we were well fortified for the search. After spending the night near Vinita, Oklahoma, we got on the road early and stopped for breakfast at the Chuckwagon in Baxter Springs, Kansas. Both the content and the price of breakfast were heart-stopping: a couple of eggs, has browns, two strips of bacon, biscuits and gravy, all for a buck forty-nine, cash money.

Halltown, Missouri, near Springfield, still looks a lot like it did decades ago when its main -- and only -- street was a link in the Main Street of America. We stopped in town to check out an antique store we'd heard about, but before we got there, we found more evidence of Route 66's international popularity. We met a German couple spending their third vacation exploring the road, and watched a young guy go flashing past with a back pack and tent bungeed on the back of his Suzuki two-stroke, right above the Japanese license plate.

Then we met Thelma White, who runs the antique shop now located in the White Hall general store, which dates from the turn of the century. Thelma taught school for 25 years, and you can still hear a bit of that background in her voice when she discusses Route 66.

"Are you riding the old road?" she asked with a smile. When we said we were, she responded, "And what you liked best?"

I only had to think for a moment of the encounters we'd had since California.

"No doubt about it," I said, "meeting the people who live and work along it."

"It's really always been that way," she said. "Route 66 has always been about nice people in small towns wanting to meet new people and help them out. I've met the nicest people from all over the world, just because I was lucky enough to have lived alongside that road."

•

Well, the last thing I remember, Doc, I started to swerve and then I saw the Jag slide into the curve."

Jan and Dean's song, "Dead Man's Curve," came vividly to mind on the way to Rolla, Missouri, where old roads and a bit of spirited riding combined to nearly end this story early,

Between the small town of Waynesville and Rolla, there's a beautiful old four-lane stretch of Route 66 that follows the meandering path of a river. And one of the highlights is a sharp turn in the river and the road ominously named Devil's Elbow.

That curve started me thinking about Jan and Dean, but it wasn't the one that almost got us. Having been warned by guide books about the Devil's Elbow, we took it easy there.

But after hundreds of miles of picking our way down old, crumbing two-lane road segments, we gave in to the temptation to pick up the tempo a bit on this rare stretch of four-lane. As a result, we were at full interstate pace as we leaned into another curve and discovered that the wide road we were on turned into a 1½-lane gravel farm path about 20 feet ahead.

All I can say is, thank goodness for luck, long-travel suspension, lack of traffic and more luck. Somehow, we both made the transition, but it was a reminder than on a road as old as Route 66, there are no guarantees.

•

The Chain of Rocks Bridge is one of the most impressive and enduring symbols of Route 66. It's also one of the most inaccessible parts of the road today.

While several bridges carried Route 66 traffic over the Mississippi River during its long run as a U. S. highway, the most famous, or infamous, was the Chain of Rocks Bridge, linking Illinois and Missouri just north of St. Louis.

Built as a money-making toll bridge in 1929 by the town of Mitchell, Illinois, the Chain of Rocks became the official Route 66 river crossing in 1930. To accommodate unusual water currents and barge traffic, the bridge was built with a 45-degree kink in it, which combined with its narrow width, earned it a reputation as the biggest bottleneck between Chicago and Los Angeles. Large trucks would sometimes get stuck trying to pass each other at the kink, and would need to back up, as would the long line of traffic behind them.

The bridge was abandoned in the '60s, but it still stands. You can see it clearly from the wide, modern Interstate 270 bridge that now takes traffic over the Mississippi.

Trying to get a closer view, we ran into a maze of obstacles on the Missouri side, where the whole bridge area is fenced off, keeping you from even seeing the towering old structure. So we crossed the river on 270, took the first exit south and discovered Chain of Rocks Road, formerly Route 66.

A few old neon signs remain, marking long-gone motels, gas stations and cafes. The road turns to gravel near the river and eventually seems to end at a fishing area with a great view of the old bridge and a classic, castle like pumping station.

On closer inspection, though, we were able to trace the old road, now choked with weeds, right up to the bridge entrance. It was worth effort. The view of the road surface disappearing into the distance on this steel-girdered landmark was moving.

•

Illinois is truly the home stretch of Route 66, and it's easy to speed along state Route 4, which exists today on much of the roadway that was 66, without paying much attention. You can just follow the line of huge grain elevators marking the approach to each small town.

But was we'd learned elsewhere, there's always more to find on old 66 if you're willing to slow down and look. We discovered literally dozens of short pieces of the old road off Route 4 just by watching for telltale concrete sections veering to the right or left. Often, these quickly dead-ended, but at times we were rewarded with great old stretches of curvy road dating from the origins of Route 66.

•

J. B. lives in Springfield, Illinois, where he sells advertising for this magazine from an office in his home. Conveniently enough, old Route 66 goes right through Springfield, so I planned a night on his couch and a visit with his family.

Actually, though, my trip to Springfield had an ulterior motive: I needed a Cozy Dog.

Way back in Hackberry, Arizona, six states and nearly a week before, J. B. and I had awakened former Springfield resident Bob Waldmire early on a Sunday morning (see our February issue) and talked to him about Cozy Dogs. In addition to being a noted Route 66 artist, historian, philosopher and dreamer in his own right, Bob is the son of a Route 66 legend -- Ed Waldmire, creator of the corn dog, aka Cozy Dog, aka hot dog on a stick.

The elder Waldmire invented this portable meal concept way back in 1946 for a booth at the Illinois State Fair in Springfield. And by 1948, his invention was so popular that he and his wife, Ginny, decided to open a restaurant.

Ed had been calling his creation the "Crusty Cut," a name that may have come up a bit short in the appetizing department. But when his wife renamed it the Cozy Dog and designed a logo showing two hot dogs in love, the business blossomed. In fact, the original Cozy Dog restaurant, right on old Route 66 in Springfield, is still run by Buzz Waldmire, one of Ed's other sons. In addition to good food, the Cozy Dog has a well stocked little museum in the back devoted to Route 66 and the history of the corn dog.

Buzz and Bob, the Cozy Dog heirs, are about as different as night and day. While they both worked in the restaurant as kids, Bob elected to drop out of college and roam the highway in his VW bus, while Buzz stayed home, enlisted in the military, and eventually took over the family business. Bob's a strict vegetarian who spends his time building a "bioregional center" in Arizona, while Buzz cooks up hot dogs, sells firearms on the side and has a business card that reads: "Go ahead, buy a gun, make my day!"

Amazingly, though, they both fit right in at their opposite ends of Route 66.

Between frying Cozy Dogs and waiting on customers ("I've got three people working for me and they all called in sick today," he told us), Buzz talked about life on Route 66.

"My wife, Sue, helped make the decision for us to take over the restaurant when I left active duty in the military after 23 years," he said. "We didn't want to do it as a lifetime career, but we're still at it today.

"It's pretty tough to stay afloat with all the regulations and the competition from the chains. I can't hire a manager to run this place and survive, so I do it. Sue helps a lot, as do the kids, and my mom still helps out at lunch, but I probably end up putting in about 60 hours a week here. We survive by serving a lot of older customers who grew up with this place, plus we have a lot of foreign travelers on the old road."

He filled two glasses with soda, dropped a basket of french fries in the deep fryer and flipped a grill full of burgers in one fluid move.

"We always have and always will serve fresh food," he said, "and people know quality. Plus, you get to watch us cook the food, and hear me and my wife bicker or joke with the customers -- all for no extra charge!"

Dishing out three more lunches, he pointed to a baby bed behind the counter.

"Our youngest child is a year old," he noted, "and sometimes the customers babysit when we get busy. Where are you going to find that at a place like McDonald's?

"Route 66," he added, "reflects the independent spirit of the American people -- the little people who want to make it on their own.

"That's what we're doing, but believe me, it's hard work."

●

There's so much more to tell. J. B. showed me a section of the old road that's now under the water of Lake Springfield, just outside of town. We visited the Dixie Truckers Home truck stop and Route 66 museum up the road in McLean, Illinois. We stopped at the site of the legendary Pig Hip restaurant near Broadwell where, for more than 50 years Ernie Edwards served pork sandwiches "always from the left hip, since when a hog has an itch he has a tendency to raise the right leg to do the scratchin', and that makes the meat tough." Sadly, the Pig Hip closed in 1991.

We ate a "burrito as big as your head" in Normal, Illinois and I can vouch for the fact that it was as big as advertised. We saw the Polka Dot Drive Inn and the green giant standing guard outside the Launching Pad Restaurant in Wilmington.

And then we arrived in Chicago, riding to the corner of Lake Shore Drive and Jackson Avenue in Grant Park. Another 50 feet east and you'd be in Lake Michigan.

There we found a sign commemorating the end (or is it the beginning?) of Route 66. After some 2,400 miles, the journey was over. There were no more tourist courts, no more drive-ins, no more roadside attractions and no more fascinating people to look forward to.

What was it Lucille Hamons told us back in Hydro, Oklahoma?

"It's a road of memories."

Yeah, that's it. ■